Revelation and the Two Witnesses

Revelation and the Two Witnesses

The Implications for Understanding John's Depiction of the People of God and His Hortatory Intent

ROB DALRYMPLE

RESOURCE *Publications* • Eugene, Oregon

REVELATION AND THE TWO WITNESSES
The Implications for Understanding John's Depiction of the People of God and His Hortatory Intent

Copyright © 2011 Rob Dalrymple. All rights reserved. Except for brief quotations in critical publications or reviews, no part of this book may be reproduced in any manner without prior written permission from the publisher. Write: Permissions, Wipf and Stock Publishers, 199 W. 8th Ave., Suite 3, Eugene, OR 97401.

Resource Publications
An Imprint of Wipf and Stock Publishers
199 W. 8th Ave., Suite 3
Eugene, OR 97401

www.wipfandstock.com

ISBN 13: 978-1-61097-138-6

Manufactured in the U.S.A.

To My Wife

Without her love and continued support this would never have been possible. I thank God for her grace, understanding, and willingness to follow the Lord's guidance for our family.

Contents

1. Introduction / 1
2. John's Portrayal of the Two Witnesses / 3
3. Issues Pertaining to the Study of the Two Witnesses / 34
4. The Main Themes Pertaining to the People of God in the Account of the Two Witnesses and the Hortatory Implications / 47
5. The Structure of Revelation in Relation to John's Depiction of the People of God / 59
6. 7:1–17 and John's Portrait of the People of God in Light of the Four Themes Present in the Account of the Two Witnesses / 86
7. 12:1–14:5 The Woman, Her Offspring, and the Four Themes / 98
8. The Seven Letters, the People of God, and the Four Themes / 112
9. The Christological Significance of John's Portrait of the People of God / 118
10. The People of God in Daniel and the OT Apocalypses, and the Apocalypses of the Second Temple / 126

Conclusion / 151

Bibliography / 153

1

Introduction

Though many works have greatly contributed to the discussions pertaining to the nuances of the text of the Apocalypse, this study seeks to examine John's account of the Two Witnesses (11:1–13) in order to ascertain the main themes pertaining to the Two Witnesses and the implications for discerning John's hortatory intent.

This work intends to provide several major contributions to scholarly research on the Apocalypse. Though much has been done on the nature of the Two Witnesses and their identity, no work has sought to examine them in terms of the manner in which they are depicted in order to discern the hortatory implications of such. This research will contend that the account of the Two Witnesses depicts those on God's side in terms of four main themes: namely, they enjoy God's sovereign protection; they are God's witnesses; they will suffer persecution and perhaps death; and, they will ultimately be vindicated. Second, this work will consider the impact of this on discerning John's hortatory intent. Third, it will be argued that an understanding of John's depiction of the Two Witnesses provides insights into other accounts relating to the people on God's side in the pre-consummation visionary section of Revelation. Fourth, this research will demonstrate that the depiction of the Two Witnesses derives from John's Christological conceptions. Finally, the results of this analysis of the people on God's side in the pre-consummation portion of the Apocalypse will be compared with the apocalypses of the ST period in order to discern how Revelation compares with the apocalyptic literature of this period.

This study, though motivated by scholarly objectives, grew out of my concerns as a teacher in the body of Christ. In a sense, I wanted to gain insights into the hortatory features of John's Apocalypse and how those features might be applied to the contemporary church. For too often discussions of the book of Revelation among Christians are vacuous, confused, or just misguided. As a result, there is little teaching in the 21st century church on Revelation. Consequently, I have endeavored to discern how John characterizes the people on God's side in the account of the Two Witnesses in order to ascertain, at least in part, the hortatory function of the book—with the goal of determining how those hortatory concerns may be applied to our contemporary understanding, teaching, and application of the book of Revelation.

WHO ARE 'THE PEOPLE ON GOD'S SIDE'?

Throughout the pre-consummation visionary section of Revelation John tends to portray an ongoing spiritual war. He depicts this war using very black and white terms to describe those who side with God and those who side with the devil. Therefore, in the early part of this work I will employ the designation "the people on God's side," or more simply "the people of God," for the Two Witnesses as a generic designation for those human beings who side with God and the holy angels in the cosmic holy war against the devil and his contingency. This generic use of "the people on God's side," though admittedly awkward, allows for the present work to focus on questions relating to *how* John characterizes them as opposed to the lengthy debates regarding *who* they are.

Once the questions pertaining to how the Two Witnesses are portrayed have been addressed, we will then examine the issues pertaining to their identity. This will remain the approach of latter chapters as well. This is necessary because the diversity of viewpoints relating to the identification of the persons in each of the relevant accounts of Revelation are so great that working through them may exhaust the entire effort of this work.[1]

---

1. For many of these differences transcend mere exegesis; encompassing entire hermeneutical schema. For example, some assume that we should read everything under the "assumption that, where expressions are not explained, they can normally be interpreted according to their natural meaning unless the context clearly indicates otherwise" (Walvoord, *Revelation*, 30). Under this 'literal' approach, Walvoord suggests that "the various judgments of God are actually poured out on the earth as contained in the seals, trumpets, and vials" (Walvoord, *Revelation*, 21). Smalley, however, proposes a reading of Revelation that ardently rejects this approach. He claims, "In my view, it is impossible to take the symbolism of the Apocalypse literally, and to do so is to misread John totally" (Smalley, *Revelation*, 14).

2

John's Portrayal of the Two Witnesses

THIS CHAPTER SEEKS TO examine the account of the Two Witnesses and John's depiction of them. In this chapter we will consider the symbolic meaning and force belonging to the various aspects of the vision of the Two Witnesses.

In preparing to look into the account of 11:1–13 we will need to consider the episode of the measuring of the Temple in 11:1–2 not only because it immediately precedes 11:3–13 and forms its immediate context, but also because it has substantive links with 11:3–13 both thematically and in terms of the structure of the accounts. In the immediate context of 11:1–13 we find a continuation of the narrative of chapter 10; which closes with John being commissioned: 'δεῖ σε πάλιν προφητεῦσαι ἐπὶ λαοῖς καὶ ἔθνεσιν καὶ γλώσσαις καὶ βασιλεῦσιν πολλοῖς' (you must prophesy again concerning many peoples, nations, tongues, and kings; 10:11). This prophetic commissioning unfolds in 11:1 with John being commanded to carry out a prophetic action: 'Καὶ ἐδόθη μοι κάλαμος ὅμοιος ῥάβδῳ, λέγων· ἔγειρε καὶ μέτρησον τὸν ναὸν τοῦ θεοῦ καὶ τὸ θυσιαστήριον καὶ τοὺς προσκυνοῦντας ἐν αὐτῷ.' (and it was given to me a reed like a staff, saying: rise and measure the temple of God and the altar and those who are worshipping in it).

MEASURING THE TEMPLE, THE ALTAR, AND THE WORSHIPPERS (REV 11:1-2)

Measuring

Revelation 11 opens with John, in accord with his prophetic commissioning, being commanded to measure the Temple, the altar, and the worshippers. This prophetic act of measuring conforms to the OT practice that signifies the destruction, restoration, or the protection of that which is measured.[1]

That the measuring of Rev 11:1 primarily conveys the divine protection upon that which is measured derives first from the metaphorical connotation of the command to 'μέτρησον' (measure) the temple in 11:1.[2] Aune defines the command to measure the temple as a "symbolic prophetic action which serves as a link between the commissioning of John as a prophet in chapter 10 and the command to carry out a prophetic mission in Rev 10:11f."[3]

The imagery of measuring has ample attestation in the OT as a metaphorical device for divine protection. This can be seen, for example, in Ezekiel 40-48,[4] which Beale suggests provides the most direct background for Rev 11:1-2.[5] Zechariah 1-2, however, also serve as a background for the measuring of the temple of God in Rev 11:1-2.[6] In Zech 1:16, after first affirming that the temple will be rebuilt, it is then declared

---

1. See: Beale, *Revelation*, 558-59, 570-71; Boring, *Revelation*, 143; Caird, *Revelation*, 131-32; Morris, *Revelation*, 142; Mounce, *Revelation*, 219; Cp. Isa 28:16-17; Jer 31:38-40; Ezek 29:6; Zech 1:6. See also; Dalrymple, 'These are The Ones ... (Rev 7)', 396-406, in which it is contended that the divine protection of the people on God's side is one of the dominate themes relating to John's portrayal of the people on God's side in Revelation.

2. For further support that 'measuring' connotes divine protection see: *Revelation*, 2.578; Boring, *Revelation*, 143; Harrington, *Apocalypse*, 155; Johnson, *Triumph of the Lamb*, 167; Michaels, *Revelation*, 137; Thomas, *Revelation*, 94; Wilcock, *Heaven Opened*, 104.

3. See: Aune, *Revelation*, 2.603-04. Cf. Smalley, *Revelation*, 271.

4. The context of Ezekiel displays several parallels with Revelation 11. See: Bornkamm, "Die Komposition der apokalyptischen," *ZNW* 36: 132-49, Harrington, *Apocalypse*, 151; The most notable parallel is the association of the measuring with that of an ideal temple. The measuring in Ezekiel, however, has even closer parallels with the measuring of Rev 21:15.

5. Cf. Beale, *Temple and the Church's Mission*, 315-320. See also: Barnhouse, *Revelation*, 193; Smalley, *Revelation*, 271; Stefanovic, *Revelation*, 339.

6. Aune contends that the measuring of Rev 11 more directly alludes to Zech 2:1-5 than to Ezek 40:3-42:20 (*Revelation*, 2.604). See also: Barnhouse, *Revelation*, 194.

that, "a measuring line will be stretched over Jerusalem" (NASB). And in 2:2, the purpose of this measuring is "to measure Jerusalem, to see how wide it is and how long it is" (NASB). The use of measuring in Zech 1–2, then, carries the notion of the divine provision for the rebuilding of the temple and the city with the result that the temple expands beyond the boundaries of the entire city. Thus, in the words of Hendriksen, "On the basis of the immediate context, the parallel expression ([Rev] 21.15), and the Old Testament background (Ezk. 40.5; 42.20; Zc. 2.1), we arrive at the conclusion that measuring the sanctuary means to set it apart from that which is profane; in order that, thus separated, it may be perfectly safe and protected from all harm."[7]

Also, supporting a metaphorical interpretation for the measuring of Rev 11:1–2 is the implausibility of measuring people.[8] Aune affirms that such a rendering, "is problematic if taken literally."[9] Thus, the use of 'ἔκβαλε ἔξωθεν' (lit.: cast it outside) in 11:2, most likely has a real-world reference to people as a result of the impracticality of casting out a temple court.[10] Furthermore, Feuillet[11] has shown that the expression 'ἐκβάλλειν ἐχω' (cast it outside) regularly applies to the expelling of people.

But divine protection is not the only possible meaning for measuring. Measuring also functions at times as a metaphorical device to connote destruction or restoration.[12] The use of 'μέτρησον' (measure) in relation to rebuilding in the OT on occasion connotes both a divine restoration and a subsequent preservation.[13] Nonetheless, in light of the context of Rev

---

7. Hendriksen, *More than Conquerors*, 126.

8. The NIV has negated the odd expression by translating the phrase "and count the worshippers there." Aune, similarly translates this phrase. He explains, "the translation 'count' is used here because 'μετρεῖν' can mean both 'measure' and 'count' (Aune, *Revelation*, 2.578). Counting is also suggested by Michaels, *Revelation*, 137; and, Thomas, *Revelation*, 94. The difficulty with this is the fact that the singular occurrence of this verb has now been rendered by two different English verbs within the same sentence.

9. Aune, *Revelation*, 607.

10. Cf. Bauckham, *Climax*, 270. This will be discussed in more detail in chapter 5.

11. A. Feuillet, "Essai D'interpretation du chapitre 11," *NTS* 4: 186. Cp. Luke 4:29; Acts 7:58; John 9:34–35; 12:31. Cf. Aune, *Revelation*, 2.607.

12. Its use in terms of destruction appears in 2 Kings 21:13, Isa 34:11, and Amos 7:7–9; and in terms of restoration, Jer 31:39, Ezek 40:1f, and Zech 1:16–2:6. In many instances, however, the notion of restoration is virtually synonymous with that of preservation. In 2 Sam 8:2, measuring is used of both destruction and preservation.

13. See: Fiorenza, *Revelation*, 77; and Mounce, *Revelation*, 213.

11 and its correspondence with the allusions to Ezekiel and Zechariah, the use of 'μέτρησον' (measure) as a metaphorical expression connoting divine protection appears to be the most natural understanding of the measuring.[14]

This analysis justifies the view that the apocalyptic vision of Rev 11:1–13 accords with the widely held perspective that the visions are symbolic rather than literal. Thus, it appears that John is primarily concerned with exhorting the people on God's side to holiness more than describing the present or future status of geographical Jerusalem. The analysis below will provide further justification for this assertion.

The Temple of God

The objects that John is commanded to measure are on the visionary level the measuring of the Temple, the altar, and the worshippers.[15] The question arises as to what these connote on the symbolic level. It has been argued that the act of measuring symbolically represents the divine protection of persons. Furthermore, that the outer court is 'ἔκβαλε ἔξωθεν' (cast outside) also symbolizes persons as well. By means of an analysis of the three items that are measured (temple, altar, and worshippers) I wish to affirm that they symbolically represent the divine protection of the people who side with God.

The phrase 'τὸν ναὸν τοῦ θεοῦ' (temple of God), which occurs eleven times in the NT,[16] connotes a spiritual application in every instance except one. The only occasion in which the phrase refers to the physical temple in Jerusalem is in Matt 26:61. However, the use of this phrase in Matthew, instead of weakening the case for a spiritual understanding throughout the NT, strengthens it. For in Matthew we have a clear indication that

---

14. See: Court, *Myth and History*, 86. Aune, in fact, argues that the notion of preservation "is obviously intended here" (Aune, *Revelation*, 2.603). Keener refers to the suggestion that measuring conveys preservation as "the most likely symbolic interpretation" (Keener, *Revelation*, 289). Walvoord agrees that it is a symbolic action, though he suggests that it conveys divine judgment (Walvoord, *Revelation*, 176). See also: Beagley, *The 'Sitz im Leben' of the Apocalypse*, 61–62; Caird, *Revelation*, 131–32; Harrington, *Apocalypse*, 151; Yeatts, *Revelation*, 191. Also, Barnhouse, *Revelation*, 194: though he applies the symbolism to the protection of Israel.

15. See Poythress, "Genre and Hermeneutics," *JETS* 36: 41–54, for a discussion of the levels of communication in apocalyptic literature.

16. Matt 26:61; 1 Cor 3:16, 17(2x); 2 Cor 6:16(2x); 2 Thess 2:4; Rev 3:12; 7:15; 11:1, 19.

the redemptive-historical era, in which Jesus is the true temple of God that supersedes the old, has arrived.¹⁷ That is, here and throughout the Gospels, Jesus is portrayed as the true temple—rebuilt via His resurrection—that has come to replace the physical Jerusalem temple. One need only reference John 2:19-21, where John parenthetically confirms that, 'ἐκεῖνος δὲ ἔλεγεν περὶ τοῦ ναοῦ τοῦ σώματος αὐτοῦ' (but He was speaking about the temple of His body; 2:21), to support the claim that Jesus, by means of His resurrection, has become the eschatological temple.

Also, such language is unequivocally applied to the people of God in both 1 Cor 3:16-17 and 2 Cor 6:16; as well as throughout the NT.¹⁸ In fact, the NT consistently uses temple and covenant language in application to the NT people of God (1 Pet 2:4-10). Furthermore, temple language was applied to the people on God's side in the seven letters of chapters 2-3. Thus, in Rev 3:12, John writes, "Ὁ νικῶν ποιήσω αὐτὸν στῦλον ἐν τῷ ναῷ τοῦ θεοῦ μου' (The one who overcomes I will make him a pillar in the Temple of My God; 3:12). Consequently, understanding the phrase 'τὸν ναὸν τοῦ θεοῦ' (temple of God) in Rev 11:1 spiritually, in application to the people who side with God, stands firmly in the redemptive-historical tradition inaugurated by the death and resurrection of Christ.

Contextual considerations also favor the conclusion that the command to measure relates to people. First, John has been exhorted: 'δεῖ σε πάλιν προφητεῦσαι ἐπὶ λαοῖς καὶ ἔθνεσιν καὶ γλώσσαις καὶ βασιλεῦσιν πολλοῖς' (it is necessary for you to prophesy concerning many peoples, nations, tongues, and kings; 10:11). Consequently, the reader is led to anticipate a depiction of persons in the narrative of the Two Witnesses.

This receives support from the location of the account of the Two Witnesses in the narrative flow of the Apocalypse. For this account resides in the midst of an intercalation.¹⁹ This intercalation, along with its counterpart in chapter 7, interjects a delay in the midst of the description of its corresponding series of judgments in order to relate the status of the

---

17. Beale observed that Matt 26:61, "provides a transitional perspective between the Old Testament prophecies of a future, eschatological temple and the way Jesus began to view those prophecies as beginning to be fulfilled" (Beale, *Temple*, 275).

18. E.g., Eph 2:19-22; 1 Pet 2:5.

19. An "intercalation" is essentially an interruption in a passage with another account. In Revelation both the intercalation of chapter 7 and chapter 11:1-13 interrupt the narrative pertaining to a series of seven judgments and provide an account of the people on God's side. See also, Bauckham, *Climax*, 9-15.

people on God's side. Thirdly, I will argue in chapter 3 that the measuring of the temple in 11:1–2 is structurally and thematically related to the account of the Two Witnesses in 11:3–13 and that 11:1–13 forms one narrative. This provides further justification for suggesting that the focal point of this narrative is the depiction of the people on God's side.

Therefore, though a modern reader may understandably conceive of the temple in 11:1 as a literal temple, the contextual factors mitigate against this approach. Thus, in light of the use of this phrase throughout the NT,[20] as well as Revelation itself,[21] I suggest that the application of 'τὸν ναὸν τοῦ θεοῦ' (temple of God) in 11:1 to the people on God's side would have been the more natural meaning to the first readers.

Therefore, the command to measure 'τὸν ναὸν τοῦ θεοῦ' (temple of God) affirms that it is the people on God's side who are the recipients of God's sovereign protection.

The Altar and the Worshippers

The questions now arise as to why John is commanded to measure 'καὶ τὸ θυσιαστήριον καὶ τοὺς προσκυνοῦντας ἐν αὐτῷ.' (and the altar and those who are worshipping [the worshippers] in it; 11:1)? Do these also designate persons? And, how does this relate to the command to measure the 'τὸν ναὸν τοῦ θεοῦ' (temple of God)? Admittedly, the inclusion of these additional items on the surface appears superfluous. For the 'τὸν ναὸν τοῦ θεοῦ' (temple of God) may well be understood as incorporating the entirety of the people on God's side. Upon closer examination these two designations may be seen to either further associate the people on God's side with the temple or to possibly specify two groups among the people on God's side.[22]

The 'τὸ θυσιαστήριον' (the altar) in Rev 11:1 is possibly an allusion to the altar of incense in the holy place.[23] This is supported first by the use

---

20. See: Bachmann, "Himmlisch: der 'Temple Gottes,'" *NTS* 40: 474–480; Beale, *Revelation*, 557–65; Caird, *Revelation*, 132; Keener, *Revelation*, 288; Metzger, *Breaking the Code*, 70; Talbert, *The Apocalypse*, 44.

21. See: Keener, *Revelation*, 288

22. Surprisingly, most commentators fail to provide even a brief discussion of these items. Some briefly address the reference to the worshippers. Those who address both include: Aune, *Revelation*, 2.593–98; Beale, *Revelation*, 553–71; Stefanovic, *Revelation*, 336–38; Thompson, *Revelation*, 124; Yeatts, *Revelation*, 191. For a nuanced approach see my: "The Use of καί in Revelation 11,1," *Biblica* 87: 387–94.

23. Mounce, *Revelation*, 214. Thompson, however, dissents (*Revelation*, 124).

of 'τὸν ναὸν' (the temple) in 11:1. For the regular use of 'ναὸς' (temple) in the NT seemingly restricts the meaning to the temple building and not the entire complex.[24] Furthermore, John's description in the latter part of 11:1b links 'τὸ θυσιαστήριον' with 'τοὺς προσκυνοῦντας' (those who are worshiping; i.e., the worshippers) 'ἐν αὐτῷ' (in it—i.e., the temple) by the connective 'καὶ' (and). Thus, the altar is more naturally the one within the temple.[25]

If 'τὸ θυσιαστήριον' (the altar) is identified with the altar of incense within the temple, it is not to be understood as literally referencing the actual altar. This follows from the fact that we have already established that 'τὸν ναὸν' (the temple) is best understood metaphorically in terms of the people of God and not a literal building. Also, 'τοὺς προσκυνοῦντας' (the worshippers), which unambiguously references the people on God's side, are to be measured. Furthermore, if 'τὸ θυσιαστήριον' (the altar) were meant to represent an inanimate entity, then one must inquire as to the purpose for asserting its being measured.[26]

But if 'τὸ θυσιαστήριον' (the altar) is best understood metaphorically to reference people, then what might it connote here? One possible suggestion is that 'τὸ θυσιαστήριον' (the altar) signifies the people on God's side who in sacrificial obedience follow the Lamb in death. This relationship stems from the association with 6:9–10 where 'τοῦ θυσιαστηρίου' (the altar) is explicitly associated with 'τὰς ψυχὰς τῶν ἐσφαγμένων' (the souls of those who were slain). If so, then John's readers are assured that the divine protection incorporates those whose fate is martyrdom.[27] This corresponds with the fact that the Two Witnesses are unable to be harmed

---

24. See: Bauckham, *Climax*, 268; Beale, *Revelation*, 560–61; Keener, *Revelation*, 288; Stefanovic, *Revelation*, 337.

25. Charles contends that 'τὸ θυσιαστήριον' (the altar) generally refers to the altar of burnt-offering (Charles, *Revelation*, 1.277). Though this is true, the context mitigates against this conclusion. For if the worshippers are 'in' the temple, then it stands to reason that the altar does as well.

26. The validity of this question is heightened when one considers the hortatory nature of Revelation: i.e., what is the purpose for encouraging the church with the assertion that the altar is to be divinely protected?

27. One may suggest that for John all of the people on God's side suffer martyrdom and that the measuring of 'the altar' serves to assure them that God is sovereignly protecting them even while they suffer. This is supported by the fact that the Two Witnesses are both killed and that they seemingly represent the entirety of the people on God's side. This, however, is perhaps guilty of reading the Apocalypse too closely to be argued with any certainty (cf 13:9–10; which seems to suggest that not all will be martyred).

until 'τελέσωσιν τὴν μαρτυρίαν αὐτῶν,' (they have finished their testimony; 11:7).[28]

The use of 'τὸ θυσιαστήριον' (the altar) in 11:1, however, may present an association with the altar and the prayers of the saints in 8:3. There is structural support for this position in that both 8:3 and 11:1 are similarly located within their corresponding intercalations. If so, then the identification of the altar with that of 6:9 and its association with martyrdom is secondary to the assurance of God's answer to the prayers of the saints as in 8:3.[29] The measuring of 'τὸ θυσιαστήριον' (the altar) would then assure the people on God's side that God's sovereign protection insures that He is answering their prayers.

John also sees that the measuring includes 'τοὺς προσκυνοῦντας' (the worshippers) (11:1). That 'τοὺς προσκυνοῦντας' (the worshippers) are to be associated with the people on God's side receives universal acclaim.[30] These worshippers are said to be the ones who are 'ἐν αὐτῷ' (in it)—the antecedent of which is most probably the temple.[31] Such worshippers, then, suggests that they are priests, for only priests were permitted in the temple proper. Moreover, in Revelation it is the people on God's side as a whole who are explicitly referred to as 'ἱερεῖς' (priests; 1:6; 5:10; and 20:6).[32] Why then would John affirm that the whole of the people on God's side are divinely protected by means of the inclusion of 'τοὺς προσκυνοῦντας' (the worshippers) when he has already affirmed that such is true by the measuring of the temple?

An answer to this may be found in a comparison with Rev 13:6. There the phrase 'τοὺς ἐν τῷ οὐρανῷ σκηνοῦντας' (those who are tabernacling in heaven) occurs appositionally to 'τὴν σκηνήν' (the tabernacle) and serves to provide the details that specify as to who/what constitutes

---

28. I will reserve further discussion of this point until chapter 4.

29. Many commentators acknowledge that the altar in 8:3 is the same as the altar of 6:9. Though it is not agreed as to whether this altar is the brazen altar in the courtyard or the altar of incense: see Aune, *Revelation*, 2.511 Beale, *Revelation*, 455; Smalley, *Revelation*, 215.

30. I have been unable to find any dissenters.

31. That 'ἐν αὐτῷ' (in it) is masculine, referring to the temple, derives most reasonably from the context in that worshippers are more naturally 'in' the temple, rather than 'in' the altar. Beale, however, suggests that the antecedent of 'ἐν αὐτῷ' (in it) is 'τὸ θυσιαστήριον' (the altar); Beale, *Revelation*, 571.

32. Though 20:6 employs a future referent.

'τὴν σκηνὴν' (the tabernacle).³³ Beale, commenting on 13:6, affirms that, "The equation of the saints with the heavenly tabernacle is virtually the same identification made in 11:1-2, where true believers living on earth were equated with the invisible, indestructible sanctuary of God."³⁴ Thus, it is not uncommon for John to provide an additional phrase or two that further identifies who it is that comprises a given reference to a temple structure.

One possibility for our understanding of the designations of 'τὸ θυσιαστήριον' (the altar) and 'τοὺς προσκυνοῦντας' (the worshippers) is that John distinguishes between those whose fate is martyrdom (the people "ὑποκάτω τοῦ θυσιαστηρίου' ; "under the altar") and those who remain faithful without suffering martyrdom ('τοὺς προσκυνοῦντας') (the worshippers). Such may be accounted for by the conception that 'τὸ θυσιαστήριον' (the altar) and 'τοὺς προσκυνοῦντας' (the worshippers) symbolize component parts of 'τὸν ναὸν' (the temple).³⁵ The measuring of the temple and its component parts would then serve to accent that they both enjoy God's sovereign protection.

Do not Measure the Outer Court; The Holy City is Trampled (11:2)

The encouraging tone that initiates the account of 11:1–13 suddenly becomes more subdued. That difficulties loom for those who are measured may have been implied in the very fact that they had a need for such protection. John now presents a more explicit depiction pertaining to the suffering of the people on God's side.

Do not Measure the Outer Court

John is next commanded, 'μὴ αὐτὴν μετρήσῃς' (do not measure it) the 'τὴν αὐλὴν τὴν ἔξωθεν τοῦ ναοῦ' (the court which is outside of the temple; i.e., the outer court 11:2). This introduces a conundrum that appears in many ways to conflict with the previous assertion regarding to the divine

---

33. Aune, *Revelation*, 2.745–46; Beale, *Revelation*, 697; Caird, *Revelation*, 166–67; Morris, *Revelation*, 163–64; Mounce, *Revelation*, 250.

34. Beale, *Revelation*, 697.

35. This contention receives support in the work of Michael Bachmann. Bachmann argues that the use of measuring in Rev 11:1 and 21:15 begin by referencing a general item and then by delineating component parts of that item. He supports this contention by further appeal to Ezek 40–48. See his: 'Ausmessung von Tempel und Stadt,' in *Das Ezechielbuch*, 61–83.

protection of the people on God's side and has consequently resulted in a variety of scholarly proposals. I will suggest that each of these designations are parallel descriptions of the suffering/persecution of the people on God's side.

First, that the 'τὴν αὐλὴν τὴν ἔξωθεν τοῦ ναοῦ' (the court which is outside of the temple) represents persons derives from the reiteration of 'μετρήσῃς' (measure) in 11:2.[36] Since, the command to 'μέτρησον' (measure) in 11:1 symbolized the divine protection afforded the people on God's side, the reiteration of the same verb in the very next sentence strongly suggests a correspondence in use.[37] In fact, assertions proposing that this court represents anything other than persons must provide strong evidence how the measuring in 11:2 might connote something entirely different from the measuring in 11:1. The lack of contextual support for disassociating the measuring of the temple (11:1) from the measuring of this court (11:2), suggests that the latter represents persons and the command 'μὴ αὐτὴν μετρήσῃς' (do not measure it) suggests that in some facet divine protection is not afforded them.[38] Johnson, in fact,

---

36. Attempts to identify this court generally fall into one of three lines of thought. Those who typically espouse a more literal interpretation generally consider the outer court to be a reference to a physical location in the ancient Jewish temple, which is rebuilt in the last days. Walvoord, for example, suggests that the nations will actually have control of this area of Jerusalem, while allowing the Israelites to have the inner courts for the reconstituting of their sacrificial system (Walvoord, *Revelation*, 177).

Secondly, many of those who allow for greater symbolism in Revelation tend to understand the outer court as representing persons who have not sided with God. Among these are those who contend that the outer court represents unfaithful members of the church who have compromised; and, therefore, are not measured/protected (Hendriksen, *Conquerors*, 128; Kiddle, *Revelation*, 341; Stefanovic, *Revelation*, 341). Others suggest that those in the outer court who are not measured constitute unbelieving Jews (Swete, *Revelation*, 132–33; Feuillet, 'L'Apocalypse' 187–88; Beagley, *The 'Sitz im Leben' of the Apocalypse*, 61–63). Swete concludes, "If the temple represents the Church, the outer court is perhaps the rejected Synagogue" (Swete, *The Apocalypse*, 1908, 1968]; Cited by Harrington, *Apocalypse*, 151).

Finally, others propose that the outer court represents the people who have sided with God but from a different perspective from that of the measuring of the temple in 11:1: namely, that 11:2 connotes them as suffering persecution (Morris, *Revelation*, 142–43; Mounce, *Revelation*, 214; Allo, *L'Apocalypse*, 130; Lohse, *Die Offenbarung*, 64; Swete, *Revelation*, 182; Beagley, *Apocalypse*, 61; Boring, *Revelation*, 143).

37. Admittedly, 'measure' in 11:2 appears in terms of a negative command in 11:2.

38. Contra Stefanovic who claims, "The outer court is evidently in contrast to the temple of God in heaven and the worshippers. It seems to represent the forces . . . that are hostile to God and the gospel, viciously persecuting God's faithful people, and are

asserts, "This prohibition shows that what is measured is placed under divine protection, and what is not measured is exposed to assault by the nations." [39] But who are those who constitute the 'τὴν αὐλὴν τὴν ἔξωθεν τοῦ ναοῦ' (the court which is outside of the temple) and why are they not granted divine protection?

That the 'τὴν αὐλὴν τὴν ἔξωθεν τοῦ ναοῦ' (the court which is outside of the temple) refers to those on God's side, and not unbelieving Jews or apostatized believers, follows from the fact that it is a part of the Temple. I have already argued that the entirety of the people on God's side are encapsulated by the designations 'τὸ θυσιαστήριον' (the altar) and 'τοὺς προσκυνοῦντας' (the worshippers) in 11:1. If 'τὸν ναὸν τοῦ θεοῦ' (the temple of God), 'τὸ θυσιαστήριον' (the altar), and 'τοὺς προσκυνοῦντας' (the worshippers), represent persons, then 'τὴν αὐλὴν τὴν ἔξωθεν τοῦ ναοῦ' (the court which is outside of the temple), which also constitutes a component of the temple, similarly should be understood as representative of persons. That the 'τὴν αὐλὴν τὴν ἔξωθεν τοῦ ναοῦ' (the court which is outside the temple) is part of the temple complex is further evident by the command to 'ἔκβαλε' (cast *it* out; 11:2). Beale affirms, "That it is an essential part of the temple complex is suggested by the assumption in v 2 that it was formerly under the protection of the temple walls but is now to be 'cast out.'"[40]

Therefore, the command not to measure 'τὴν αὐλὴν τὴν ἔξωθεν τοῦ ναοῦ' (the court which is outside the temple) serves to inform John's readers that though they are divinely protected they are still subject to opposition and suffering. This serves to exemplify the flexibility inherent within the vision and as a reminder that a proper exegesis must account for a measure of fluidity.

The Holy City is Trampled

The assertion that the 'τὴν αὐλὴν τὴν ἔξωθεν τοῦ ναοῦ' (the court which is outside the temple) references persons is further evidenced by an examination of the next clause in 11:2 where John suggests that 'καὶ τὴν πόλιν τὴν ἁγίαν πατήσουσιν' (and they will trample the holy city).[41]

---

excluded from the kingdom" (*Revelation*, 341).

39. Johnson, *Triumph of the Lamb*, 167.
40. Beale, *Revelation*, 568–69.
41. Cf Dan 8:10, 13; Luke 21:24.

I suggest that the designation 'τὴν αὐλὴν τὴν ἔξωθεν τοῦ ναοῦ' (the court which is outside the temple) parallels the 'τὴν πόλιν τὴν ἁγίαν' (the holy city); and that both of these represent persons who side with God.[42] Aligning 11:2, as I have done below, suggests that the 'τὴν αὐλὴν τὴν ἔξωθεν τοῦ ναοῦ' (the court which is outside the temple) parallels 'τὴν πόλιν τὴν ἁγίαν' (the holy city); while the command to ἔκβαλε ἔξωθεν (cast out) similarly parallels 'πατήσουσιν' (they will trample).

καὶ τὴν αὐλὴν τὴν ἔξωθεν τοῦ ναοῦ ἔκβαλε ἔξωθεν καὶ μὴ αὐτὴν μετρήσῃς,
ὅτι ἐδόθη τοῖς ἔθνεσιν,
καὶ τὴν πόλιν τὴν ἁγίαν πατήσουσιν μῆνας τεσσεράκοντα [καὶ] δύο.

Supporting the conclusion that by not measuring 'τὴν αὐλὴν τὴν ἔξωθεν τοῦ ναοῦ' (the court which is outside the temple) John has in view the suffering/persecution of the people on God's side is the fact that the nations 'πατήσουσιν' (will trample) on the 'τὴν πόλιν τὴν ἁγίαν' (the holy city). The presence of the verb 'πατέω' (tread on; trample on: 11:2) corresponds with the reiteration of this verb in 14:20 and 19:15. Admittedly, the verb 'πατέω' (trample) is employed in the context of the punishment of the wicked in the latter two instances. This verb, however,—which appears only these three times in the Apocalypse (11:2; 14:20; and 19:15)—appears to invoke the principle of *lex talionis* in the context of the latter two occurrences.[43] That is: God punishes the wicked by "trampling" on them, because they "trampled" on the people who side with God. This is further evidenced by the fact that the latter two passages (14:20; 19:15) function as parallel accounts depicting the final judgment upon the wicked. Both, in fact, contain the identical expression: 'ἐπατήθη ἡ ληνὸς' (the winepress was trodden). Therefore, it appears that John may have employed 'πατέω' (trample) in 14:20 and 19:15 in order to affirm

---

42. Contra Seiss who contends, "we understand it by what the Scriptures always mean by the phrase, and interpret it with confidence of *Jerusalem*" (Seiss, *The Apocalypse*, 205–206).

43. John notes several times in Revelation the justness of God's wrath based on the principle of *lex talionis*. For example, in chapter 16 each of the seven angels are said to have 'ἐξέχεεν' (poured out; 16:2, 3, 4, 8, 10, 12, 17) their bowls. This is interrupted by an angel who then announces the justice of God's retributive acts: He is righteous, 'ὅτι αἷμα ἁγίων καὶ προφητῶν ἐξέχεαν καὶ αἷμα αὐτοῖς [δ]έδωκας πιεῖν, ἄξιοί εἰσιν' (because they have *poured out* the blood of the saints and prophets and you have given them blood to drink, they are worthy; 16:6). Perhaps, further evidence that correlates 11:2 with 14:20 is the presence of the preposition 'ἔξωθεν' (outside), which appears only in these two verses.

that God has invoked the *law of retaliation* upon those who "trampled" on the people on God's side in 11:2.

Also, that the 'τὴν πόλιν τὴν ἁγίαν' (the holy city) references the people on God's side derives also from the fact that this expression applies only to such people in Revelation.[44] Thus, the 'τὴν πόλιν τὴν ἁγίαν' (the holy city) is the New Jerusalem in 21:2, 10, 22:19, and is also the bride in 21:9–10).[45] Some may object at this point because they prefer to read the reference to 'τὴν πόλιν τὴν ἁγίαν' (the holy city) literally; applying to Jerusalem.[46] It appears best, however, to understand the 'τὴν πόλιν τὴν ἁγίαν' (the holy city) as designating those who side with God in parallel to 'τὴν αὐλὴν τὴν ἔξωθεν τοῦ ναοῦ' (the court which is outside the temple) and in correspondence with the designation of 'τὴν πόλιν τὴν ἁγίαν' (the holy city) in reference to persons in the consummation.

Furthermore, designating the people on God's side in 11:2 in terms applicable to the future eschatological New Jerusalem is not inappropriate for John. For in 13:6 he proleptically identifies them as, 'τοὺς ἐν τῷ οὐρανῷ σκηνοῦντας' (those who dwell in heaven; 13:6). This also is in accord with the teaching of the NT in terms of an already-not-yet eschatology. Hence, the author of Hebrews claims, 'προσεληλύθατε Σιὼν ὄρει καὶ πόλει θεοῦ ζῶντος, Ἰερουσαλὴμ ἐπουρανίῳ' (you have come to Mount Zion and to the city of the living God, the heavenly Jerusalem; 12:22).

FORTY TWO MONTHS AND 1,260 DAYS AS THE PERIOD OF PERSECUTION (11:2–3)

The account of the Two Witnesses employs the Danielic designation of three-and-one-half years. This era applies to both the period in which the Two Witnesses minister and the time of the cosmic war with the dragon. Thus, John employs, "μῆνας τεσσεράκοντα [καὶ] δύο' (forty-two months) in 11:2 and 13:5; 'ἡμέρας χιλίας διακοσίας ἑξήκοντα' (one thousand two

---

44. Admittedly, this expression is used throughout the Old and New Testaments for the literal city of Jerusalem. But Revelation clearly employs imagery throughout and in the case of this expression never uses it literally. Thus, the use of this designation in Revelation itself must be determinative for its application here. See: Beale, *Revelation*, 568.

45. Beagley notes that "John himself uses the term 'holy city' exclusively of the 'new Jerusalem.'" He adds that John "calls the present earthly Jerusalem 'Sodom' and 'Egypt.'" *Apocalypse*, 60. See also, Johnson, *Triumph*, 169–70; Thomas, *Revelation*, 93.

46. See also, Beagley, *Apocalypse*, 62; Cohen, *Understanding Revelation*, 133; Thompson, *Revelation*, 125.

hundred and sixty days) in 11:3 and 12:6); and "καιρὸν καὶ καιροὺς καὶ ἥμισυ καιροῦ" (time, times, and half a time) in 12:14.

That John's use of differing expressions of time derive from Daniel is evidenced by the fact that John employs the variant expression: 'καιρὸν καὶ καιροὺς καὶ ἥμισυ καιρου' (time, times, and half a time; Rev 12:14).[47] This phrase corresponds directly to the period of tribulation set forth in Daniel 7:25 and 12:7.[48] The use of "three and one-half years"—in all the variant forms—serves primarily as an indication of the era in which the people on God's side are persecuted. Stefanovic affirms, "the phrase exclusively refers to the period of the activities of the symbolic little horn in oppressing and persecuting the saints of God."[49]

The use of the Danielic time frame to mark the period in which the people on God's side are persecuted conforms to a classic apocalyptic style. This Danielic time designation appears throughout the literature of the second temple period in reference to a time of tribulation: either in relation to a general period of trial,[50] or in relation to the travails of the nation of Israel, both past and future.[51] Therefore, the various references to the "three and one-half years" in Revelation are alternative ways of referencing the apocalyptic period during which the people on God's side suffer.[52]

---

47. The proposed backgrounds of this time frame include the suggestion that this period corresponds to Israel's forty-two encampments in the wilderness (Num 33:5–49; see: Morris, *Revelation*, 147); or the forty-two years of the Israelites' wandering in the wilderness (Farrer, *Revelation*, 132; he proposes this based on the inference that the forty year punishment was not imposed on the Israelites until two years had passed). These suggestions adhere to the pronounced influence of Exodus throughout the book of Revelation, which receives confirmation from the correlation of the wilderness and the use of three and one-half years in 12:6 and 14.

48. Thomas suggests, "The time periods are identical in length and have similarities to their usage in the book of Daniel. It might even be the case that John was reading and re-reading the second half of Daniel as he wrote this book!" (*Revelation*, 93). See also: Beale, *Revelation*, 565–68; Caird, *Revelation*, 132; Fiorenza, *Revelation*, 77; Harrington, *Apocalypse*, 152; Hendriksen, *Conquerors*, 129, 143–44; Hengstenberg, *Revelation*, 396; Hughes, *Revelation*, 122; Keener, *Revelation*, 292; Morris, *Revelation*, 142–43; Mounce, *Revelation*, 215 Stefanovic, *Revelation*, 337–38.

49. Stefanovic, *Revelation*, 337–38.

50. E.g., *Midr. Ps.* 10:1.

51. E.g., *B. Sanhedrin* 97b-98a.

52. Aune, *Revelation*, 2.587.

That this 'καιρὸν καὶ καιροὺς καὶ ἥμισυ καιροῦ' (time, times, and half a time) designates the same era as the 'ἡμέρας χιλίας διακοσίας ἑξήκοντα' (one thousand two hundred and sixty days) of Rev 11:3 derives support from the reiteration of 1,260 days in 12:6, which functions in a parallel context to 12:14. For both 12:6 and 12:14 describe the divine protection accorded the woman. And, each makes mention of her having a 'τόπος' (place) in the 'ἔρημος' (wilderness).

The use of these time designations as the era in which the people on God's side suffer finds further support in the work of Richard Bauckham. Bauckham has convincingly argued that John has employed a numerical schema throughout Revelation.[53] He has demonstrated that John uses square numbers[54] to represent the people on God's side (144), triangular numbers[55] to represent the forces of evil that are opposed to the people on God's side (666), and rectangular numbers[56] to represent the period of time during which the forces of good and evil oppose one another (42; 1,260).[57] Thus, according to Bauckham, John's use of the Danielic era conforms to the apocalyptic conception that it represents the time during which the people on God's side are persecuted.

I would suggest, however, that the three and one-half years in Revelation 11 also appears to designate the time during which the beast

53. Bauckham, *Climax*, 384–407.

54. Square numbers are the result of adding successive odd numbers (1 + 3 + 5 . . .).

55. Triangular numbers are the result of adding successive numbers (1 +2 + 3 . . .).

56. Rectangular numbers are the result of adding successive even numbers (2 + 4 + 6 . . .).

57. Bauckham's analysis explains one of the more puzzling elements related to John's designation of the three and one-half years. For Daniel the three and one-half years is numerically designated as '1,290' days (12:11). John, however, though employing the Danielic designation of a 'time, times, and half a time' uses the numerical equivalent of 1,260 days. One can easily reconcile how each of these numerical designations could equate to three and one-half years. The outstanding question, however, is why John varies the numerical designation. Beale, in fact, asserts, "Why some of the periods in Daniel and Revelation are not stated with precisely the same formula is not clear" (Beale, *Revelation*, 565). Bauckham's insight seemingly provides the explanation. He suggests, "John preferred rectangular numbers" (Bauckham, *Climax*, 401). It appears that John consistently adhered to his numerical schema (i.e., that of utilizing numbers in accord with recognizable patterns) more strictly than he did the OT context in which he was alluding. Bauckham's proposal provides a long sought for explanation regarding the use of '1,260' days and in doing so provides further support for his thesis that the type of numbers (i.e., square, triangular, or rectangular) applies to the people on God's side, the wicked, or the eschatological time frame.

reigns and persecutes the people on God's side. For there is reason to suggest that this period of three and one-half years as the duration of the Two Witnesses ministry serves to link them with the prophets of the past: primarily Moses and Elijah. For, though 1 Kings 18:1 limits the time of Elijah's drought to less than three years, the Second Temple period traditions commonly transformed this time to either three or three and one-half years.[58] This connection, however, admittedly appears secondary at this point of the narrative. The relationship between the Two Witnesses and the great prophets of the past does, however, become explicit as the narrative proceeds.

MY TWO WITNESSES (11:3A, 7)

Revelation 11:3 turns its attention specifically to a description of the Two Witnesses and their function. The first and most obvious feature pertaining to the description of the Two Witnesses relates to the fact that they are characterized as witnesses. This facet of their role appears to be such a significant characteristic that 'τοῖς δυσὶν μάρτυσίν μου' (my two witnesses; 11:3) may even serve as a title for them. In the least, this description unequivocally depicts them, as with much in the following verses, as carrying out a prophetic witness.

In its usage elsewhere within the NT the noun 'μάρτυς' (witness) entails a legal dimension in terms of the context of one who establishes a legal testimony.[59] The term occurs primarily in the context of anyone bearing witness—especially God—or testifying to anything.[60] BDAG, in fact, notes, the "strong focus in all the NT passages in this classification is on the fact of witness."[61] Thus, 'μάρτυς' (witness) expresses the function of humans as witnesses—primarily in a passive sense.[62] In Revelation, this prophetic testimony is often stressed as a testimony to Jesus.[63]

In light of its contextual use in Revelation 'μάρτυς' appears to connote a more refined sense that also incorporates suffering, and perhaps death, as the consequence of bearing witness. In fact, it is likely that the

---

58. Cf. Luke 4:25; Jas 5:17; *Liv. Pro.* 21:5.
59. Cp. Acts 6:13; 7:58; 2 Cor 13:1; 1 Tim 5:19; Heb 10:28.
60. Cp. Rom 1:9; 2 Cor 1:23; Phil 1:8; 1 Thess 2:5, 10.
61. BDAG, 620.
62. Cp. 1 Thess 2:10; 1 Tim 6:12; 2 Tim 2:2.
63. Cf. especially 1:9; 2:13; 12:11, 17; 17:6.

association of this term in Revelation with the proclamation of the Gospel and the accompanying persecution that led to the application of this term in a more technical sense of "martyr" in the early church.

The prominence of this designation for the Two Witnesses is evident in that the use of 'μάρτυς' (witness) in 11:3 is followed by the use of the cognate 'τὴν μαρτυρίαν' (testimony; 11:7) to describe their conduct. Together these form a sort of an inclusio.[64] That is, the ministry of the Two Witnesses begins with their being designated as 'τοῖς δυσὶν μάρτυσίν' (the two witnesses) and closes only 'ὅταν τελέσωσιν τὴν μαρτυρίαν' (when they have finished their testimony).[65] Therefore, the account of the public ministry of the Two Witnesses begins in 11:3 with the declaration that "προφητεύσουσιν" (they will prophesy) and closes in 11:7 with a reiteration of this calling by reference to when 'τελέσωσιν τὴν μαρτυρίαν αὐτῶν' (they finish their testimony: 11:7).

That 'τὴν μαρτυρίαν' (the testimony) refers to their proclamation is contextually demanded by the use of the pronoun 'αὐτῶν' (their: 11:7). For, if μαρτυρία (testimony) here meant strictly 'martyrdom' it would be non-sensical—for how does one finish their own martyrdom? Hence, "testimony"—as found in most English translations[66]—must be an essential component of 'τὴν μαρτυρίαν' (the testimony) and, consequently, provides us with what is an insight into John's depiction of the Two Witnesses.[67]

This is further supported by the designation of them as 'δυσὶν' (two; 11:3). The use of *two* in referring to the number of witnesses likely derives its primary import from the OT law of legal witness.[68] This feature, which reappears in the following verses, serves as a confirmation that a leading feature of the Two Witnesses is that they are those who carry forth a valid legal testimony.

---

64. Evidence of the inclusio, also, includes that fact that each verse begins with an identical use of 'καὶ': See Aune, *Revelation*, 2.580.

65. That is, the description of their public ministry actually closes with their deaths in 11:7b.

66. The NJB actually uses "witnessing" instead of "testimony."

67. That their "testimony" results in their deaths may well be entailed in the context of Rev 11; as well as in the nuance of *marturia*. But, this will be reserved for discussion in the next chapter.

68. Cf Deut 17:6; 19:15. See: Hengstenberg, *Revelation*, 398; Johnson, *Triumph*, 170; Morris, *Revelation*, 143; Seiss, *Apocalypse*, 175.

THEY WILL PROPHESY CLOTHED IN SACKCLOTH (REV 11:3)

Prophesy (11:3, 6, 10)

The second half of Rev 11:3 continues the description of the Two Witnesses as functioning in a witnessing role by depicting them as engaged in prophetic activity. In 11:3, 6, 10, John depicts them as engaged in the act of prophesying. That the Two Witnesses serve as prophets is confirmed by the explicit reference to them as 'οὗτοι οἱ δύο προφῆται' (these two prophets) in 11:10.

Though some have contended that the grammar of 11:3 warrants the consideration that the Two Witnesses have a two-fold commission of both having "authority" and "prophesying," it appears that such is unnecessary. This suggestion results from the apparent need to insert an object for the verb 'δώσω' (give; 11:3)—such as "authority" or "power."[69] A proper understanding of the function of the two *kai*'s (and) in 11:3, however, renders this insertion as questionable. The Greek text of 11:3a reads: 'καὶ δώσω τοῖς δυσὶν μάρτυσίν μου καὶ προφητεύσουσιν' (And I will give[70] to my Two Witnesses and they will prophesy). As all recognize, the first *kai* (and) merely serves to continue the narrative of 11:1-2. It is my suggestion, however, that the second 'καὶ' (and) in 11:3 serves to introduce a result or consequence clause.[71] If so, 11:3 may be understood: "And I will give to my Two Witnesses in order that they will prophesy . . . ."[72] This renders as unnecessary the insertion of an object for 'δώσω' (give)—in accord with the lack of such in the Greek text. In fact, the fronting of the verb in 11:3 strongly suggests that the stress is on the divine issuance and not what is issued. Omitting "power" or "authority" from an English translation, though admittedly leaving a moderately awkward reading,

---

69. Most English translations add either 'authority' or 'power' as the object of 'δώσω' (I will give) in order to facilitate an easier reading of 11:3. The ESV, NAS, and NRS add "authority"; while the KJV, NIV, NLT, and RSV add "power."

70. Aune translates the verb 'δώσω' as 'permit' (*Revelation*, 2.577–78). I prefer the more common use of 'give' due to contextual indicators, which suggest that the Two Witnesses are empowered by God: note the divine passive 'ἐδόθη' in 11:1, which introduces the whole section.

71. Aune, *Revelation*, cxciii. See also: Aune, *Revelation*, 1.198; 1.231; 2.579; 2.787; 3.1074. Aune cites Ljungvik, *Syntax*, 82–83: who "provides examples of this use of paratactic καί as a substitute for a "ἵνα' clause or an inf." *Revelation*, 2.579.

72. The translation I have offered reflects that found in the NAB and NJB, as well as Aune: *Revelation*, 2.577.

serves to best accent this stress. The result of the divine issuance is the prophesying activity of the Two Witnesses.

Why, then, did John refer to them as finishing their "testifying" and not their "prophesying"?[73] I suggest that at least four factors may have influenced John's choice of terms. First, as mentioned above the use of 'τὴν μαρτυρίαν' (the testimony) forms an inclusio with the cognate 'μάρτυσίν' in 11:3. Secondly, 'τὴν μαρτυρίαν' (the testimony) would likely have been understood as parallel with 'προφητεύσουσιν' (they will prophesy). Thirdly, the choice of 'τὴν μαρτυρίαν' (the testimony) may have been influenced by the parallel account in 6:9–11; where the souls under the altar were killed 'διὰ τὴν μαρτυρίαν ἣν εἶχον' (on account of the testimony they had; 6:9).[74] Finally, it appears that John may have been more concerned to portray the Two Witnesses as those who provide a legal witness for God. And this is accomplished more directly by the use of 'τὴν μαρτυρίαν' (the testimony).[75] All this suggests that John had multiple reasons for preferring 'τὴν μαρτυρίαν' (the testimony).

Though determining the precise nature of their prophetic activity—whether it entails future predictions or simply the proclamation of the gospel—is the subject of much contention amongst Revelation scholars, one may well assert that it in the least comprises witnessing activity. That it here connotes far more than merely foretelling of the future derives from the nature of biblical prophecy. For, even in the OT, prophesy did not exclusively entail foretelling. Aaron was to be Moses' prophet, which was later affirmed to incorporate his role as the mouthpiece or spokesman for Moses.[76] Seiss asserts that, 'to prophesy is not simply to foretell the future events; but to exercise the functions of a witness for God.'[77] Boring affirms, "'Prophesy' means 'speak and act for God.'"[78]

---

73. That 'prophesying' is used in 11:3 is accounted for in that the Two Witnesses are depicted in terms of the great prophets of the OT (see below). Thus, 'prophesy' serves to connect them with the biblical tradition; while "testimony" links them with the legal element of trustworthy in their testimony.

74. See Beale, *Revelation*, 587–88.

75. See: Trites, Allison A, "Μάρτυς and Martyrdom in the Apocalypse: A Semantic Study," *NovT* 15 (1973): 72–80.

76. Seiss, *Apocalypse*, 2.154

77. Seiss, *Apocalypse*, 2.154.

78. Boring, *Revelation*, 144.

Clothed in Sackcloth

Next we see that the Two Witnesses wear the garb of the prophets.[79] The wearing of sackcloth may first conjure up an association with the proclamation of mourning on account of judgment and possibly repentance.[80] Swete has noted that in the *Ascension of Isaiah* 2:9-11 the garb of the prophets is sackcloth.[81] The most significant link with the wearing of sackcloth, however, is to that of the persons of Elijah and John the Baptist: both of whom were considered prophets.[82] This would suggest that their garb further associates them with their prophetic calling. A significant element of the prophetic ministry of the OT prophets was related to their role as witnesses in the covenant lawsuit.[83] The language of the lawcourt is prominent in Isaiah 41–50 and 56–66. Trites notes, "In Isa. 53:3-13 some of the formal elements of a controversy appear in the summoning, interrogation, accusations, resumption of interrogation and threats."[84] Such legal contexts among the prophets appear also in Amos 2; Hosea 2, 4, 5, and 12; Isaiah 1, 3, 5, 41–50; Micah 2 and 6; Jeremiah 2, 12, and 15; Ezekiel 17 and 20; and, Malachi 3.

Thus the donning of the garb of the prophets likely associates the Two Witnesses with their prophetic ministry in relation to the covenant lawsuit. Though this aspect of witness transcends the notion of witness of in the Apocalypse, it nonetheless serves to associate the Two Witnesses with the prophetic traditions.

THESE ARE THE TWO OLIVE TREES AND THE TWO LAMPSTANDS THAT STAND BEFORE THE LORD OF THE EARTH (11:4)

Revelation 11:4 begins without a conjunction and serves to further John's description of the Two Witnesses. Thus John continues, ʽοὗτοί εἰσιν αἱ

---

79. See; Beale, *Revelation*, 576; Hendriksen, *Conquerors*, 129; Morris, *Revelation*, 143-44; Stefanovic, *Revelation*, 345-46; Yeatts, *Revelation*, 193.

80. Cf. Jon 3:4-10; Matt 11:21; Luke 4:13. See: Bauckham, *Climax*, 277. Beale notes that twenty-seven of forty-two occurrences of sackcloth in the OT are associated with mourning alone, while an additional thirteen include repentance (*Revelation*, 576). See: Stefanovic, *Revelation*, 347-48.

81. Swete, *Revelation*, 184.

82. Cf. 2 Kings 1:8; Mark 1:6.

83. See: Trites, *Witness*, 33.

84. Trites, *Witness*, 33.

δύο ἐλαῖαι καὶ αἱ δύο λυχνίαι αἱ ἐνώπιον τοῦ κυρίου τῆς γῆς ἑστῶτες· (these are the two olive trees and the two lampstands who stand before the Lord of the earth). This imagery serves to further identify them as witnesses but also as those who serve a priestly function.

The use of 'λυχνίαι' (lampstands) appeared previously in Revelation in chapters 1–2 where the churches were specifically designated as 'ἑπτὰ λυχνίας χρυσᾶς' (seven golden lampstands; 1:12; cf also 1:13, 20; 2:1, 5). Though the designation of the Two Witnesses as 'λυχνίαι' builds upon John's identification of the seven churches, it is more likely that John has Zechariah 4 in mind in the account of the Two Witnesses.

Though a notable distinction between Revelation 11 and Zechariah 4 is present in that only one lampstand appears in Zechariah, it is beyond question that John's imagery derives from this OT passage.[85] In fact, an awareness of John's use of this imagery and its relationship to his use of Zechariah 4 will enhance our understanding of his use of 'λυχνίαι' both in this account and that of the seven letters. That Zechariah 4 is more prominently in view in John's account of the Two Witnesses derives first from the fact that they are designated as both, 'αἱ . . . ἐλαῖαι καὶ αἱ . . . λυχνίαι' (the olive trees and the lampstands; cf Rev 11:4; and Zech 4:2, 3, 11–14). This receives further support by means of the use of the anaphoric article 'αἱ' (the); which is best accounted for in terms of referencing the lampstand and olive trees of Zechariah. Briggs suggests, rightly I believe, that the presence of the articles before each of the items confirms that, "'*the* olive trees and *the* menorot which stand before the Lord of the earth' cannot help but lead the reader to identify them with the ones in Zechariah 4."[86] The declaration in Rev 11:4 in fact appears emphatic: 'οὗτοί εἰσιν αἱ δύο ἐλαῖαι καὶ αἱ δύο λυχνίαι' (these are the two olive trees and the two lampstands). Smalley observes, "Both images, olive trees and lampstands, appear in verse 3 with the definite article; . . . and this suggests that the metaphors and their significance would be well

---

85. See: Bauckham, *Climax*, 162–66; Beale, *Revelation*, 576–79; Caird, *Revelation*, 134; Hendriksen, *Conquerors*, 129; Keener, *Revelation*, 289–93; Morris, *Revelation*, 144; Mounce, *Revelation*, 218; Poythress, *The Returning King*, 126–27; Smalley, *Revelation*, 277.

86. Briggs, *Jewish Temple Imagery*, 65, n. 75. emphasis original. See also: Aune, *Revelation*, 2.612. Seiss, in fact, affirms, "all agree that the allusion is to Zechariah's vision" (*Apocalypse*, 2.202). See: Caird, *Revelation*, 134; Collins, *Jewish Temple Imagery*, 21; Court, *Myth and History*, 91; Johnson, *Triumph*, 170; Michaels, *Revelation*, 139; Stefanovic, *Revelation*, 345, 348; Thompson, *Revelation*, 126; Yeatts, *Revelation*, 193–94.

known to John's audience."⁸⁷ Aune affirms that it is articular, "because it is an allusion to the well-known menorah of Zech 4:2–3, 11."⁸⁸

In Zechariah, the two olive trees are identified as "the two anointed ones" (Zech 4:14), which, as most commentators affirm, was thought to represent the king (Zerubbabel) and the high priest (Joshua).⁸⁹ Thus, such imagery in Revelation would naturally have been understood by John's readers as applicable to the people of God (cf 1:6).

In Zechariah the lampstand has also long been recognized as symbolizing Israel.⁹⁰ The lamps on the lampstand are then understood as symbolizing God's Spirit which was to empower Israel in the completion of the construction of the Temple (Zech 4:6; cf Rev 4:5). Thus, the stress in Zechariah was on the sufficiency of the Spirit to accomplish the rebuilding of the Temple.

John's use of the imagery of 'αἱ δύο λυχνίαι' (the two lampstands) and 'αἱ δύο ἐλαῖαι' (the two olive trees), therefore, serves to associate the work of the Spirit in the life of the people on God's side in their priestly functions.⁹¹ Their priestly activity, however, appears to connote their witnessing activity. For in Acts 1:8, the commissioning of the people on God's side, 'ἔσεσθέ μου μάρτυρες' (you will be my witnesses) even to the remotest part of the earth, is directly linked with the empowerment of the Spirit. That the use of 'λυχνίαι' (lampstands) conveys the call to witnessing receives further support from the use of *lamp* in the OT and NT, the

---

87. Smalley, *Revelation*, 277.

88. Aune, *Revelation*, 612.

89. Smith goes so far as to suggest that this passage provides evidence for a diarchic structure between the king and priest in Israel at this time (Smith, *Micah-Malachi*, 207). Beagley, "The 'Sitz im Leben' of the Apocalypse," 65; Beale, *Revelation*, 577; Beasley-Murray, *Revelation*, 184; Caird, *Revelation*, 134; Court, *Myth and History*, 154, 192; Harrington, *Apocalypse*, 154; Hendriksen, *Conquerors*, 129 (with reservation); Keener, *Revelation*, 290; Mounce, *Revelation*, 217, n. 80; Seiss, *Apocalypse*, 203; Stefanovic, *Revelation*, 343, 348; Thompson, *Revelation*, 126; Walvoord, *Revelation*, 180; Yeatts, *Revelation*, 193.

90. See Beale, *Revelation*, 208; Motyer, *Zechariah*, 2003), 92. Cf *Midr*. Ps. 16.12; *Midr. Rab.* Lev. 30.2; 32.8; *Midr. Rab.* Num 13.8; *Midr. Rab.* Eccles. 4.1; *Midr. Rab.* Songs 4.7; *Sifre* Deut. 10; *Pesitka de Rab Kahana*, Piska 27.2; *Pesitka Rabbati* 7.7; 8.4; 51.4 all identify the lampstands of Zech 4 with Israel.

91. Beale affirms, "Despite resistance, the Christian community's successful establishment as God's temple throughout the church age is assured by means of the Spirit's empowerment of the church's faithful prophetic witness" (*Revelation*, 578).

Apocrypha, and non-biblical writings.[92] Even more prominent than this is the association of light with witness as found in the synoptics.[93]

John, therefore, employs Zechariah's imagery of the lampstands in application to the people on God's side (both the seven churches in chapters 1–2 and the Two Witnesses of chapter 11) in order to affirm the success of the witnessing activity of the people on God's side. Beale concludes, "So new Israel, the church, is to draw its power from the Spirit, the divine presence, before God's throne in its drive to stand against the world's resistance. . . . Consequently, the 'lampstand' (the church) is given power by the seven lamps on it, a power primarily to witness as a light uncompromisingly to the world."[94]

The question arises at this juncture as to why John envisions two lampstands when Zechariah presents only one? The suggestion that John's foremost concern was to demonstrate the legal validity and trustworthiness of the Two Witnesses' testimony provides an explanation for this modification. In fact, I would suggest that the use of *two* corresponds to the theme of witnessing and the legitimizing their testimony as was made explicit in 11:3. It appears that the central objective of the use of *two* continues to reiterate their prophetic functions.

The argument that John has a priestly conception derived from Zechariah 4 in mind is further strengthened by the assertion that the 'αἱ δύο ἐλαῖαι καὶ αἱ δύο λυχνίαι' (these are the two olive trees and the two lampstands) are 'αἱ ἐνώπιον τοῦ κυρίου τῆς γῆς ἑστῶτες' (who stand before the Lord of the earth) (11:4). This is a direct allusion to Zechariah 4:14.[95] That the Two Witnesses 'αἱ ἐνώπιον τοῦ κυρίου τῆς γῆς ἑστῶτες' (who stand before the Lord of the earth) further suggests a priestly function.[96] There is reason to suggest that this parallels Lev 24:4 where the "pure gold lampstand" is said to be "before the Lord."[97]

---

92. Cf., Zech 4:2–6; Matt 5:14–16; John 5:35; Sirach 48:1; *Targ. Ps.-J.* Zech 4:7. See Beale, *Revelation*, 574, who references *Sifre* Deut 10 and *Pesitka Rabbati* 51.4. Within this literature lampstand imagery also serves as a figurative expression for the Word of God, the message of the prophets, and the presence of God.

93. Cf., Mark 4:21–22; Matt 5:14–16; Luke 8:16–17.

94. Beale, *Revelation*, 207.

95. Cf Aune, *Revelation*, 2.612; Smalley, *Revelation*, 277.

96. Cp Exod 27:21; 30:8; Lev 24:3: where the priests 'stand before the Lord' in the tabernacle. See: Beale, *The Temple*, 321.

97. Note: the lampstand in Zech 4:2 is similarly said to be 'golden,' further strengthening the parallel. See: Beale, *Temple*, 321.

Therefore, it appears that John has designated the Two Witnesses as lampstands and olive trees in accord with a priestly function as associated with Zechariah. John, however, does so in a manner that accents their roles as witnesses.

ANYONE DESIRES TO HARM THEM; FIRE PROCEEDS FROM THEIR MOUTHS (11:5)

The fact that the Two Witnesses are divinely protected does not necessitate that they are exempt from suffering and persecution. Now John informs his readers that the Two Witnesses have an ability to defend themselves. The logical implication of this is that the ability to defend themselves is necessary because their opponents are attempting to inflict suffering upon them. Therefore, as the narrative proceeds, John now begins to make known the source of their suffering and persecution: namely, those who oppose them will try to harm them.

That the Two Witnesses suffer at the hands of their opponents is implied in the conditional statement, 'εἴ τις αὐτοὺς θέλει ἀδικῆσαι' (if anyone wants to harm them; 11:5). Though there is a basis for hesitation as to whether or not the conditional statement presupposes an actual attack against the people on God's side,[98] several contextual factors favor the conclusion that persecution is directly implied. First, that the statement implies at the referential level a real condition of the suffering of the Two Witnesses derives from the presence of suffering throughout the episode of the Two Witnesses: both implicit and explicit.[99] Secondly, it is reasonable, though not absolutely necessary, to suppose that if the Two Witnesses can "κατεσθίει τοὺς ἐχθροὺς αὐτῶν" (devour their enemies; 11:5), then such enemies must be conceived as attempting to inflict sufferings upon them. Bauckham, in fact, who also affirms that the Two Witnesses are subject to attack, notes, "The power of the two witnesses to call down fire to consume their enemies (11:5) indicates their immunity from attack for as long as—but no longer than—they need to complete

---

98. Wallace references this as a 'potential indicative' (Wallace, *Greek Grammar*, 451–52). Aune, however, suggests, "This is a typical first-class conditional sentence in which the conditional particle εἰ + indicative in the protasis (here the present indicative), with any tense of the indicative or imperative in the apodosis (BDF 371–72), emphasizes the reality of the condition; i.e., it is taken to be a real instance" (*Revelation*, 2.613).

99. The most explicit indication of their suffering is found in 11:7 where they are killed.

their testimony."[100] Finally, though a basis exists for viewing the powers of the Two Witnesses in terms of the effectiveness of their testimony, and not in terms of an ability to defend themselves, it appears that John predicates their powers upon the OT principle of *lex taliones*.[101] Consequently, the depiction of the Two Witnesses as 'κατεσθίει τοὺς ἐχθροὺς αὐτῶν' (devour their enemies) provides a measure of assurance to John's readers that amidst their sufferings it is the proclamation of the Word that serves as their defense.

The ability to spew fire out of their mouths ('πῦρ ἐκπορεύεται ἐκ τοῦ στόματος αὐτῶν': fire proceeds out of their mouth; 11:5), however, also serves as further attestation to their character as witnesses in the prophetic tradition.[102] This imagery serves to signify that at least a component of their message is one of judgment.[103] That 'ἐκ τοῦ στόματος αὐτῶν' (out of their mouths) primarily connotes their message derives from the use of fire proceeding from the mouth outside of the Apocalypse.

Jeremiah 5:14 provides a background for understanding the fire from the mouth of the Two Witnesses as representative of their message. It says, "because you have spoken this word, Behold, I am making My words in your mouth fire and this people wood, and it will consume them."[104] A. A. Trites proposes, "Their fire is the actual testimony which they must give in a Roman court of law."[105] Josephus, similarly, claims that Elijah's calling down fire from Heaven served to prove he was a true prophet.[106]

The figurative use of 'ἐκ τοῦ στόματος αὐτῶν' (out of their mouth) for words is evident in 4 Ezra 13. There the "man from the sea" is said to have no weapons of warfare, "but I saw only how he sent forth from his mouth as it were a stream of fire, and from his lips a flaming breath,

---

100. Bauckham, *Climax*, 277.

101. Cp. Deut 19:15; Num 35:30; Lev 24:17–21. See also the earlier discussion of 'trampling.' Cf. also, Rev 16:1, 2, 3, 4, 6, 8, 10, 12, 17; where the verb "ἐκχέω" is used for the *pouring out* of God's wrath in response to the *pouring out* of the blood of the saints. Cf. Ford, *Revelation*, 171.

102. Beagley, *Apocalypse*, 66; Thompson, *Revelation*, 126; Yeatts, *Revelation*, 193.

103. See: Beale, *Revelation*, 580–81; Caird, *Revelation*, 134; Hendriksen, *Conquerors*, 130; Keener, *Revelation*, 291; Mounce, *Revelation*, 218–19; Smalley, *Revelation*, 278.

104. NASB. Cp., also, Isa. 11:4; 1:16; 2:12, 16; 19:15, 21. Beagley, *Apocalypse*, 66; Hughes, *Revelation*, 124; Ladd, *Revelation*, 155; Sweet, *Revelation*, 185.

105. Trites, *Witness*, 167.

106. Josephus, *Ant.* 9.23.

and from his tongue he shot forth a storm of sparks" (4 Ezra 13:10).[107] This imagery is figuratively understood as connoting his "reproving" and "reproaching" the people (4 Ezra 13:37, 38). Also, this ability of the Two Witnesses likely contrasts with the demonic hordes in 9:17, 18; 13:5; and 16:13.[108] The references to the mouths of demonic, or demonically empowered entities (as in 13:1-10), and the reiteration of the deceptive aims of these beings (cp 13:14) form a stark contrast with the testimony of the Two Witnesses.

Furthermore, there is likely a contrast between the mouths of the demonic beings and the sword that proceeds from Christ's mouth (1:16; 2:12, 16; 19:15, 21). That the 'ῥομφαία δίστομος ὀξεῖα' (sharp two-edged sword; 1:16) represents His words parallels both Heb 4:12 and 2 Thess 2:8. In the latter passage, Christ 'ἀνελεῖ' (will slay) his enemies with the 'πνεύματι τοῦ στόματος αὐτου' (breath of his mouth). A combination of these passages and Revelation affirms that Christ defeats his enemies by His very proclamation; which the Apocalypse represents by a sharp two-edged sword.

Therefore, the portrayal of the Two Witnesses as able to defend themselves by means of spewing fire from their mouths serves to indicate both that they will suffer persecution and that their testimony is effective. It cannot escape notice, however, that implicit in this is another assurance of the divine protection of the Two Witnesses. For their powers of defense are assuredly not innate.

THESE MEN HAVE AUTHORITY (11:6)

The depiction of the Two Witnesses continues in 11:6 with the note that: 'οὗτοι ἔχουσιν τὴν ἐξουσίαν' (these men have authority/power). This description further points to their prophetic functions. This depiction, in fact, corresponds with the prophetic ministries of the OT prophets: in particular that of Moses and Elijah.[109] Most commentators, in fact, affirm

---

107 Charlesworth, *The Apocrypha and Pseudepigrapha*, 551.

108. The same phrase ("πῦρ ἐκπορεύεται ἐκ τοῦ στόματος αὐτῶν") (fire comes out of their mouth) occurs in 9:17, 18.

109. See: Barnhouse, *Revelation*, 199-203; Boring, *Revelation*, 146; Bousset, *Offenbarung*, 318-19; Collins, *Apocalypse*, 71; Court, *Myth and History*, 93; Fiorenza, *Revelation*, 78; Harrington, *Apocalypse*, 155; Hendriksen, *Conquerors*, 130; Keener, *Revelation*, 290-91; Kraft, *Offenbarung*, 1974), 156; Lohmeyer, *Offenbarung*, 90; Morris, *Revelation*, 143; Seiss, *Apocalypse*, 180-205; Stefanovic, *Revelation*, 348-49; Thomas,

John's Portrayal of the Two Witnesses 29

that the Two Witnesses are depicted in terms of the prophetic tradition of Moses and Elijah.[110] That the Two Witnesses are depicted in terms of the prophetic tradition of Moses and Elijah is well acknowledged.[111] Depicting them in such prophetic terms, of course, supports the contention that the Two Witnesses function as witnesses.

The allusions to the prophetic ministries of Moses and Elijah occur primarily in terms of the power of the Two Witnesses. For the Two Witnesses are empowered to 'κλεῖσαι τὸν οὐρανόν, ἵνα μὴ ὑετὸς βρέχῃ' (close the heavens, in order that it might not rain; 11:6) and 'ἐπὶ τῶν ὑδάτων στρέφειν αὐτὰ εἰς αἷμα' (over the waters to turn them into blood; 11:6). The first of these reminds one of the ministry of Elijah (cf 1 Kings 11). The latter alludes to the first of Moses' miracles in Egypt (cf Exod 7:14–25). What is perhaps of even greater significance to the overall message of Revelation is that each of these miracles were the responses of the great prophets to pagan rulers. In this regard Bauckham notes,

> Moses' contest with Pharaoh and his magicians and Elijah's with Jezebel and the prophets of Baal were the two great Old Testament contests between the prophets of Yahweh and pagan power and religion, in which Yahweh's power and authority were vindicated against the claims of pagan gods and rulers. The same is to be true of the beast, though vindication will take a different form and have greater consequences.[112]

Beale notes that these powers "do not demonstrate outwardly their prophetic legitimation but indicate rather God's protection of them."[113]

Revelation, 95; Wilcock, *Heaven Opened*, 105; Walvoord, *Revelation*, 180; Yeatts, *Revelation*, 193–95.

110. See: Aune, *Revelation*, 600, 603; Bauckham, *Climax*, 275–77; Beale, *Revelation*, 582–85; Beasley-Murray, *Revelation*, 180; Caird, *Revelation*, 135; Charles, *Revelation*, 283; Court, *Myth and History*, 98; Hopkins, "Historical Perspective of Apocalypse 1–11," 45; Mounce, *Revelation*, 216; Poythress, *The Returning King*, 129; Walvoord, *Revelation*, 180; Wilcock, *Heaven Opened*, 105.

111. See: Beale, *Revelation*, 573. For a discussion as to why John appears to depict them in terms of Moses and Elijah see: Bauckham, *Climax*, 276–77. See also, Tan, "The Identity of the Two Witnesses in Revelation 11," 31–58.

112. Bauckham, *Climax*, 277.

113. Beale, *Revelation*, 579.

THE BEAST WILL KILL THEM (11:7)

With 11:7 the narrative suddenly turns. The positive affirmation appears in that they will successfully complete their ministry ('ὅταν τελέσωσιν'; when they finish). But now John suddenly introduces a shocking notion: 'τὸ θηρίον τὸ ἀναβαῖνον ἐκ τῆς ἀβύσσου ποιήσει μετ' αὐτῶν πόλεμον καὶ νικήσει αὐτοὺς καὶ ἀποκτενεῖ αὐτούς' (the beast that comes up out of the abyss will make war with them and will conquer them and will kill them; 11:7). This explicit statement of opposition provides a measure of affirmation for the earlier conclusion that the Two Witnesses, though divinely protected, are not exempt from harm.

The deaths of the Two Witnesses are explicitly noted to occur only 'ὅταν τελέσωσιν τὴν μαρτυρίαν αὐτῶν' (when they have finished their testimony; 11:7). That their deaths do not occur until 'τελέσωσιν τὴν μαρτυρίαν αὐτῶν' (they have finished their testimony) does not necessarily imply that they do not suffer until the end of their ministries, but only that they do not die until they have completed their ministerial calling. The focus, I suggest, resides not with the conception that they are immune from suffering until they have completed their ministries, but on the time of their deaths.

Finally, there appears to be an implicit measure of encouragement in this pronouncement. For the opposition of this beast will not result in their deaths until their ministries are complete!

BODIES WILL LIE IN THE STREET OF THE GREAT CITY (11:8)

That the Two Witnesses are murdered provides the most explicit statement of the opposition to them. Though they endure persecution, John's account of the deaths of the Two Witnesses suggests that their suffering transcends death. In doing so, John further associates their suffering in accord with the prophets of old.

The association of the Two Witnesses with the suffering of the great prophets of the past is accentuated by John's note that after their deaths their bodies lay, "ἐπὶ τῆς πλατείας τῆς πόλεως τῆς μεγάλης, ἥτις κᾶλεῖται πνευματικῶς Σόδομα καὶ Αἴγυπτος, ὅπου καὶ ὁ κύριος αὐτῶν ἐσταυρώθη" (in the street of the great city which spiritually is called Sodom and Egypt, where also their Lord was crucified; 11:8).[114] That this

---

114. Identifying whether this city is actually Rome, Jerusalem, the Roman Empire, etc., is not pertinent to this investigation; and, therefore, will not be addressed here.

city is deemed 'Σόδομα καὶ Αἴγυπτος' (Sodom and Egypt) serves to associate it with places in which the people on God's side have suffered at the hands of their enemies. That this city is identified as 'ὅπου καὶ ὁ κύριος αὐτῶν ἐσταυρώθη' (where also their Lord was crucified) directly links the suffering of the Two Witnesses more directly with the suffering of Christ. The use of 'Αἴγυπτος' (Egypt) may derive from the association of it as the paradigm for the nation who mistreats God's people (cf Joel 3:19). Such usage is also found in some of the rabbinic writings. R. Jose b. Chalaphta notes, "All kingdoms are called by the name Egypt because they enslave Israel."[115] The inclusion of 'Σόδομα' (Sodom) also suggests a city that was known for its ill treatment of the people on God's side (cf Gen 19:1–29; Deut 32:32). Thus, Trites postulates that, "This city is called 'Sodom' because it is devoted to evil and destined to destruction. . . . It is termed' Egypt' because in it the people of God are persecuted and oppressed."[116] Beale affirms that the description of 'Sodom and Egypt' suggests, "places where the saints lived as aliens under persecution."[117]

Thus, John's note that their bodies lie in the street of a city that is figuratively called 'Σόδομα καὶ Αἴγυπτος' (Sodom and Egypt) and 'ὅπου καὶ ὁ κύριος αὐτῶν ἐσταυρώθη' (where also their Lord was crucified) serves to relate the suffering of the Two Witnesses with that of the prophets of the past and with Christ.

THREE AND A HALF DAYS (11:9, 11)

Next John notes that the bodies of the Two Witnesses were allowed to remain unburied for 'ἡμέρας τρεῖς καὶ ἥμισυ' (three and one-half days; 11:9, 11). A first reading of three and one-half may strike the reader as something unexpected. For one may expect John to have employed "three days" or "three days and three nights" in accord with the Gospel tradition. Aune attempts to explain it by noting that, "The statement that the two prophets were lying dead in the public square for *three and one-half* days suggests a partial parallel to the three-day period between the death and resurrection of Jesus."[118] I would contend, however, that the use of 'ἡμέρας τρεῖς καὶ ἥμισυ' (three and one-half days) does not associate as directly

---

115. Str. B. 3.812. (Court, 101).
116. Trites, *Concept of Witness*, 168.
117. Beale, *Revelation*, 591.
118. Aune, *Revelation*, 2.587.

with the death of Christ, but continues Johns preference for associating the Two Witnesses with the prophetic tradition.

John's preference, as noted above, for three and one-half (cf 11:3; 12:6, 14; 13:5)—especially as it relates to the Danielic era of suffering—and the possible association with the three and one-half years of Jesus' ministry appear to provide a more substantive explanation for his use of 'ἡμέρας τρεῖς καὶ ἥμισυ' (three and one-half days). Bauckham concludes,

> The parallel continues with the resurrection and ascension of the witnesses after three and a half days (11:9, 11). John has converted the 'third day' of the Gospel tradition into 'three and a half days,' just as the tradition he followed with regard to Elijah's drought converted the 'third year' of 1 Kings 18:1 into 'three and a half years'. The fate of the witnesses is given an apocalyptic period appropriate to the allusion to Daniel 7:21 in 11:7, but the Danielic allusion is interpreted by reference to the history of Jesus which provides the model for his faithful followers.[119]

RESURRECTED AND ASCEND INTO HEAVEN IN A CLOUD (11:11-12)

John closes his account of the Two Witnesses with an affirmation that though they appear to have been defeated, it is indeed they who are the true victors. Just as the readers may have been surprised by the sudden intrusion of the beast (11:7) into the narrative and his killing of the Two Witnesses, so now the narrative affirms the resurrection and ascension of the Two Witnesses in the presence of their enemies (11:11-12). This likely served as an encouragement to John's readers that it is the people on God's side who are the vindicated.[120]

Validating the conception that the Two Witnesses are the true victors is the presence of the confirming voice: 'φωνῆς μεγάλης ἐκ τοῦ οὐρανοῦ' (great voice from heaven: 11:12), which was said to be heard by the inhabitants of the earth! This affirmation of the victory of the people on God's side is intensified in that it occurs even while, 'ἐθεώρησαν αὐτοὺς οἱ ἐχθροὶ αὐτῶν' (their enemies beheld them; 11:12). Thus, Beale concludes,

---

119. Cf. Bauckham, *Climax*, 280.

120. Ladd affirms that it serves as a "sign to those whom they had been witnesses that they were truly prophets" (Ladd, *Revelation*, 159). Ladd, however, contra the view presented here, suggests that the entire chapter is predictive of the final salvation of the Jewish people (cf. 151f).

God restores the witnesses to himself after their apparent defeat at the end of the church age. The restoration consists in an overturning of their vanquished condition. The portrayal of the restoration depicts God raising the witnesses from the dead before the eyes of their enemies. . . . It seemed that God had deserted the witnesses by leaving them in a subdued condition. . . . But he vindicates them by delivering them and demonstrating that he is their covenantal protector. . . . At the least, the ascent of the witnesses figuratively affirms a final, decisive deliverance and vindication of God's people at the end of time.[121]

This exegesis has attempted to examine how John portrays the people on God's side in the account of the Two Witnesses. This work will now address the issues surrounding the identity of the Two Witnesses.

---

121. Beale, *Revelation*, 596–97.

3

Issues Pertaining to the Study of the Two Witnesses

AFTER EXAMINING THE VISION of Rev 11:1–13, this work now seeks to determine the implications of the exegesis of the account of the Two Witnesses both in terms of understanding John's depiction of those who side with God and the hortatory implications. This chapter will address three preliminary issues that must be addressed before we may derive conclusions from the previous exegesis of Rev 11:1–13. First, we must attempt to determine the identity of the Two Witnesses. Second, we must consider the narrative relationship between the measuring of the Temple (11:1–2) and the Two Witnesses (11:3–13). The third issues relates to the portrayal of the Two Witnesses as participants in 'holy war.'

THE TWO WITNESSES AS CORPORATE REPRESENTATIVES OF THE PEOPLE OF GOD

One of the key questions pertaining to the account of the Two Witnesses relates to their identity—who are these Two Witnesses? Many efforts have been undertaken to identify them. Some have determined that they reference two literal individuals. The most common propositions identify them with Enoch and Elijah[1] or Moses and Elijah.[2] A plethora of other

---

1. Enoch and Elijah: Virtually the unanimous conclusion of Patristic exegesis after Irenaeus and Tertullian: Tertullian, *De anima* 50; Hippolytus, *de Ant.* 46.3-4; *Comm. in Dan.* 4.35.3; 4.50.1-2; Augustine, *Ep.* 193.3, 5; *De Gen. ad litt.* 9.5; Jerome, *Comm. In Evang.* Mt. 3.57; Lang, *Revelation*, 185; Seiss, *Apocalypse*, 242–68.

2. Moses and Elijah: Charles, *Revelation*, 1.281; Hal Lindsay, *New World Coming*, 149–50.

alternatives have also been set forth along these lines.³ Others have suggested an allegorical approach to determining the referents of the Two Witnesses. Among these proposals are the suggestions that the Two Witnesses represent symbolically the law and the prophets; or the Old and the New Testaments.⁴ Aune proposes that a mythological approach. He contends that they represent a mythological prophet of God.⁵ Still others have argued that they represent a corporate entity.⁶ Those who view the Two Witnesses as a corporate depiction of the people of God often differ as to whether or not they represent a component of the people of God or the entirety of them.⁷ It is my contention that they represent the entirety of the people of God.

---

3. E.g., Jeremiah and Elijah: Victorinus, *Comm. In Apoc.* XI.3 (ed Haussleiter, *Victorinus*, 98); Peter and Paul: Court, *Myth and History*, 90–104; Giet, *L'Apocalyse et l'Historie*, 40; J. Munck, *Petrus und Paulus in der Offenbarung Johannis*, 33–34; James and John: considered by Kraft, *Die Offenbarung*, 156; James the Apostle and James the Lord's brother, or Stephen: considered by Kraft, *Offenbarung*, 156; John the Baptist and Jesus: considered by Kraft, *Offenbarung*, 156; Two Jewish High Priests murdered in 68 A.D.: Alford, *The Greek Testament* IV, 659; Leivestad, *Christ the Conqueror*, 228–30; Two Christian prophets predicting the fall of Jerusalem prior to 70 A.D.—James and Peter: Russell, *The Parousia*, 430–44; Purely eschatological prophets: Beckwith, *Apocalypse*, 595; Walvoord, *Revelation*, 179; Zahn, *Introduction to the NT* III, 424–28.

4. A) Law and the Prophets: Feuillet, "Essai," 196. B) Law and the Gospel C) Old and New Testaments: view held by Tyconius, Primasius, Beatus, Bede. D) Israel and the Church E) Israel and the Word of God

5. He claims that they represent a mythological account of a prophet of God (doubled by John) who is confronted by a godless, evil tyrant: Aune, *Revelation*, 2.603.

6. See also; Allo, *L'Apocalypse*, 160–61; Aune, *Revelation*, 2.602; Beale, *Revelation*, 574–75; Boring, *Revelation*, 146; Farrer, *Revelation*, 133; Johnson, *Triumph*, 170; Keener, *Revelation*, 291–97; Metzger, *Code*, 70–71; Stefanovic, *Revelation*, 349; Swete, *Revelation*, 134; Wilcock, *Heaven Opened*, 105.

7. Those who identify them corporately include: A) Part of the Christian community: Bauckham, *Climax*, 273–83; Caird, *Revelation*, 134–38; Johnson, "Revelation", 504; Kiddle and Ross, *Revelation*, 183; Minear, *New Earth*, 99; Morris, *Revelation*, 147–48; Rissi, "Das Judenproblem", 49–50; Trites, *Witness*, 164–70. B) All Christians: Allo, *L'Apocalypse*, 160–61; Beale, *Revelation*, 572–73; Beasley-Murray, *Revelation*, 183–84; Boring, *Revelation*, 145–46; Hendriksen, *Conquerors*, 110; Metzger, *Breaking the Code*, 70–71; Lacy, "The Two Witnesses", 55; Smalley, *Revelation*, 275; Swete, *Revelation*, 134; Strand, "The Two Witnesses", 134; Wall, *Revelation*, 143–44; Wilcock, *Heaven Opened*, 105–106.

The Two Witnesses are 'Lampstands'; and they Represent the People of God

That the Two Witnesses represent a corporate entity composed of the entirety of the people of God may be evidenced by a number of features. First, the Two Witnesses are specifically designated as 'λυχνίαι' (lampstands: 11:4). We noted in chapter 2 that this imagery explicitly referenced churches in Rev 1:20. Since, however, the Two Witnesses are represented as only two of the seven lampstands, Caird, among others, contends that they represent only a fraction of the people of God. He claims, "The two lamps, then, are a proportion of the church in all parts of the world; and they provide the clearest possible evidence that John did not expect all loyal Christians to die."[8] On the surface Caird's argument is compelling. It is widely acknowledged, and I concur, that the seven lampstands of Rev 1–3 are representative of the whole of the people on God's side.[9] And since the Two Witnesses are both killed, it stands to reason that they must not represent all of the people on God's side, or John would then be suggesting that all of the people of God suffer martyrdom.

But Caird's argument may weaken when we consider the fluidity of the visionary elements in the Apocalypse. We must consider the immediate context of each account before assuming that the imagery necessarily conveys a one to one correspondence in meaning. For it may well be that John has chosen to reference the Two Witnesses as 'αἱ δύο λυχνίαι' (the two lampstands) not because he was concerned to demonstrate that only a portion of the people of God suffer martyrdom,[10] but because, in the

---

8. Caird, *Revelation*, 134. Emphasis original.

9. See: Bauckham, *Climax*, 274; Beasley-Murray, *Revelation*, 184; Caird, *Revelation*, 134; Keener, *Revelation*, 291; Mounce, *Revelation*, 218. I do think that the seven lampstands at the same time literally represent the actual seven churches of Asia and symbolically represent the whole of the people on God's side.

10. As suggested by Caird, *Revelation*, 134; Yeatts, *Revelation*, 193. I do concur with the understanding that Revelation does not depict the entire community of the people of God as suffering martyrdom, but I do not accept the argument that only two-sevenths of the people of God are martyred because only two of the seven lampstands are present in the account of chapter 11. This argument, however, does have the added appeal that it alleviates a difficulty attached with the position that I have taken; namely, if the Two Witnesses represent the entire community of the people of God, then does not this account depict the entire people of God community as suffering martyrdom? I will respond to this argument below. Allow me to add here the thought that though such a quandary arises with the position I have taken, this does not demand that we impose on the context of Rev 11 a reading that is foreign to the account in order that we may have less trouble in our exegesis.

context of the account of the Two Witnesses, the *two* certified the legitimacy of their testimony in accord with the OT law of legal witness. This is supported by the appeal in both passages to Zechariah 4, where, as we noticed previously, only one lampstand was present. Therefore, the best explanation as to why John has envisioned *two* lampstands, even though as we have established that he has Zechariah in mind, is that John is concerned to portray them in accord with the Deuteronomic requirement for the verification of an authentic testimony. That is, only "two" lampstands are referenced may be accounted for simply by appeal to the law of legal witness. The significance of the numerical designations in each passage (seven churches; two witnesses), thus, are best understood in terms of their immediate contexts. The Witnesses are only two in 11:1–13 because that is the minimum requirement for a valid legal testimony.

Therefore, though the appeal to the presence of only two witnesses as evidence that only a fraction of the church is martyred—in an effort to maintain the symmetry between the presence of the lampstands in chapters 1–3 and chapter 11—is understandable, it is likely not warranted in Rev 11:4. Caird, in fact, himself shows a measure of hesitancy in justifying the view that the Two Witnesses represent only a fraction of the church: "We might have concluded from this that John expected only two of the seven churches of Asia to suffer martyrdom (perhaps the blameless churches of Smyrna and Philadelphia), were it not that in each of the seven letters there was a promise to the Conqueror."[11]

Consequently, the context of 11:4 favors the identification of the Two Witnesses as a corporate reference to the people of God. Bauckham supports this conclusion:

> John is nothing if not consistent in his very precise use of imagery. If the seven lampstands are churches, so must be the two lampstands. But it would be better to say that, if the seven lampstands are representative of the whole church, since seven is the number of completeness, the two lampstands stand for the church in its role of witness, according to the well-known biblical requirement that evidence be acceptable only on the testimony of two witnesses.[12]

---

11. Caird, *Revelation*, 134.
12. Bauckham, *Climax*, 274.

The Beasts Wages War with Them

Second, that the Two Witnesses are portrayed as corporate representatives for the entirety of the people of God is evidenced by the fact that the beast makes "war" against them. John states, 'τὸ θηρίον τὸ ἀναβαῖνον ἐκ τῆς ἀβύσσου ποιήσει μετ' αὐτῶν πόλεμον' (the beast, who comes up out of the abyss, will make war with them; 11:7). It has long been noted that one hardly makes war against only two persons.[13]

Their Deaths are Viewed by All

Third, an identification of the Two Witnesses as encompassing a community and not two individuals may be evidenced by the fact that their dead bodies are said to be viewed by all the inhabitants of the earth (11:9). This imagery naturally suggests to the reader that they represent far more than two individuals. The suggestion that this occurs by means of the use of a global television network (e.g., CNN) is incredible.[14] For John, and God speaking through John, knowing his readers' conceptual world, would have taken into account their conceptualizations. Thus the awareness that such could some day be possible by means of modern communication media must be pronounced alien to the original meaning. Furthermore, we have established through our exegesis of Rev 11:1–13 that Revelation employs symbolic imagery. That John's readers would have understood the whole world viewing the bodies of these two men as a figurative depiction of the world contemplating a corporate entity provides the best reading.[15]

---

13. Tan acknowledges the strength of this argument but counters, "granted, it seems difficult to imagine a war against just two people, but these individuals will have extraordinary powers" (Tan, *Identity*, 12).

14. See: Barnhouse, *Revelation*, 204; Lindsay, *New World Coming*, 151; Tan, "Two Witnesses," 25.

15. We must recognize that we are embroiled in the midst of a hermeneutic debate and not merely an exegetical one. I would contend at this juncture that adhering to a strict grammatical-historical methodology results in the reading I have proposed. That God could have asserted His authorial intent and inspired this verse with the knowledge that CNN would broadcast their deaths is wholly plausible. However, such a reading is not necessary when there is ample reason to acknowledge that John's readers would have understood this passage in terms of the corporate identity of the Two Witnesses. Consequently, there is no reason to look elsewhere for a more scientific answer.

Two Witnesses are Described as a Unity

That the Two Witnesses are best understood as corporate representatives of the people of God is found in that, as we have seen, they are always depicted in unified terms. Thus, their powers, attributes, titles, and fate are shared equally. For example, it is said that fire proceeds out of 'αὐτῶν τοῦ στόματος' (their mouth; 11:5); and when they have finished 'αὐτῶν τὴν μαρτυρίαν' (their testimony; 11:7). In both verses the pronouns are plural but the accompanying nouns are singular.

In fact, the suggestion that the Two Witnesses are two particular individuals encounters a significant difficulty when, after John notes in 11:7 that the Beast 'ποιήσει μετ' αὐτῶν πόλεμον' (will make war with them) and 'νικήσει αὐτοὺς' (will overcome them) and 'ἀποκτενεῖ αὐτοὺς' (will kill them), he then continues in 11:8 with reference to the fact that 'τὸ πτῶμα αὐτῶν' (their body) will lie in the street. This use of the singular noun (τὸ πτῶμά; 'body') in conjunction with the plural pronoun (αὐτῶν; 'their') strongly contends for a corporate understanding of the Two Witnesses. John, in fact, utilizes precisely the same construction in 11:9.[16] In 11:9b, however, John employs the plural noun alongside the plural pronoun (τὰ πτώματα αὐτῶν; 'their bodies'). Many commentators propose that the two singular nouns should be read as collective singulars.[17] This leaves unanswered why John employed the plural 'τὰ πτώματα' (bodies) in 11:9b? Swete suggests that the use of the plurals derives from the association with burial, which necessitates separate reference to the bodies.[18] This explanation, though suspect,[19] may account for the plural in 11:9b but it leaves us perplexed as to why the singulars in 11:8–9a. Beale suggests, "The likely reason for the change in number is to connote the corporate nature of the witnesses. They are one 'body' of Christ who witness, but they are also many witnesses scattered throughout the earth."[20]

---

16. Though there are text critical issues with the singular nouns in both 11:8 and 11:9. The textual evidence for the singular in 11:8 is strong (A and C; though P47 and a both support the plural 'τα πτωματα' 'bodies'). The textual evidence for the singular in 11:9a is unambiguous (with A, C, P47, and a all having the singular).

17. See: Beale, *Revelation*, 594; Beckwith, *Apocalypse*, 601; Swete, *Apocalypse*, 137.

18. Swete, *Apocalypse*, 138–39.

19. Beale concludes that Swete's answer "is not convincing" (*Revelation*, 594).

20. Beale, Revelation, 594. The presence of a plural noun is easily accounted for by the fact that they are 'two'. If they were to be viewed as individual persons, then the presence of the singular nouns remains unaccounted.

The Two Witnesses serve as Kings and Priests which Reference all of the People of God in Rev 1:6.

Finally, we have seen that the Two Witnesses are depicted in terms of kingly and priestly functions. Such designations also support a corporate identification of them.[21] Though one may well consider the Two Witnesses as referencing individual Christians who function as kings and priests in accord with John's earlier depiction of the people of God as 'βασιλείαν καὶ ἱερεῖς' (a kingdom and priests; 1:6; 5:10), it is my suggestion that we are equally, if not more, justified in viewing the account of the Two Witnesses as in accord with these earlier corporate references. This conclusion receives support from the fact that every other occurrence of the kingly and priestly functions of the people of God in Revelation relate to the entirety of the people of God.

One may, however, simply contend that the Two Witnesses function as individuals who corporately represent the entirety of the people of God. This position, however, essentially corresponds with that represented in this work. For in the same way that the calling of the twelve apostles serves as an outstanding example of the general calling of all believers, so also what is characteristic of the Two Witnesses is likewise characteristic of the community as a whole.

RELATIONSHIP BETWEEN 11:1–2 AND 11:3–13

Another important questions pertaining to the account of the Two Witnesses relates to its proper starting point. I argued briefly in chapter 2 that the measuring of the Temple in 11:1–2 serves to at least provide a foundation for our understanding of the context of 11:3–13. In chapter 4, I will assess the portrait of the people of God in each of these sections. There, it will be argued that the thematic considerations warrant the viewing of 11:1–2 and 11:3–13 as a whole. However, I desire first to examine the structural evidence in favor of viewing 11:1–13 as a literary unit in which John extends the thoughts relating to the measuring of the Temple and applies them to the activities of the Two Witnesses.[22] Another way of phrasing this is that the depiction of the Two Witnesses attempts both

---

21. Beagley, *Apocalypse*, 65; Boring, *Revelation*, 145; Court, *Myth and History*, 92; Johnson, *Triumph*, 170; Keener, *Revelation*, 292–93; Swete, *Revelation*, 185.

22. See; Court, *Myth and History*, 85; Johnson, *Triumph*, 169; Minear, *New Earth*, 99; Stefanovic, *Revelation*, 343; Thompson, *Revelation*, 125.

to continue the episode of the measuring of the temple and to develop in greater detail the implications of such an act. Hence, Minear can refer to 11:1–13 as, "One of the longest unbroken speeches in the entire book."[23] And Caird affirms that, "The object of measuring the Temple was to ensure that God's Two Witnesses should have free scope to complete their testimony without hindrance from inner doubts or outward coercion."[24] The evidence for viewing the measuring of the Temple (11:1–2) and the account of the Two Witnesses (11:3–13) as a coherent unit is multifaceted.[25] Such a conclusion will only add force to the conclusions relating to the thematic similarities in the two accounts.

11:1–2 and 11:3–13 Utilize the Same Danielic Time Period

First, there is the reiteration of the Danielic time period of three and one-half years in each section.[26] For the time-frame of forty-two months during which the city is to be trampled (11:2) corresponds with the 1,260 days during which the Two Witnesses are empowered (11:3). The juxtaposition of these references to the three and one-half years establishes the correspondence between the measuring of the Temple and the account of the Two Witnesses. Fiorenza suggests, "The time of persecution and suffering caused by the monster coincides with the time of the two witnesses . . . as well as with the duration of the woman's (12:6, 10) and the true worshipper's protection (11:2). These narrative symbolizations prophetically illuminate in different ways the same 'last time' of tribulation."[27]

11:1–2 and 11:3–13 Both Apply Temple Imagery to the People of God

The introduction to the Two Witnesses (11:3–4) parallels the measuring of the Temple in 11:1–2 by employing Temple imagery in each account. In regard to these parallels, Court suggests, "the parallelism may be contrived . . . in order to express more clearly and emphatically the connec-

---

23. Minear, *New Earth*, 95.
24. Caird, *Revelation*, 133.
25. See: Aune, *Revelation*, 585; Boring, *Revelation*, 143.
26. Bauckham suggests that the references to the time frame provide the only link between these two sections (*Climax*, 267). See: Keener, *Revelation*, 340.
27. Fiorenza, *Revelation*, 84. See also: Caird, *Revelation*, 166–67; Considine, "The Two Witnesses,": 386; Court, *Myth and History*, 87; Johnson, *Triumph*, 171; Stefanovic, *Revelation*, 407; Wilcock, *Heaven Opened*, 125; Yeatts, *Revelation*, 244.

tion we have observed already between the episode of the measuring and trampling and the episode of the witnesses."[28] For this reason, Beale asserts that, "Verses 3–6 explain the primary purpose of the 'measuring' in vv 1–2. That is, God's establishment of his presence among his end-time community as his sanctuary is aimed to ensure the effectiveness of their prophetic witness."[29]

Such parallels are evident in that both accounts employ temple imagery in application to the people of God. We have shown that the reference to the 'τὸν ναὸν τοῦ θεοῦ' in 11:1 best reads as a referent to the entirety of the people of God. This corresponds with the account of the Two Witnesses, which as I have already argued symbolizes corporately the whole of the people of God.

Also, the Two Witnesses are depicted as 'αἱ δύο ἐλαῖαι καὶ αἱ δύο λυχνίαι' (the two olive trees and the two lampstands; 11:4) in accord with Zechariah 4. This use of lampstand imagery in application to the Two Witnesses affirms correspondence between the episode of the measuring of the temple and the account of the Two Witnesses. But, as noted in chapter 2, this imagery in Zechariah was understood as symbolic of the people of God. Therefore, the account of the Two Witnesses begins by applying Temple imagery from Zechariah 4 that corresponds with the people of God in parallel with the use of Temple imagery for the people of God in Rev 11:1–2. Consequently, the presence of this temple imagery in reference to the people of God in the account of the Two Witnesses serves to note that correspondence between 11:1–2 and 11:3–13.

Furthermore, as noted in chapter 2, the Two Witnesses 'αἱ ἐνώπιον τοῦ κυρίου τῆς γῆς ἑστῶτες' (those who are standing before the Lord of the Earth). This designation also suggests a priestly function and further associates the Two Witnesses with the Temple of 11:1–2. In light of the application of all this temple imagery and the allusions to Zech 4 in the account of the Two Witnesses, Beale concludes:

> The establishment and preservation of the true temple despite opposition has been introduced in Revelation 11:1–2, and Zechariah 4:14 is a climax to a section concerning the very same topic. Just as the priest and king were the key vessels used by the Spirit for the establishment of the temple against opposition, so here the

---

28. Court, *Myth and History*, 88.
29. Beale, *Revelation*, 572. See: Fiorenza, *Revelation*, 77.

two witnesses are likewise empowered by the Spirit to perform the same role in relation to 11:1–2.[30]

Others contend, based on a literalistic reading of Revelation, that there is a distinction between the focus of 11:1–2 and 11:3–13. That is, 11:1–2 references a literal Temple, while 11:3–13 references two literal persons who will function as God's eschatological evangelists.[31] I have already established that the Temple represents the whole of the people of God and that this corresponds with the Two Witnesses as corporate representatives of the whole of the people of God. If true, then an identity exists between the people of God in 11:1–2 and the Two Witnesses of 11:3–13. This identity holds true regardless of the position taken as to whom the Two Witnesses represent. That is, even if we held to the position that the Two Witnesses are two distinct eschatological people of God, they would still be a component of the people of God symbolically represented by the imagery of the Temple in 11:1–2.

The Unity of 11:1–13 in Response to Source Critical Claims

Some, however, suggest that the measuring of the Temple in 11:1–2 should be disassociated from the account of the Two Witnesses (11:3–13). This notion is based on several suppositions. First, some have contended that 11:1–2 derive from a different source than 11:3–13. The most popular theories set forth that contend for a different source for 11:1–2 were proposed by Wellhausen,[32] Bousset,[33] Charles,[34] and others;[35] as well as more recently by Collins[36] and Aune.[37] Wellhausen claimed that 11:1–2 was originally a fragment of a "Zealot pamphlet" written prior to the destruction of the Temple in A.D. 70. This hypothetical reconstruction contends that the original intent of the scene was that of a prophecy designed to assure the Jerusalemites that the Temple would not be destroyed even if

---

30. Beale, *Temple*, 323.
31. E.g., Wong, "The Two Witnesses,": 344–54.
32. Wellhausen, *Offenbarung*, 15.
33. Bousset, *Offenbarung*.
34. Charles, *Revelation*, 1.270.
35. This view also received support from Beasley-Murray, *Revelation*, 176–77; Beckwith, *Apocalypse*, 586–87; Kraft, *Offenbarung*, 152–54; Lohse, *Offenbarung*, 64.
36. Collins, *Combat Myth*, 195 n. 60.
37. Aune, *Revelation*, 2.593–97; see also, Boring, *Revelation*, 143.

the city were to be occupied. One must wonder, however, why John would incorporate into his work a failed prophecy! Charles responds to this allegation by proposing that John reinterpreted the prophecy so that he viewed it as affirming a preservation from spiritual dangers.[38] Bauckham responds, "It is highly unlikely that in Revelation 11:1–2 John intends to speak literally of the temple which had been destroyed in A.D. 70 and the earthly Jerusalem, in which he nowhere else shows any interest."[39]

But, even if we were to give credence to the suggestion that 11:1–2 existed independently of John's writing, this in no way demands that John could not have woven disparate accounts into a cohesive narrative. As Boring suggests, "Whatever its past, the picture of measuring the temple is now an integral part of the whole visionary scene of 11:1–13."[40]

THE PEOPLE OF GOD AS HOLY WARRIORS

Several works has discussed the use of holy war and its relation to the book of Revelation.[41] The impact of this aspect of the Apocalypse's imagery will be evidenced throughout this work. At this point we merely want to establish the reality of its presence in Revelation and the account of the Two Witnesses in particular.

Two recent works have discussed the role of holy war in Revelation. The work of Tremper Longman focuses primarily on Christ as a 'divine warrior.'[42] Longman notes five features in the depiction of the return of Christ in Rev 19:11–16 that impress the reader to view Christ as a holy warrior. First, Christ is wearing a robe dipped in blood (19:13). He is leading a heavenly army (14). He has a sharp sword in his mouth (15).

---

38. Charles, *Revelation*, I.274.

39. Bauckham, *Climax*, 272.

40. Boring, *Revelation*, 143. Mounce adds, "Since we recognize by now that John makes use of his sources with a sort of sovereign freedom, it is far more important to understand what *he* is saying than to attempt a reconstruction of the originals" (*Revelation*, 212).

41. Cf. esp. Bauckham, *Climax*, 210–37; Longman, "The Divine Warrior." Holy war has also been the subject of Collins, *Combat Myth*; Ford, *Revelation*; Giblin, *Revelation*. This holy war, however, is an ironic war. For the weaponry of the Two Witnesses is not that of traditional warfare, nor is their goal the death of their opponents. Instead, they fight by means of their 'testimony' and their intended outcome is the conversion of their enemies. Their victory is secured not in the death of their opponents, but in their own deaths.

42. Longman, *Warrior*, 290–307.

He is treading the wine press (15). And, He is presented as the, 'Βασιλεὺς βασιλέων καὶ κύριος κυρίων' (King of Kings and Lord of Lords; 16).

The people of God as holy warriors is argued persuasively in the work of Richard Bauckham.[43] Bauckham contends that Revelation metaphorically portrays holy war in terms of *"human participation."*[44] He notes that among the extent Jewish apocalypses the participation of the people of God in holy war is essentially unique to Revelation; paralleled only by the War Scroll in Qumran. In the Jewish apocalypses, holy war is waged either by God alone, or by God and His heavenly armies. Bauckham argues that the account of the 144,000 in Rev 7 and 14 depict the righteous as a 'messianic army.'[45] The primary strength of Bauckham's position is the numbering of the 144,000 as 12,000 from each of the twelve tribes, which bears the marks of a census. Consequently, he asserts, "That the 144,000 Israelites are those called to serve God in battle is clear from the form of 7:4–8: a *census* of the tribes of Israel. In the Old Testament a census is always the counting up of the *military* strength of the nation."[46] This contention receives further justification from the fact that the 144,000 are said to be males of military age in 14:4. Therefore, Bauckham concludes, "As we have seen, human participation in the eschatological war is not rejected in Revelation, but emphasized and, again, *depicted* in terms drawn from traditions of holy war, which are then carefully reinterpreted in terms of faithful witness to the point of death."[47]

That the righteous, by participation in this holy war, are depicted as suffering follows naturally. Bauckham in fact notes:

> Therefore, instead of simply repudiating apocalyptic militancy, he *reinterprets* it in a Christian sense, taking up its reading of Old Testament prophecy into a specifically Christian reading of the Old Testament. He aims to show that the decisive battle in God's eschatological holy war against all evil, including the power of Rome, has already been won—by the faithful witness and sacrificial death of Jesus. Christians are called to participate in his war

---

43. Bauckham, *Climax*, 210–38.
44. Bauckham, *Climax*, 212.
45. Bauckham, *Climax*, 215–32.
46. Bauckham, *Climax*, 217.
47. Bauckham, *Climax*, 233.

and his victory—but by the same means as he employed: bearing the witness of Jesus to the point of martyrdom.[48]

Though a thorough analysis of these works and the issue of holy war in general extend beyond the parameters of this work, a cursory look into this issue appears to provide a measure of confirmation to the suggestion that Revelation incorporates holy war themes and depicts the righteous as persecuted.

CONCLUSION

Consequently, I suggest that we have strong reason for understanding the narrative of 11:3–13 as an expansion upon the episode of the measuring of the Temple in 11:1–2. That is, John utilizes the depiction of the ministry of the Two Witnesses in order to develop his understanding of the people of God. The relationship between 11:1–2 and 11:3–13 is one in which John utilizes the account of the measuring of the Temple (11:1–2) in order to highlight the divine protection that is granted the people of God. The nature of their prophetic ministry for which they are called and the corresponding persecution that inevitably follows, though hinted at in 11:1–2, are then detailed in 11:3–13.

The Two Witnesses represent the entirety of the people of God amidst holy war. Therefore, we may now examine the results of our exegesis of 11:1–13 in terms of the manner in which John portrays the whole of the people of God.

---

48. Bauckham, *Climax*, 234.

4

The Main Themes Pertaining to the People of God in the Account of the Two Witnesses and the Hortatory Implications

This chapter intends to summarize the varying imagery associated with the people of God in the account of the Two Witnesses (11:1–13) based on the exegesis of chapter 2. The goal of this inquiry is to ascertain the features pertaining to the people of God in this account in order to gain insights into John's hortatory intent. The observations here are derived strictly from the exegesis of 11:1–13.

THE FOUR THEMES PERTAINING TO THE PEOPLE OF GOD PRESENT IN THE ACCOUNT OF THE TWO WITNESSES

In working through the exegesis of the account of the Two Witnesses it appears that four themes dominate John's depiction of the Two Witnesses. These four themes are: they are divinely protected; they are called as witnesses; they are persecuted; and, they are ultimately vindicated. Are these the only features present in the account of the Two Witnesses? Not necessarily. But though other features pertaining to John's depiction of the people of God are present it appears that these features most often function as subsidiary components of the four themes that are clearly present.

For example, the Two Witnesses are depicted in terms of engaging in a prophetic ministry. Thus, they wear the garb of the prophets, as well as perform miracles in accord with the prophetic ministries of Moses and Elijah. The portrayal of them as prophets, however, corresponds with the first theme that they function as God's witnesses. Furthermore, their ability to defend themselves corresponds both to their being divinely protected and their enduring persecution. Thus, the four themes that I presented here are essentially designations of larger categories that subsume almost every aspect of John's portrayal of the people of God in the pre-consummation visionary section of Revelation.[1] Furthermore, since other features pertaining to the people of God are not consistently reiterated, it will be determined that these four themes provide the most helpful insights pertaining to John's depiction of the people of God in the pre-consummation section of the Apocalypse.[2]

Divine Protection of the People of God

The first of the four themes relates to the divine protection of the people of God. The account of 11:1–13, in fact, opens with an emphatic announcement of the divine protection of the Two Witnesses. In fact, several features pertaining to the account of the Two Witnesses affirm that the people of God are divinely protected emissaries.

John opens this account with the prophetic commission to measure the Temple (11:1). It was affirmed in our exegesis that this act serves as a metaphorical, prophetic act (in accord with John's prophetic commissioning in 10:11) that conveys the assurance of divine protection for that which was measured. This meaning corresponds with Zechariah 1 and 4, where the measuring of the Temple served to affirm its protection. That it was the 'τὸν ναὸν τοῦ θεοῦ' (temple of God) (11:1), which we have seen spiritually applies to the people of God, that was measured confirms the

---

1. Admittedly, one may well find other 'themes' pertaining to the people of God in the pre-consummation visionary section of Revelation (e.g., they cry out before God in 7:10; and they sing in 14:3). Since, however, they do not find repeated emphasis in the extended narratives that concern the people of God, they will not be examined in this work.

2. When I speak of 'themes' relating to John's portrait of the people of God, I am not referring to the titles or the imageries associated with the people of God, but to the significance of such designations. Thus, the use of 'lampstands' accords with the theme of witnessing. Furthermore, the designation of the 144,000 as 'sealed' relates the truth that they are divinely protected. Consequently, the use of differing imagery in application to the people of God in two corresponding accounts may nonetheless connote varying expressions of the same themes and bolster the contention that the portrayal of the people of God in one account accords with that of another. Thus, for example, I will argue in the body of this work that the 'sealing' of the 144,000 in Rev 7 corresponds with the 'measuring' of the Temple in Rev 11.

suggestion that the account of Two Witnesses opens with the assurance of the divine protection for the people of God.

The divine protection of the people of God also appears in that the Two Witnesses have divine powers to defend themselves (11:5–6). Though this ability supports the themes relating to their call to witness and that they suffer persecution, we must not overlook the fact that the power to defend themselves implies a means of divine protection over them.

Also, the fact that they are not killed until 'ὅταν τελέσωσιν τὴν μαρτυρίαν αὐτῶν' (when they have finished their testimony; 11:7) implicitly affirms that God sovereignly protects them during the course of their ministry. Thus, we may surmise, during the course of their ministry the Two Witnesses are afforded divine powers to defend themselves and will not suffer martyrdom until they have completed their ministry.

The Two Witnesses as Witnesses

Perhaps the most apparent feature pertaining to John's account of the Two Witnesses relates to theme of their prophetic commissioning as God's witnesses. Much of this narrative is concerned to demonstrate that not only do the Two Witnesses function as prophetic mouthpieces of God, but that they do so effectively.

First, we noticed that the Two Witnesses receive the explicit title of "τοῖς δυσὶν μάρτυσίν" (the Two Witnesses; 11:3). We noted that in its usage elsewhere within the NT the noun 'μάρτυς' (witness) often entails a legal dimension in terms of the context of one who establishes a legal testimony and that it therefore essentially related to anyone who bore a witness—especially God. The importance of this designation is highlighted by the use of the cognate 'τὴν μαρτυρίαν' (testimony) in 11:7 to describe their conduct and that these two nouns form a sort of an inclusio relating to the ministry of the Two Witnesses. Thus, the ministry of the Two Witnesses opens and closes with a description of their function as God's witnesses.

Also, the importance of their task as witnesses is exemplified in the care that John takes to portray them as effective heralds of God's truth. This is evident by the designation of them as 'δυσὶν' (two; 11:3) witnesses; which recalls the OT law of legal witness.

Second, that the Two Witnesses specifically function as witnesses receives affirmation in that their commissioning is that, 'προφητεύσουσιν' (they will prophecy; 11:3). In fact, we noted numerous elements in the account of the Two Witnesses that linked them with the great prophets of the past. They are 'περιβεβλημένοι σάκκους' (clothed in sackcloth; 11:4) as with the prophetic traditions of Elijah and John the Baptist. Their powers link them with the great prophets of the past; especially that of Moses and Elijah. That 'πῦρ ἐκπορεύεται ἐκ τοῦ στόματος αὐτῶν' (fire proceeds out of their mouth; 11:5) has been shown to associate them with Elijah. In fact, the parallel with Jeremiah 5:4 and Elijah's calling fire from heaven also serve to indicate that the 'πῦρ' from the mouths of the Two Witnesses symbolically conveys the effectiveness of their message.

Third, John identifies the Two Witnesses as the "αἱ δύο λυχνίαι" (the two lampstands; 11:4), which we argued recalled the imagery from Zechariah. The declaration of the Two Witnesses as the lampstands was rather emphatic: 'οὗτοί εἰσιν' (these are: 11:4). We have shown that the imagery in Zechariah and throughout the NT affirms that the lampstands are empowered by the Spirit in their role as witnesses (cf Acts 1:8).

The account of the Two Witnesses also suggests that they are engaged in a holy war and that they serve as priests. John's conception of their participation in holy war and their priestly service, however, appears to correlate with role as covenant witnesses.

Though the Two Witnesses role in holy war is not explicitly stated, the fact that they are engaged as holy warriors is implied by the fact that the beast is said to wage war against them (11:7). One may surmise that the Two Witnesses engage in this war with 'τὴν ἐξουσίαν' (the power) of 11:5. However, we have seen that the powers that they possess associate them with a prophetic tradition as heralders of truth. Thus, their participation in this war is primarily by means of their prophetic witness.

The depiction of the Two Witnesses as priests, which is slightly more explicit than the use of holy war imagery, also accords with their function as witnesses. We have shown that John derived his priestly conceptions of the Two Witnesses from Zechariah and that he understood their role as primarily engaged in bearing witness. Thus, the Spirit's empowering the lampstands is understood as the One who equips the Two Witnesses to be effective proclaimers.

Finally, that the Two Witnesses are primarily depicted as witnessing is further supported by the fact that from 11:3a to 11:7 no further characteristics are listed as part of the mission of the Two Witnesses. For 11:3 concludes with the reference to the Danielic time period of three and one-half years (1,260 days) as the duration of their prophetic ministry. Verse 4, then, forms an emphatic clause clarifying the identity of the Two Witnesses. Verse 5 continues the narrative—note the identical use of 'καὶ' (and) as in 11:3a³—with a conditional clause indicating the immunity of the Two Witnesses from harm during the course of their ministry. Verse 6 provides more details pertaining to the powers granted them. These powers, mimicking the great prophets of the past, serve to confirm that the Two Witnesses are engaged in prophetic activities. The Two Witnesses, therefore, are described not only as prophesying, but perhaps even solely in this capacity.

The People of God as Suffering Persecution and Perhaps Martyrdom

Thirdly, John depicts the Two Witnesses as those who must suffer persecution and possibly martyrdom. This theme appears throughout the narrative and climaxes with the death of the Two Witnesses.

The most direct confirmation of the suffering of the Two Witnesses appears in the explicit statement that: 'τὸ θηρίον τὸ ἀναβαῖνον ἐκ τῆς ἀβύσσου ποιήσει μετ' αὐτῶν πόλεμον καὶ νικήσει αὐτοὺς καὶ ἀποκτένει αὐτούς' (the beast that comes up out of the abyss will make war with them and will conquer them and will kill them; 11:7). Though the Two Witnesses suffering of martyrdom confirms that thesis that they suffer persecution, other aspects of the narrative also suggest that they suffer persecution during the time of their ministry.

The suffering of the Two Witnesses was evidenced to be the meaning behind the somewhat enigmatic commands for John to 'ἔκβαλε ἔξωθεν' (cast out) and not to 'μετρήσῃς' (measure), 'τὴν αὐλὴν τὴν ἔξωθεν τοῦ ναοῦ' (the court outside the Temple; 11:2). It was argued in the exegesis that this court must also reference persons in accord with the symbolic meaning of the Temple in 11:1. Furthermore, the casting out of this court and the failure to measure it suggests that divine protection was provided for it. This is further suggested by the declaration that 'τὴν πόλιν τὴν ἁγίαν πατήσουσιν' (they will trample the holy city; 11:2).

Furthermore, that the Two Witnesses suffer persecution is evidenced by the use the Danielic time period for the duration of their ministry. The use of "three and one-half years"—in all the variant forms—we argued served primarily as an indication of the era in which the people of God

---

3. See Aune, *Revelation*, 2.579.

are persecuted. It was noted that John uses this designation in accord with classic apocalyptic style. The association of "three and one-half" with the Danielic era of suffering was also seen to provide the best explanation for the use of 'ἡμέρας τρεῖς καὶ ἥμισυ' (three and one-half days; 11:9, 11) in reference to the period of their death and non-burial. One would more naturally expect a reference to "three days" or "three days and three nights" in accord with gospel tradition. Nonetheless, John appears to have been more concerned on this point with associating the Two Witnesses with the suffering of God's people in the past.

Furthermore, John notes that the suffering of the Two Witnesses transcend their deaths. For after their deaths John notes that their bodies lay, "ἐπὶ τῆς πλατείας τῆς πόλεως τῆς μεγάλης, ἥτις καλεῖται πνευματικῶς Σόδομα καὶ Αἴγυπτος, ὅπου καὶ ὁ κύριος αὐτῶν ἐσταυρώθη" (in the street of the great city which spiritually is called Sodom and Egypt, where also their Lord was crucified; 11:8). This we suggested served to thoroughly associate them with the suffering of the people of God in history. The designation of the city as "Σόδομα καὶ Αἴγυπτος" (Sodom and Egypt) we have seen served as a reference to places in which the people of God have suffered at the hands of their enemies.

The designation of the Two Witnesses as "witnesses" not only accords with the theme that they serve as prophetic covenant witnesses, but also with their suffering. For the use of the 'μάρτυς' (witness) word group and the fact that the consequence of one's witness appears to be persecution and possibly even death, suggests that 'μάρτυς' (witness) may have also suggested a connotation that included suffering. Aune, in fact, concludes, "The term occurs just three times elsewhere [i.e., in application to the righteous] in Revelation, always in connection with those who die for their faith (2:13; 11:3; 17:6), suggesting the possibility that 'μάρτυς' (witness) here connotes the faithful witness who has sealed his testimony through *death*."[4] Charles likewise affirms that 'μάρτυς' (witness) is closely related to martyrdom: "For the seer expects all the faithful to seal their witness with their blood."[5]

It is true that by the second century 'μάρτυς' (witness) and its cognates were used widely in the sense of martyrdom.[6] Strathmann associ-

---

4. Aune, *Revelation*, 1.37.

5. Charles, *Revelation*, 1.62.

6. Polycarp (19.1); Melito of Sardis (*H.E.* 4. 26. 3). Polycrates in his letter to Victor of Rome about the paschal question.

ates this transition of the term to its use in the "church of Asia Minor."[7] It is possible that *martureo* (the cognate verbal form) was utilized in the context of martyrdom as early as Clement of Rome in the late first century. In fact, the strong association of witness and persecution, conveyed not only by the use of 'μάρτυς' (witness), but perhaps also by the constant association of the righteous throughout Revelation as witness bearers who suffer as a result of their testimony, likely influenced the development of 'μάρτυς' (witness) in the early church so that it came to expressly connote martyrdom. Court may have best summarized the situation: "If the technical term for 'martyr' is not yet established, this is the situation out of which that usage was born."[8]

Finally, we should note that the powers of the Two Witnesses to defend themselves against 'τοὺς ἐχθροὺς αὐτῶν' (their enemies; 11:5) implies that they have enemies who are opposing them and perhaps causing suffering. Admittedly, we have already noted that these abilities relate primarily to the effectiveness of their testimony. Nonetheless, they also appear to predicate that the Two Witnesses suffer persecution.

How can the People of God be Divinely Protected and yet Persecuted?

Admittedly, the thought that the Two Witnesses are divinely protected as well as exempt from martyrdom until their ministries are completed, and the presence of the power to defend themselves, which certainly implies that the Two Witnesses will suffer persecution, creates a tension. For what does this divine protection entail if it fails to eliminate all suffering? At this point we may first state the obvious: whatever the divine protection entails, it does not exclude the possibility of persecution nor even eventual martyrdom.[9]

---

7. Strathmann, *TWNT*, 4.506.

8. Court, *Myth and History*, 90.

9. Contra Aune, who states, "The view that protection in Revelation means not security against physical suffering and death but rather support in and through suffering and death and support from spiritual danger seems to me to subvert the meaning of the text" (*Revelation*, 2.604). Aune, however, from this writer's perspective grants too much authority to source critical analyses of Revelation, and, consequently, views this passage in isolation from the whole of the Apocalypse. If this episode of measuring were viewed in light of the whole of Revelation, then there is ample evidence to suggest that though the people of God enjoy divine protection, they, nonetheless, are not immune to suffering (cp 2:10; 3:10; 13:10). Of course, in the account of the Two Witnesses one may contend that martyrdom occurs only after the protection is removed; i.e., they are killed only after they have finished their testimony. This contention, however, would be mitigated by

The conclusion that the measuring of the Temple connotes the divine protection of the people of God, while both the failure to measure the outer court and the trampling of the holy city, as well as the martyrdom of the Two Witnesses entails their persecution and martyrdom, results in an apparent incongruity. This apparent inconsistency is alleviated only when the true nature of the divine protection has been delineated. For I suggest that God's sovereign protection of the people of God relates primarily to their true spiritual status.[10]

That Revelation portrays the people of God as recipients of persecution should not surprise the student of the Bible. Jesus warned his disciples, 'ἐν τῷ κόσμῳ θλῖψιν ἔχετε' (in the world you have tribulation; John 16:33). And Paul emphatically declared, 'πάντες δὲ οἱ θέλοντες εὐσεβῶς ζῆν ἐν Χριστῷ Ἰησοῦ διωχθήσονται' (all who desire to live a godly life in Christ Jesus will be persecuted; 2 Tim 3:12). In fact, the conception that the people of God suffer is so prevalent throughout the Bible that I would suggest that John's readers would never have understood their being divinely protected as an exemption from all harm.

In all, the contextual indicators suggest that the divine protection of the people of God does not exempt them from harm and even death. Therefore, this protection is best understood as a spiritual preservation of their souls. Beale comments, "They may undergo bodily, economic, political, or social harm, but their eternal covenant status with God will not be affected. One reason they were measured was so that they would prosper in their prophetic witness despite persecution."[11] That the measuring suggests on a literary level physical protection, after all they cannot be killed

---

a comprehensive analysis of the portrait of the people of God throughout Revelation—which naturally extends beyond our limitations. Also, if we are able to establish that the divine protection afforded the Two Witnesses entails the divine presence, then we have reason for doubting that this protection is ever removed (Collins, *Apocalypse*, 53).

Collins, in commenting on the relationship of the 'sealing' in Rev 7 and Ezek 9 suggests that John has altered the use of sealing from that of Ezekiel. For, "it does not symbolize divine protection from physical harm and death. Rather, it symbolizes divine protection within and in spite of suffering and death" (*Apocalypse*, 52).

10. Commentators view the notion of divine protection throughout Revelation in the following manner: spiritually (Beale, *Revelation*, 409–410; Hughes, *Revelation*, 93–94); protection from demons (Charles, *Revelation*, 269); or, as some form of physical protection (Mounce, *Revelation*, 218–19; Walvoord, *Revelation*, 140; Lindsay, *New World*, 107–08). On the other hand, Caird claims that it is "ambiguous, since it does not protect them from death" (*Revelation*, 97).

11. Beale, *Revelation*, 579.

until they have finished, is true. Nonetheless, the primary connotation is that of a spiritual preservation.

The People of God as Vindicated

That John portrays the Two Witnesses as those who are ultimately vindicated serves as the conclusion to the narrative of 11:1–13. The resurrection of the Two Witnesses in the presence of their enemies serves as an explicit indication of their vindication (11:11-12).[12] Further validating the Two Witnesses as the true victors is the presence of the confirming voice: 'φωνῆς μεγάλης ἐκ τοῦ οὐρανοῦ' (great voice from heaven: 11:12), which was said to be heard by the inhabitants of the earth! The vindication of the Two Witnesses is intensified in that it occurs even while, 'ἐθεώρησαν αὐτοὺς οἱ ἐχθροὶ αὐτῶν' (their enemies beheld them; 11:12). Thus, Beale concludes,

> God restores the witnesses to himself after their apparent defeat at the end of the church age. The restoration consists in an overturning of their vanquished condition. The portrayal of the restoration depicts God raising the witnesses from the dead before the eyes of their enemies. . . . It seemed that God had deserted the witnesses by leaving them in a subdued condition. . . . But he vindicates them by delivering them and demonstrating that he is their covenantal protector. . . . At the least, the ascent of the witnesses figuratively affirms a final, decisive deliverance and vindication of God's people at the end of time.[13]

THE HORTATORY IMPLICATIONS OF JOHN'S DEPICTION OF THE TWO WITNESSES

John's portrayal of the Two Witnesses in accord with these four themes carries tremendous implications for discerning his hortatory intent. It must be acknowledged that the conclusions presented at this point pertaining to John's hortatory intent are based solely on our exegesis of

---

12. Ladd affirms that it serves as a "sign to those whom they had been witnesses that they were truly prophets" (Ladd, *Revelation*, 159). Ladd, however, contra the view presented here, suggests that the entire chapter is predictive of the final salvation of the Jewish people (cf. 151f).

13. Beale, *Revelation*, 596–97.

11:1–13. It is hoped, however, that they will gain further merit when examined in light of the rest of the Apocalypse.

First, John begins his account with the assurance to his readers that the Two Witnesses are divinely protected. It is my suggestion that John's objective in alerting his readers that they enjoy God's sovereign protection was to comfort them with the assurance that, though they will indeed endure much tribulation, their eternal destiny resides in God's control. It is conceivable that this sentiment served to alert them that despite the fact that they enjoy God's sovereign protection the reality is that this does not exempt them from harm. But the fact that this narrative begins with the act of measuring, which signifies the divine protection of the people of God, suggests to me that John's purpose was more in line with encouraging them.

Furthermore, that John depicts them as those who worship in the Temple of God (11:1) suggests that he went to great lengths to assure them that their final destiny was secure. The force of this assurance is heightened when the text is read for a second time. For when the reader is aware of the fate that awaits the Two Witnesses there is a measure of confidence gained when they recall that their destiny is in God's sovereign control. Thus, the measuring of the temple serves to encourage the people of God that regardless of what befalls them the right hand of God protects them. This measuring also conveys the notion of God's presence upon the people of God in order that they may effectively witness.[14] Therefore, after arming them with the understanding of this security, John now exhorts them to persevere in their witness.

Perhaps the most significant feature of this narrative resides with the prophetic commission of the Two Witnesses. That this may well be their sole function according to this account, stresses the significance of this task. We may even speculate at this juncture that John's readers were negligent of their duties in proclaiming the good news; or, that they needed encouragement that their proclamation will ultimately be

---

14. Metzger, in fact, summarizes Rev 11: "There is presented here an almost bewildering interweaving of symbols suggested by Old Testament history and prophecy. We find reference to the temple and the altar, to Moses and Elijah, to the wild olive trees and the lampstand seen by Zechariah, to the plagues sent upon Pharaoh, to the tyrant predicted by Daniel, and to Sodom and Egypt and Jerusalem. Perhaps the most that can be said with confidence is that the author views the people of God as bearing faithful testimony" (*Breaking the Code*, 68).

effective; or, perhaps John wanted to remind them of the essential task of the people of God.

That the Two Witnesses suffer harm and eventual death provides John's readers with an awareness of the fate of those who faithfully adhere to their calling. Perhaps, this awareness reminded his readers of the words of Christ in the Sermon on the Mount, 'μακάριοι οἱ δεδιωγμένοι ἕνεκεν δικαιοσύνης' (blessed are the ones who are persecuted on account of righteousness; Matt 5:10). Or, perhaps John employed this theme in accord with the words of Jesus to His apostles on the night of His betrayal, 'Ταῦτα λελάληκα ὑμῖν ἵνα μὴ σκανδαλισθῆτε' (these things I have said to you in order that you may be kept from stumbling; John 16:1). Perhaps, even both of these truths would have reminded John's readers that the lot of the Christian life is suffering and those who suffer for Him are accordingly blessed.

The suffering of the Two Witnesses climaxes with the announcement that the beast will kill them. Even here, there appears to be an implicit measure of encouragement in this pronouncement. For we are told that the opposition of this beast will not result in their deaths until their ministries are complete! The readers can be assured, not that they may be spared martyrdom, but that martyrdom will only come when God has deemed their ministries complete!

Finally, by means of the theme of vindication John also seeks to encourage his readers. For, though the account of the Two Witnesses details the apparent defeat of the righteous in the midst of a war with the Beast (11:7), John, nonetheless, seeks to exhort his readers that their defeat is indeed only apparent. That is, from a temporal perspective the murdering of the Two Witnesses conveys to the world the notion that the righteous have been defeated: hence, the rejoicing and gift giving (11:10). John, however, informs his readers that it is indeed the people of God who are vindicated. As Boring concludes, the people of God have won, "from the heavenly perspective of the Lamb's redefinition of winning," even though, "on earth they have been killed."[15]

This work now seeks to compare our understanding of the people of God with John's portrait of the people of God throughout the pre-consummation sections of Revelation in order to determine the force of these conclusions. That is, we seek to compare our understanding of the

---

15. Boring, *Revelation*, 131.

people of God in the account of the Two Witnesses with his depiction of the people of God. In doing so, we wish to determine the force of our understanding of John's hortatory intent as derived from the exegesis of the Two Witnesses. Before doing so, however, we must examine the structure of Revelation in order to determine the parameters of our investigation.

5

The Structure of Revelation in Relation to John's Depiction of the People of God

IT IS THE OBJECTIVE of this chapter to set forth a proposal that delineates where in the pre-consummation section of Revelation the narratives pertaining to the people of God reside. Though I intend to incorporate an overview of the structure of the entire book, the primary goal of this analysis is to provide a foundation for the investigation of John's portrait of the people of God in the pre-consummation visionary section. Thus, I intend first to determine the overall structure of the Apocalypse in order to delineate precisely where the accounts pertaining to the people of God in the pre-consummation era (4:1–19:10) occur within the overall framework of Revelation. This determination will then allow the following chapters to compare the portrait of the people of God in these narratives with the depiction of the Two Witnesses.

VARIOUS APPROACHES FOR DETERMINING THE STRUCTURE OF REVELATION

The complexity of the literary design of Revelation continues to confound commentators.[1] Efforts to delineate the structural composition of the book of Revelation fall within the parameters of three main ap-

---

1. I assume in this work the unity of Revelation: an assumption that space does not afford me to defend. Such an assumption is, nonetheless, the overwhelming consensus among scholars today. Regardless, my intent is to analyze the structure of Revelation as it stands today. See: Bauckham, *Climax*, 1–37; Beale, *Revelation*, 108–51; Smalley, *Revelation*, 19–21.

proaches.² First, a plethora of chiastic arrangements have been set forth.³ Secondly, many prefer to read the Apocalypse in a linear-sequential or chronological arrangement.⁴ Finally, a variety of proposals exist that suggest that portions of Revelation recapitulate⁵ earlier sections.⁶ Of course, many of the proposals noted above combine two or even all three of these approaches.⁷ For it is not uncommon that one who advocates a linear approach might also allow for the presence of chiasms and/or recapitulations. And, visa versa, those who suggest that the accounts are recapitulatory, or arranged chiastically, often acknowledge that a progression of events occurs.⁸ After all, nearly everyone acknowledges that Revelation winds its way toward the visible return of Christ and the consummation of His kingdom.⁹ Hendriksen observes, "We notice that the final sections of the Apocalypse, though synchronous with the other sections and applicable to the entire course of history, describe especially what will happen

---

2. These three represent the main line approaches to the issue of chronology in the narrative of Revelation. Other approaches, which favor more radical theories relating to the literary structure, are beyond the purview of this work. E.g., M. D. Goulder's linking of Revelation with the lectionary calendar ("The Apocalypse as an Annual Cycle of Prophecies,": 342–67).

3. Note: some commentators actually incorporate elements of two or more of these approaches. See: Beagley, "The 'Sitz im Leben' of the Apocalypse," 28–31, 181; Fiorenza, *Revelation*, 175–76; Lioy, *Revelation*; Shea, 'The Chiastic Structure of Revelation 12:1–15:4: 269–92; Strand, *Interpreting the Book of Revelation*, 43–52; Strand, "The Eight Basic Visions in the Book of Revelation": 107–21; Strand, "The Two Witnesses of Rev 11:3–12": 127–35; Strand, "Chiastic Structure and Some Motifs in the Book of Revelation": 401–08.

4. See: Beasley-Murray, *Revelation*; Cohen, *Understanding Revelation*; Seiss, *Revelation*; Thomas, *Revelation*; Thompson, *Revelation* ; Walvoord, *Revelation*. Keener notes that "this view is not widely held today" (*Revelation*, 34).

5. I use the term 'recapitulate' in terms of a literary feature. Whether or not recapitulation infers that John is describing the same series of historical events or not is beyond the scope of this investigation.

6. Though not all prefer the term 'recapitulation.' See: Beale, *Revelation*, 39, 108–51; Bauckham, *Climax*; 199–209; Beckwith, *Apocalypse*, 318; Collins, *The Combat Myth*, 32–44; Feuillet, *The Apocalypse*; Steinmann, "Tripartite Structure"; Giblin, "Recapitulation and the Literary Coherence of John's Apocalypse": 81–96; Hendriksen, *Conquerors*; Johnson, *Triumph*, 44–47; Keener, *Revelation*, 34–35; Mounce, *Revelation*, 31–45; Talbert, *Apocalypse*; Thomas, *Revelation*; White, "Reexamining the Evidence for Recapitulation in Revelation 20:1–10": 319–44.

7. See: Smalley, *Revelation*, 19;–20; Stefanovic, *Revelation*.

8. The latter is the position of Michaels, *Revelation*, 26–32.

9. Keener simply states: "It seems to end with the end of the age" (*Revelation*, 34).

in connection with the final judgment. . . . The book reveals a gradual progress in eschatological emphasis."[10]

An Evaluation of Chiastic Proposals

Due to the large number of efforts to discern a chiastic arrangement to the Apocalypse it seems worthy to give a brief appraisal of them. Supporting any chiastic arrangement is the fact that Revelation is a highly integrated work in which material is often both recapitulated and presented in terms of a promise/anticipation and fulfillment. However, since both of these features serve to integrate material throughout various sections of the Apocalypse, the inevitable result is a vast array of chiastic arrangements.

Encumbering any chiastic arrangement within Revelation is the necessary task of defending why any two thematic parallels serve as chiastic counterparts over and above other such parallels—i.e., why are other viable parallels not seen as counterparts?[11] Another difficulty with proposed chiastic arrangements relates to the measure of "forcing" that is occasionally required. Though Revelation's highly integrated language provides much evidence for chiasms, the language also serves to integrate sections for which chiastic proposals are unable to account. That is, Revelation has chiastic elements, especially in its exterior sections, but it has much more. It is this "much more," for which the chiastic efforts cannot account, that serves to deflate every chiastic effort that seeks to encompass the whole of the Apocalypse.

Of the various chiastic proposals offered one of the most recent is that presented by Dan Lioy.[12] His arrangement sets forth the chiastic structure of Revelation in a terms of a customary ABCDC'B'A' format. This suggestion has the advantage of viewing the book in terms of a heptadic structure. In light of the proliferation of the number seven in the Apocalypse there is much to be said for such a proposal.[13] Lioy adds to his

---

10. Hendriksen, *Conquerors*, 35.

11. E.g., the repetition of the phrase, "gathering them for war" (16:14; 19:19; 20:8) provide evidence for either recapitulation or a strong thematic parallel. However, none of the chiastic proposals relate these sections in such a manner. Surely, one could contend that other parallels are present that mitigate for a chiastic arrangement between these sections and others, but one must still account for the strong relationship between these accounts.

12. Lioy, *Christological Focus*.

13. Cp. Lohmeyer, *Offenbarung*. Contra Strand, who criticizes views that set forth

structural arrangement of the Apocalypse Strand's supposition that each of the major literary sections of Revelation are introduced by a throne room scene.[14] In favor of this thesis, is the fact that the heavenly scenes do appear to introduce each of the major sections of Revelation.[15] Lioy and Strand, however, fail to give an adequate account of the fact that many of these heavenly scenes serve a double function of both concluding previous units as well as introducing that which follows.[16]

Commentators and scholars have long noted the parallels that abound between John's prologue (1:1–8) and his closing (22:6–21): or A and A' in Lioy's arrangement.[17] A difficulty, however, with this arrangement is the presence of the overlapping technique in 22:6–9, which I will delineate below.[18] Furthermore, the demonstrative 'Οὗτοι' (these) in 22:6 might be best understood as referencing the previous section and not the entire book as Lioy supposes.[19] Thus, though I affirm the appropriateness of placing 22:6–9 as the introduction to the closing section, one should not ignore its ancillary function as the conclusion to the New Jerusalem episode.

From Lioy's second set of chiastic counterparts (the seven churches, 1:9–3:22, and the account of the New Jerusalem, 19:1–22:5) arise some formidable objections to his overall presentation. First, though Lioy correctly observes numerous parallels between the two sections, most of them derive from the latter portion of 19:1–22:5.[20] Secondly, I question

---

a seven-fold structure of Revelation on the basis that authors have simply assumed the importance of seven ("Eight Basic Visions," 108–09). Instead, Strand proposes that there are eight basic visions to the structure of Revelation (See also his: "Chiastic Structure"). In light of the proliferation and importance of seven throughout Revelation it seems more reasonable that, assuming such an arrangement, John would have utilized seven rather than eight. Of course, such is by no means necessarily the case.

14. Strand, "Eight Basic Visions," 107–21.

15. As suggested by Strand who prefers the referent 'throne room scenes.' See: Strand, "Eight Basic Visions."

16. See the discussion below.

17. See: Bauckham, *Climax*, 3.

18. The presence of overlapping throughout the Apocalypse provides a formidable objection to any chiastic proposal. One could, however, envision a chiastic arrangement that takes this technique into account—though I have yet to find such an attempt.

19. Lioy, *Christological Focus*, 55, 59. Beale, *Revelation*, 1123–24.

20. Only the use of "rule all nations with a rod of iron" derives from the earlier part (cp. 2:26–27 and 19:15).

The Structure of Revelation

Lioy's proposition that 19:1–10 is a natural break in the narrative flow that inaugurates a new section. He claims, regarding 19:1–10, "The choice of sectional divisions seems to fit together well with the naturally occurring breaks in the narrative flow of the book."[21] Instead, as Bauckham has shown, 19:1–10 functions as the conclusion to the previous narrative.[22] This is supported by the linguistic parallels between 19:9–10 and 22:6–9, which suggests that they both function as conclusions to their corresponding narratives of Babylon (17:1–19:10) and the New Jerusalem (21:9–22:9). Further evidence that 19:1–10 serves primarily to conclude the narrative of chapter 18 derives from the explicit statement that the occasion for the rejoicing in heaven (19:1–6) is that God has 'ἔκρινεν τὴν πόρνην τὴν μεγάλην' (judged the great harlot: 19:2). Also, the rejoicing of the saints in 19:1–6 appears to function as the carrying out of the exhortation in 18:20.

The third set of chiastic counterparts (4:1–8:1 and 16:18–18:24) contains, perhaps, the greatest difficulties for Lioy's presentation. Lioy suggests that they function as parallel sets.[23] But, they contain contrasting elements as well. These include the scene of heavenly worship and the contrasting scenes of idolatry and blasphemy, as well as the parallel shouts of praise offered by the Great Multitude of 7:10 and the corresponding Great Multitude of 19:1. It is true that these sections indeed begin similarly with John being urged to "come up here" (4:1; 17:1). However, the linguistic parallels are not as strong as Lioy presents. For in 4:1 John uses the imperative 'Ἀνάβα' (come up) followed by the adverb 'ὧδε' (here). Whereas, in 17:1 he employs only the imperative 'Δεῦρο' (come here). Bauckham, however, has demonstrated that John utilizes verbatim recitation in order to identify structural indicators. Thus, one must question whether or not John intended for his readers/hearers to understand these sections as parallel.

Lioy's fourth set of chiastic counterparts (8:2–11:18 and 15:1–16:17) incorporate the seven Trumpets and the seven Bowls, along with their corresponding throne room scenes. This arrangement, present in nearly all chiastic proposals, is surely the strength of Lioy's proposal. The parallels with these two sections are so well noted that they need

---

21. Lioy, *Christological Focus*, 59.
22. Bauckham, *Climax*, 4–7.
23. Lioy, *Christological Focus*, 57.

not be repeated here. In criticism of Lioy's chiastic structure I only wish to note that his arrangement fails to grapple completely with the complexity inherent in the overall structure of Revelation. This is evident in this passage in that the technique of overlapping occurs at the beginning of each of these sections and serves to confirm that these sections are more integrated into the overall structure of the Apocalypse. More importantly, is the question pertaining to the parallel structure of each of the three sets of septets (Seals, Trumpets, and Bowls). If all three function as parallel descriptions, then a chiastic arrangement that includes only the latter two comes up short.

Finally, according to Lioy's proposal the central unit and, consequently, the most authoritative is that of the episode of the Woman, the Dragon, and the Offspring of the Woman (11:19—14:20).[24] As Lioy himself states, "Revelation 11:19-14:20 is seen as the core, or center, of the book."[25] Such a sentiment is affirmed by Shea.[26] In general, I affirm Lioy's positing of a central role for the narrative of this section. However, I will contend below that this section also serves to highlight the opposition to God's people presented in an abbreviated form in 11:5, 7. Therefore, this section—though in many ways it serves as the climax of the story and thus as the core and focal point of the narrative—also carries forward the themes presented in the account of the Two Witnesses and Lioy's chiastic arrangement fails to account for this.

Consequently, Lioy's suggestion that 11:19—14:20 posits the climatic center of Revelation illustrates one of the most significant problems inherent in any proposed chiastic arrangement: namely, the failure to comprehensively bring to the fore thematic elements, which are developed throughout each of the sections of the Apocalypse. Smalley, in fact, affirms, "My own view is that the content of Revelation . . . is theologically and thematically conceived."[27]

---

24. Many efforts have viewed this section as the center of the Apocalypse—though some prefer to begin with 12:1, while others may wish to include up to 15:4. I suggest that the section begins in 12:1; but, such a fine tuning is not pertinent here. See: Shea, "Chiastic Structure."

25. Lioy, *Christological Focus*, 65.

26. Shea, "Chiastic Structure," 269. Shea further suggests that this section consists of a triad of chiasms (270f). In essence, his evaluation of this section is profound; though his failure to grapple with the thematic developments—as presented and defended below—illustrates its shortfalls.

27. Smalley, *Revelation*, 19.

As a result, though chiastic efforts have enlightened many features within Revelation, it appears that no chiastic proposal is able to comprehensively account for the complexity of the structure of the entirety of Revelation. Furthermore, the examination of the structure of Revelation that follows will affirm the presence of overlapping and recapitulatory features. The presence of recapitulatory features provides a measure of explanation as to why some have attempted to encapsulate the entirety of Revelation in accord with a chiastic arrangement. That some sections, which no chiastic arrangements affirm as parallel, are recapitulatory strongly contends against the presence of an all-encompassing chiastic arrangement within Revelation. Furthermore, I will contend below that many sections of Revelation serve a dual purpose of introducing one scene and concluding another. If so, this would virtually eliminate the possibility of aligning Revelation in a purely chiastic sense.

The Structure of Revelation Adhered to in this Work

The structure of Revelation adhered to in this work largely corresponds with the recent work of Richard Bauckham.[28] Bauckham's work thoroughly analyzes the nuances of Revelation and captures in a comprehensive system the structure of the Apocalypse. Consequently, the section that follows incorporates my own reflections, but derives in large part from his proposal.

Before beginning, however, three principles that control Bauckham's presentation are worthy of note. First, he suggests that Revelation was written in such a fashion that John's readers would have gained a measure of understanding not only from their initial reading, "but also progressively" by means of a "closer acquaintance and assiduous study."[29] Secondly, Bauckham claims that John sought to "integrate the various parts of his work into a literary whole."[30] Finally, Bauckham contends that John wrote in such a manner that the "essential structure of the book . . . must have been intended to be perceptible in oral performance."[31] Thus, Bauckham insists that the structure of the book "is intimately connected

---

28. Bauckham, *Climax*, 1–37.
29. Bauckham, *Climax*, 1.
30. Bauckham, *Climax*, 2.
31. Bauckham, *Climax*, 1–2.

with the meaning his work conveys, but we must expect it to be signaled by linguistic markers."[32]

The focal point of Bauckham's proposal in regard to determining the structure of Revelation is this third principle that Revelation was initially intended for oral performance. Consequently, he contends that John employed verbatim repetition as the means of identifying structural indicators. Bauckham, thus, asserts, "precise verbal repetition is virtually limited to structural markers."[33] This has been affirmed by Beale who notes: "John used verbal repetition to indicate these broad divisions of the book because oral recitation would require such structural markers so that the hearers would be enabled better to perceive these divisions."[34] Therefore, for Bauckham, when John repeats a phrase in a variant form that serves as a strong indication that John did not intend the phrase to serve as a structural indicator. Only verbatim repetition and explicit indicators, such as enumeration of the seven Seals, serve as structural indicators. In all, Revelation utilizes both verbatim repetition and the variation of key phrases in order to create "a complex network of textual cross-references, which helps to create and expand the meaning of any one passage by giving it specific relationships to many other passages."[35]

PRELIMINARY OBSERVATIONS IN DETERMINING THE STRUCTURE OF REVELATION

I would add several preliminary observations designed to enhance our insights into the structure of Revelation as set forth by Bauckham. First, in terms of the structure of the Apocalypse, I suggest that Revelation tends to display a literary growth in which the general pattern is for latter accounts to develop and expand upon previous themes—oftentimes making explicit what was previously only implicit.[36] Thus, when two accounts

32. Bauckham, *Climax*, 3.

33. Bauckham, *Climax*, 23.

34. Beale, *Revelation*, 111. Fiorenza affirms, "Revelation as a whole makes quite a different impression when it is heard" ("Composition and Structure": 345).

35. Bauckham, *Climax*, 22. Though Bauckham accounts for some of the exceptions in this fashion, part of the modifications to his overall presentation that will be offered later in this work will attempt to explain their thematic significances and how they integrate and enhance the story in accord with Bauckham's structural conclusions, beyond what Bauckham has noted.

36. Vern Poythress suggests that Revelation displays a literary growth in which early

parallel one another—parallel in terms of function and/or theme—the second likely builds upon the first so that it serves to clarify and amplify the earlier.[37] On some occasions, a latter section may parallel an earlier one in terms of a promise, or anticipation, and a fulfillment scheme: such as in the depiction of Christ in 1:12–18 and then in 19:11–16.[38] In such cases, the general pattern is for later events to be depicted in greater detail.[39] Hendriksen, whose first proposition[40] claims that each of the sections in Revelation "are parallel and each spans the entire new dispensation,"[41] nonetheless, qualifies this statement in his fourth proposition, which he labels "progressive parallelism."[42] In this proposition he suggests, "*The final judgment is first* announced, *then* introduced, *and finally* described."[43]

on the author "doesn't want to give away too much" ("Revelation," Class lecture given on May 8th, 2003, Westminster Theological Seminary). Hendriksen claims that Revelation reveals, "a glorious unity and gradual blossoming of thought.' Later he adds, 'The book reveals a gradual progress in eschatological thought" (*Conquerors*, 33, 35). Since, however, it is well beyond the purpose of this paper to thoroughly defend this assertion, I will attempt a partial defense in the analysis below.

37. In some cases, what is said to have been implied is so obscure that one may hardly justify its presence without an appeal to a secondary passage. E.g., the 144,000 are said to be witnesses, yet, the context of Rev 7:1–8 alone lacks any explicit features that express such a connotation. Yet the suggestion that the 144,000 function as witnesses is widely accepted among commentators. Many who advance the suggestion that the 144,000 represent witnesses or evangelists fail to provide any textual argumentation for this suggestion. Walvoord, for example, puts forward the suggestion that the 144,000 are ethnic Israelites who are converted in order to bear witness for the gospel during the tribulation period. In his commentary, however, he does not mention any exegetical evidence for this assertion. However, the fact that the account of the Two Witnesses is structurally and thematically parallel, and that in the latter account the people of God are explicitly depicted as witnesses seemingly suggests that the 144,000 of Rev 7 are indeed sealed in order that they might bear witness.

38. Fiorenza refers to this as "pre-announcements" ("Composition and Structure," 359). Allo refers to this as '*loi de l'emboitement*' (*L'Apocalypse*, LXXXII–LXXXV), which Collins suggests "refers to the technique of preliminary allusion to what will be described in further detail later in the work (*Combat Myth*, 49, n. 64).

39. Johnson labels this 'anticipation' and notes: "Symbolic figures and events that are to be disclosed in greater detail later in the book are often introduced briefly at an earlier point" (*Triumph*, 43).

40. Hendriksen lists nine 'propositions' that he suggests will aid the reader in understanding the book of Revelation. See: *Conquerors*, 22, 23, 33, 36, 40, 43, 45, 49, 50.

41. Hendriksen, *Conquerors*, 22. Such a proposition accords with the traditional understanding of recapitulation.

42. Hendriksen, *Conquerors*, 34–36.

43. Hendriksen, *Conquerors*, 36.

Secondly, John complicates any effort to delineate the overall structure of Revelation by means of the insertion of intercalations and by employing the technique of overlapping. The intercalations serve to interrupt the narrative flow of the book and present a dramatic pause.[44] Within them, John interjects a glimpse at the people of God into the narrative.[45] Since the concern in this work relates to John's portrait of the people of God in the pre-consummation era, the two intercalations, which John introduces in the midst of the accounts of the seven Seals and the seven Trumpets, will be of primary interest.

Third, the task of identifying the structure of Revelation is eased given Bauckham's suggestion that major structural indicators are evidenced by verbatim repetition. Yet this not a simple exercise. For one must ask how long a phrase or clause must be in order to determine if it has structural import? For example, Bauckham does not accept the repetition of 'καὶ εἶδον' (and I saw: 5:1, 2, 6, 11; 6:1, 2, 5, 8, 12; 7:2; 8:2, 13; 9:1; 10:1; 13:1, 11; 14:1, 6, 14; 15:1, 2; 16:13; 17:3, 6; 19:11, 17, 19; 20:1, 4, 11, 12; 21:2) as a formal indicator of major structural import. And rightfully so, for its shear abundance, especially within clearly unified sections (e.g.,

---

44. I.e., 7:1–17; and 10:1–11:13. There is some ambiguity in the use of the term "intercalation." Essentially, most scholars understand 'intercalation' in the sense with which it is employed here: an intercalation interrupts a section by means of introducing an entirely new topic (e.g., the account of the 144,000 and the Great Multitude in 7:1–17 amidst the seven Seals narrative). Fiorenza, however, prefers to call these interludes, which would be acceptable, except that she refers to what others have deemed John's technique of 'overlapping' as "intercalations" (Fiorenza, "Composition and Structure," 360f). In regards to John's use of 'overlapping,' Bauckham suggests that Fiorenza, "confuses this technique, by which the end of one section is interlocked into the beginning of the next section, with the quite different technique of intercalation, in which a section is interrupted by the intercalation of a passage of different character" (Bauckham, *Climax*, 9, n.15). Hall prefers the name 'hooking' or 'hook interlock'; but, again his description applies more to the phenomenon of overlapping discussed below. (Mark Seaborn Hall, "The Hook Interlocking Structure of Revelation: The Most Important Verses in the Book and How They may Unify its Structure," *NovT* 44 [2002]: 7–19). In addition to Bauckham, those who affirm the presence of intercalations are abundant: Beale, *Revelation*, ; Boring, *Revelation*, 102–21, 27, 39; Fiorenza, *Revelation*, 171; Goulder, "The Apocalypse," 353; Hendriksen, *Conquerors*, 16; Ladd, *Revelation*, 110–111; Lenski, *Revelation*, 244; Lohmeyer, *Offenbarung*, 67; Lohse, 50, 61; Mounce, *Revelation*, 47; Prigent, *L'Apocalypse*, 117, 149; Steinmann, "Tripartite"; Strand, "Eight Basic Visions," 112; Swete, *Apocalypse*, 95.

45. This is especially the case in the two intercalations that most interest this study: namely, those of 7:1–17 and 10:1–11:13. Strand proposes that the interludes—which he finds in each of the middle six of his eight visions—"enhance or intensify the thrust of the immediately preceding material" ("Visions," 111).

5:1, 2, 6), demonstrates that it does not mark major transitions within Revelation.

Finally, not enough attention is given to thematic issues that pervade the book of Revelation. Beale questions whether the structure of Revelation is "according to a chronological scheme, a thematic scheme, or a combination of the two."[46] It is my contention that John employs the story itself in order to convey his message, and that the story unfolds in a highly complex fashion through the use of recapitulation and a gradual development of the plot.[47]

Overlapping Sections

Any attempt at a comprehensive determination of the structure of Revelation must account for John's use of overlapping or interlocking.[48] Overlapping occurs when a sentence or paragraph performs a dual role of concluding a previous section and introducing the one that follows. Utilization of this technique serves as the structural means by which John weaves his entire account into a cohesive whole, allowing him to link later sections with previous ones. The presence of overlapping, however, presents the single greatest difficulty for any attempt to provide a comprehensive, orderly outline of Revelation.[49]

An example of overlapping is found in the introduction to the seven Trumpets.[50] In 8:2, seven angels appear with seven trumpets. Yet the narrative of the seven Trumpets does not actually commence until 8:6. For

---

46. Beale, *Revelation*, 108.

47. Fiorenza adds; "An analysis of the specific form-content *gestalt* of Revelation should focus on how theology and form are interrelated as well as on the tradition-history of each. Against the old dichotomy between content and form the so-called New Criticism maintains that the form is not a container for the content but the patterning and arrangement of it. If one changes the order of a text one changes its meaning. However, one has to see the difference between a work of literature and the NT writings. Whereas a work of art is considered as a system or structure of signs serving esthetic purpose, the NT literature is not written with such a goal. Since the NT books are theological and historical writings, one has not only to analyze the literary patterns and structure of a writing but also their relation to its theological perspective and its historical setting" ("Composition and Structure," 344).

48. See Collins, *Combat Myth*, 16–19; Bauckham, *Climax*, 9–15.

49. See: Fiorenza, "Composition and Structure," 361.

50. See: Bauckham, *Climax*, 8–9; Collins, *Combat Myth*, 16–18; Fiorenza, "Composition and Structure," 360f.

in 8:3–5 a heavenly liturgy intervenes. This heavenly liturgy, however, appears to continue the description of the seventh Seal (8:1) and, thus, functions as the conclusion to the seven Seals.[51] Consequently, 8:3–5 serves in part to close the narrative of the seven Seals. The introduction of the seven Trumpets in 8:2, however, leads the reader to expect that the Trumpets narrative has begun. Even in the introduction to the seven Trumpets, however, there is a link backwards. This is evidenced by the allusion to the prayers of the saints (cf. 6:9–11) in 8:3, which suggests that perhaps the seven Trumpets provide an answer to the saints' request. This suggests that 8:3–5 also functions as part of the introduction to the seven Trumpets, which commences in 8:6.[52]

Why overlap these sections? Perhaps, John wished to associate both the Seals and the Trumpets with the prayers of the saints. At the very least, the overlapping of the heavenly liturgy in 8:3–5 with the seven Seals and the seven Trumpets serves to strengthen the literary connection of the two series.[53]

Other instances of overlapping include the references to the throne at the close of each of the three septets.[54] For in the theophany of chapter

---

51. Beale, *Revelation*, 460–64.

52. This correlates with U. Vanni's observation that conclusions to major literary units from 4:1 onwards are not delimited but open-ended (Beale, *Revelation*, 110; C. H. Giblin, "Structural and Thematic Correlations in the Theology of Revelation 16–22," *Biblica* 55 [1974]: 491).

53. The closing unit (22:6–9) within the visionary section of Revelation (4:1–22:9) also serves as a primary example of John's technique of overlapping. According to Bauckham's proposal 22:6–9 serves as both as a conclusion to the prior section or sections (21:9–22:9; or, 1:9–22:9) as well as an introduction to the epilogue (22:6–21). Evidence for the inclusion of 22:6–9 with the epilogue derives in part from the strong verbal parallels with the opening unit of 1:1–3. The parallels include: an angel is sent (1:1; 22:6); the phrase 'ἃ δεῖ γενέσθαι ἐν τάχει' (what must soon take place: 1:1; 22:6); John's naming of himself (1:1; 22:8); A blessing for the keepers (1:3; 22:7); and references to the 'τῷ δούλῳ αὐτοῦ' (servants: 1:1; 22:6). Furthermore, the verbal links between the entire prologue and whole of the epilogue include: the phrase 'ὁ γὰρ καιρὸς ἐγγύς' (the time is near: 1:3; 22:10); references to 'χάρις' (grace: 1:4; 22:21); and, the identification of the 'τὸ ἄλφα καὶ τὸ ὦ' (the Alpha and the Omega: 1:8; 22:13). That 22:6–9 serves a secondary function of concluding the section of the vision proper (1:9–22:9) receives justification in the light of the following. First, 22:6–9 is verbally parallel with both 19:9–10 (which closes the section on the destruction of Babylon), and the prologue of 1:1–3. Yet, though 22:6–9 concludes the vision of the descent of the New Jerusalem, it also serves as an appropriate conclusion to the entire vision.

54. See: Bauckham, *Climax*, 7–8.

4 it was stated that from the throne proceeded 'ἀστραπαὶ καὶ φωναὶ καὶ βρονταί' (lightning, sounds, and thunder; 4:5). This expression, though not in identical form, perhaps because it does not serve as a major structural indicator, recurs in expanded form at the close of each of the three septets (8:5; 11:19; 16:18–21).[55]

Recapitulation

Recapitulation suggests that in instances of parallel accounts the latter account often reflects the same events or themes as an earlier one; either from a different perspective, or, perhaps, by adding greater detail. Several factors support the contention that recapitulations are present in the Apocalypse. First, there are the parallels within the accounts of three septets of judgments.[56] Also, Revelation repeatedly inserts descriptions of the consummative judgment. Beale suggests that,

> the strongest argument for the recapitulation view is the observation of repeated combined scenes of consummative judgment and salvation found at the conclusions of various sections throughout the book. The pattern of these scenes is always the same, consisting of a depiction of judgment followed by a portrayal of salvation.[57]

Other examples include the repetition of the phrase 'συναγαγεῖν αὐτοὺς εἰς τὸν πόλεμον' (to gather them for war: 16:14; 19:19; 20:8—though variant in 19:19). Beale adds that this repetition:

> is a strong hint that 15:1–16:21; 17:1–19:10 and 19:11–21:8 refer to the same time and episode. It is also striking that the three occurrences of this clause come in the descriptions of the judgment of Babylon, of the beast, and of the dragon. Probably the reference is to one war in which all three evil figures are defeated together."[58]

Finally, the references to the fall of Babylon scattered throughout the Apocalypse (14:8; 16:19; 17:16; 18:2, 10, 17, 19–21; 19:2–3) appear to depict the same event. These examples, among others, have led many to conclude that the narratives within Revelation recapitulate one another.

---

55. See Bauckham, *Climax*, 202–04.
56. E.g., all make use of Exodus imagery.
57. Beale, *Revelation*, 121.
58. Beale, *Revelation*, 132.

The question, however, unfortunately not asked often enough, relates to the implications of such repetition. Does the fact that the latter passages recapitulate the former (assuming for a moment that such is true in these accounts) mean that the latter always provide a different perspective on the same events?[59] This is the conclusion of Beale. He contends, for example, that the presence of recapitulation "suggests that chs. 11 (vv 1–13), 12, and 13 do not follow one another chronologically but refer to the same events."[60] Granted, such a conclusion is a natural assumption. Johnson, however, cautions against drawing too hasty a conclusion and alerts us to another option. He suggests that though, "repetition in visions sometimes provides a second or third camera angle on the same person, historical event, or institution," it may also signal "that different historical events or ages participate in a common pattern that comes to expression at different points in the great cosmic conflict between God and Satan, Christ and the beast, the bride and the harlot."[61]

The presence of recapitulatory features, whether they were intended to convey the notion that the latter accounts always restate the former, or they merely depict later events in similar terms, suggests that John has incorporated literary features within the Apocalypse that warrant the reading of parallel accounts, whether wholly recapitulatory or not, in light of one another. In fact, I would contend that since the latter accounts are consistently more detailed, they often serve to clarify earlier texts.

OVERVIEW OF THE STRUCTURE OF REVELATION ACCORDING TO THIS WORK

Major Divisions in the Structure of Revelation

The three major divisions in Revelation include the prologue (1:1–8), the vision proper (1:9–22:9), and the epilogue (22:6–21).[62] As mentioned earlier, the strong correlations between the prologue and the epilogue provide some measure of justification for those who attempt a chiastic

---

59. E.g., Strand proposes that the difference between the Seals and Trumpets is one of emphasis. He concludes, "We have found that the seals septet emphasizes victory through the blood of the Lamb and that the trumpets septet places its emphasis upon victory through the prophetic word" (Strand, "'Overcomer': 245).

60. Beale, *Revelation*, 132.

61. Johnson, *Triumph*, 44.

62. As discussed above, the technique of overlapping justifies the inclusion of 22:6–9 in both the vision proper and the epilogue.

arrangement.⁶³ As one should expect, the prologue contains an epistolary opening (1:4–6), while the epilogue contains an epistolary conclusion (22:21). Both sections contain prophetic oracles and each serves to mark the letter as an epistle.

In terms of the structure of the visionary section comprising 1:9–22:9 Bauckham argues that the entirety of it "is recounted as a single visionary experience which took place on Patmos on the Lord's day."⁶⁴ He suggests that the use of 'ἐγενόμην ἐν πνεύματι' (I was in the spirit: 1:10) serves as the structural beginning of the vision, while the abbreviated form 'ἐν πνεύματι' (in the spirit) in 4:2, 17:3, and 21:10, indicates transitions within the vision.⁶⁵ Consequently, the fourfold divisions within the visionary sections are 1:9–3:22; 4:1–16:21; 17:1–21:8; and 21:9–22:9. For the purpose of this investigation, the survey of the visionary section of Revelation (1:9–22:9) will be subdivided at 1:9–3:22 (the introductory vision of Christ and the seven letters), 4:1–16:21 (the throne room scene and the three septets of judgments), and 17:1–22:9 (the judgment of the Harlot and the reward of the Bride).⁶⁶

Overview of the Primary Divisions within the Visionary Section of Revelation

1:9–3:22: Introductory Vision of Christ and the Seven Letters

The section comprising 1:9–3:22 is composed of the introduction (1:9–20) and the corresponding messages to the seven churches (2:1–3:22). Again, Revelation resists a simplistic outline. For though there is little dissent from the contention that 1:9 introduces this section, there is similarly ample evidence for accepting 1:9 as introducing the entire visionary section (through 22:9).⁶⁷

---

63. The chiastic parallels between the letters to the seven churches (2:1–3:21) and the description of the New Jerusalem (19:1–22:5) present an even stronger case for chiasms. The structure defended here, however, will contend that these passages fail to function comprehensively as counterparts.

64. Bauckham, *Climax*, 3.

65. Bauckham, *Climax*, 3. See also: Michaels, *Revelation*, 26.

66. The justification for combining 17:1–21:8 and 21:9–22:9 here is twofold: first, as will be evident in the analysis below, this section is easily read as a whole; secondly, this section lies beyond our focus of the portrayal of the people of God in the pre-consummation era; hence, it is not necessary to subdivide and scrutinize its structure.

67. See: Minear, *New Earth*, 27.

Of importance is the correlation of earlier sections of the Apocalypse with later ones. For example, the concluding message to the church in Laodicea closes with the promise that the overcomer will sit, 'μετ' ἐμοῦ ἐν τῷ θρόνῳ μου' (with me on my throne; 3:22). This final note appears to function in correlation with the vision of chapters 4–5 by directly anticipating the revelation of the 'τοῦ καθημένου ἐπὶ τοῦ θρόνου' (the one sitting on the throne) in 5:1f. Further confirmation that 4:1f is linked with the opening vision (1:10–3:21) derives from the fact that the voice that speaks to John in 4:1 is identified as the same voice as that in 1:10–11: 'ἡ φωνὴ ἡ πρώτη ἣν ἤκουσα ὡς σάλπιγγος' (the first voice which I had heard like a trumpet). The significance of these types of connections is the confirmation of the intricacy of the presentation of Revelation.[68]

4:1–16:21: The Throne Room Scene and the Three Septets of Judgments

Structurally, the main visionary section of Revelation begins in 4:1. In terms of the structure of this section, Bauckham, suggests, "Chapters 6–16 is the most structurally complex part of the book, but precisely for that reason John has made his structural markers prominent and emphatic."[69]

The section commences with an inaugural vision of heaven (4:1–5:14).[70] This section, however, should not be viewed in isolation from the previous section as evidenced by the presence of the "first voice" from 1:10.[71] It is on the basis of the theophany presented in chapters 4–5 that the whole series of judgments follow (6:1–16:21) in the form of three series of sevens and two intercalations. There can be no mistaking the explicit numbering of each of the septets as indicative of their structural import.

---

68. Fiorenza suggests that the letters form one of the four series of sevens. She affirms that, "A primary means chosen by the author to achieve an interwoven structure and unitary composition is the use of *numbers* and *numerical structures*" ("Composition and Structure," 360). The objection to this is that the seven letters, though indeed numbering seven and thus of significance, are not explicitly numbered and therefore do not serve as a structural device. See: Bauckham, *Climax*, 9–10.

69. Bauckham, *Climax*, 7.

70. As mentioned previously, Strand suggests that each of the major units of Revelation begin with a heavenly scene. In part, this observation holds true.

71. See: Minear, *New Earth*, 66.

The Three Septets of Judgments

The three series of seven judgments (Seals, Trumpets, and Bowls) are a central component of the main visionary section. As for the importance of these septets in terms of the overall structure of the Apocalypse, Court proposed:

> The three plague sequences, the seven seals, the seven trumpets and the seven bowls, have an important role to play in any interpretation of the structure of the Book of Revelation. Upon the critical appraisal of their function within the Book depends a judgement about the chronological order and historical nature of the events described. Is the divine process, which John sees to be at work, moving forward through these sequences of events, taken consecutively; or do these sequences reiterate, in a scheme of recapitulation, a single set of circumstances?

It is my contention that the question as to whether or not the septets are sequential (i.e., they reflect the course of events that are to occur in a sequential order: typically construed to follow the order of the Apocalypse—Seals, Trumpets, and Bowls),[72] or, whether the latter septets merely recapitulate the former, is not vital to this thematic investigation of the portrait of the people of God in the Apocalypse. In terms of my objective to determine the John's portrait of the people of God in Revelation the point of import relates to the literary aspect. That is, is there a development within other parallel portions of Revelation that may provide insights into the relations between passages that depict the people of God?

The relationship of the three septets is far too complicated to expect a thorough analysis here. Nonetheless, a few observations are appropriate. It is my contention that the debates as to whether or not the three septets are sequential or recapitulatory often miss the mark. Occasionally this results from the failure to distinguish whether John's primary intent was literary, or to express conditions pertaining to reality in the physical realm (with the realization that many prefer a position in the middle).

Those who tend to favor a more literal reading of Revelation typically deny that any such distinction is present. For them, John's intent was strictly to depict the events of the end-times as he saw them. Thus, they contend that the three septets are sequential and that each series displays characteristics that distinguishes it from the others. The

---

72. See: Cohen, *Revelation*, 83–126.

presence of distinguishing features, of course, is undeniable. The question that must be raised in regard to the disparities is whether these differences serve primarily a literary purpose, or whether they intend to express physical realities.

For example, the effects of both the second Trumpet and the second Bowl dramatically affect the sea (8:8, 9; 16:3). As a result of the second Trumpet one-third of the sea life are killed. As a result of the second Bowl, however, all of the sea life are killed. For the sequentialist, this means that the remaining two-thirds which survived the effects of the second Trumpet are destroyed as a result of the second Bowl. But, from a literary perspective, the Bowl series may be viewed as narrated in terms that express a more comprehensive and catastrophic judgment.

One may, however, read the accounts in terms of sequential judgments—albeit ones in which the latter are modeled on the former—that function literarily. Thus, while favoring a more literal reading (i.e., that the plagues depict reality), one may still affirm a literary relationship between the three septets (e.g., the presence of Exodus imagery). Others, while denying that Revelation provides details about actual plagues and suggesting instead that it depicts the true spiritual state of affairs, may acknowledge that John was not, in his delineation of the three septets, merely recapitulating.

My contention is that a middle ground is most warranted. That is, I suggest that a literary aspect is present in which a development occurs within the series of three judgments (e.g., one-third are killed—all are killed). This development links the three septets so that one is compelled to view them in light of each other. This conclusion stands regardless of whether or not we are to view the septets as recapitulatory or sequential. Consequently, the brief analysis of the three septets that follows will attempt to observe the interrelationship of each series.

That the series of the seven Trumpets (8:2—11:19) parallels the series of seven Bowls (15:1—16:21) is widely recognized.[73] For each of the series can be described as affecting, in order, the earth, the sea, the inland waters, the heavenly bodies, pain, enemies from near the Euphrates, and the second coming of Christ. Other features further suggest that each of the three septets parallel one another.[74] Bauckham has noted that each of the

---

73. This does not mean to imply that nearly all commentators view them as merely recapitulatory.

74. It is noteworthy to mention parenthetically that the septets do not correspond

final members of each series links with the heavenly vision of chapters 4–5 by means of a formula alluding to the Sinaitic theophany and Exodus 19:16: "The formula serves to anchor the divine judgments of chapters 6–16 in the initial vision of God's rule in heaven in chapter 4."[75] He adds that, "the formula indicates that it is the same final judgment which is reached in the seventh of each of the three series."[76] This is further supported by the fact that each series makes ample use of the Egyptian plagues and Exodus imagery.[77]

Yet the seven Trumpets also parallel the series of the seven Seals. For both conform to a four plus three structure. This four plus three structure of the seven Seals is marked by the description of the first four as horses. The series of seven Trumpets, though not as explicitly marked as the series of Seals, also displays a four-three structure in that the last three are narrated as the three "woes."[78] Strongly contending for the literary comparison of the Seals and Trumpets is the fact that each includes an intercalation following the sixth item in each series. Both of these intercalations introduce a delay into their respective series that address the fate of the people of God.

Therefore, I affirm the position that the three septets correspond literarily to one another but are not merely recapitulations. That is, each successive judgment reiterates, supplements, and intensifies the earlier depictions. The emphasis resides with the stress upon the increase in intensity. Hughes suggests, "The seven trumpet blasts are in effect a recapitulation of the seven unsealings of the scroll."[79] While Boring asserts, "The second cycle is not a chronological continuation of the first but a

---

structurally to the seven letters. This is evidenced by the fact that the septets are all explicitly numbered; while the seven letters are not. Also, the seven letters have a three plus four structure, while the series of judgments have a four plus three structure. Furthermore, the seven Seals correspond closely to the 'Little Apocalypse' in the Synoptics. This, however, extends beyond our present interests. See: Court, *Myth and History*, 47–54.

75. Bauckham, *Climax*, 8.
76. Bauckham, *Climax*, 8.
77. See: Court, *Myth and History*, 74.
78. Joseph S. Considine notes the similarities here, but suggests, "There is something more than a difference in symbolism, however, because the general import is different. The visions of the seals are the preludes to the visions of the trumpets. In the seals, we behold God's plan; in the trumpets, we see the execution of that plan" ("Two Witnesses," 377).
79. Hughes, *Revelation*, 105.

retelling of the first cycle at a more intensive level."[80] Thus, from a literary perspective the three series are not merely recapitulatory. Instead, the latter two series serve to amplify the former by means of providing greater detail. That is, a literary expansion has occurred. This expansion suggests that the latter judgments do not merely recapitulate the former.

The Two Intercalations (7:1–17 and 10:1–11:13)

The structure and relationship of the two intercalations (7:1–17; 10:1–1:13) are of the most significance for this work, since the latter contains the account of the Two Witnesses. Both focus on the people of God and serve as the two key narratives depicting the people of God in the pre-consummation era. Four factors, in fact, strongly support the contention that the intercalation of 10:1–11:13 parallels 7:1–17.

First, both sections serve functionally similar roles. That is, they are both intercalations (interludes, or parentheses) in the midst of their accompanying series of judgments.[81] In fact, in both instances these intercalations occur after the disclosing of the sixth item in each series.

Second, both of the intercalations are closely related to the sixth item in their corresponding series. Thus, 7:1–17 relates directly to the sixth Seal by answering the question of 6:17: 'τίς δύναται σταθῆναι' (who is able to stand?: cp. 7:9; and perhaps 7:1).[82] The relationship of the intercalation of 10:1–11:13 and the sixth judgment is less clear. A good case, however, exists that it relates directly to the words in the closing of the sixth Trumpet, which reiterates the people's failure to repent.[83] Bauckham, in fact, argues that it is the ministry of the Two Witnesses that results in the conversion of the nations (cp. 11:13).[84]

Third, both of these intercalations present a delay in their respective series of judgments. Thus, the intercalation of 7:1–17 suspends the series of seven Seals—that resumes in 8:1—and the intercalation of 10:1–11:13 serves to suspend the series of seven Trumpets. This delay would have

---

80. Boring, *Revelation*, 135. See also, Collins, *Apocalypse*, 56.

81. Fiorenza, comments on chapters 10–11, "they have the same structural function within Revelation as the interlude of chapter 7" (*Revelation*, 74). See also: Hughes, *Revelation*, 92.

82. Fiorenza, *Revelation*, 65–66. Hughes, *Revelation*, 95.

83. In fact, the announcement of the end of the sixth Trumpet and second woe occurs in 11:14.

84. Cf. Bauckham, *Climax*, 12, 238–337.

been enhanced in an oral enactment. In fact, this would have been particularly heightened in the account of the six Seals; since the first four Seals follow one another with a measure of rapidity.[85]

Finally, each of these intercalations depict the state of the people of God during their respective delays.[86] An analysis of the thematic depiction of the people of God in these accounts follows in the body of this work. Consequently, at this point, I only note that the two intercalations interrupt their corresponding series of judgments in order to relay the status of the people of God amidst the judgments.

It is appropriate at this juncture in the discussion of the structural import of the two intercalations to note the literary links among both of the intercalations and the vision of the Lamb in chapter 5. First, in chapters 5 and 7 the motifs of "hearing" and "seeing" are both present.[87] Also, both chapters 5 and 7 have beings "standing."[88] The parallels within chapters 5 and 10 include the fact that they are both introduced with references to 'ἄγγελον ἰσχυρὸν' (a strong angel) with a scroll.[89] Also, chapters 5 and 10 are seemingly modeled on Ezekiel 2:9–10 and 3:1–2. Consequently, since both intercalations—which address the people of God—contain allusions to the vision of the Lamb, there is a strong implication to the Christological element within John's portrayal of the people of God.

Structurally, though not pertinent to this thesis, I suggest that the account of the Two Witnesses (11:1–13) details both what was written on the scroll as well as the contents of John's prophecy. Thus, John, after digesting the scroll, then proclaims the contents. That chapter 11 functions as the expression of the contents of the scroll follows from the charge that closes chapter 10: 'δεῖ σε πάλιν προφητεῦσαι' (you must prophesy again; 10:11). Aune, in fact, categorizes 11:1–13 as a "narrative prophecy focusing on the two witnesses."[90]

---

85. See: Bauckham, *Climax*, 12.

86. See: Bauckham, *Climax*, 12. Fiorenza adds to other parallels. Namely, that both passages refer to the same time period and that each section may be viewed as an introduction to the sections that follow (*Revelation*, 74).

87. Cp 5:5–14 and 7:4–14 (See: Hall, "Hook Interlocking Structure," 284).

88. Cf. 5:6 and 7:1, 9.

89. Cf. 5:2 and 10:1

90. Aune, *Revelation*, 2.585; see also, Bauckham, *Climax*, 267.

The Woman, Her Offspring, the Dragon, the Beasts, and the 144,000 (12:1–15:4)

The narrative of the Woman and her offspring, and the opposition to them on the part of the Dragon and the Beasts (12:1–15:4), provides us with Revelation's longest narrative pertaining to the people of God in the pre-consummation era. Despite its length, however, it is my contention that this account builds upon the narrative of the Two Witnesses in terms of its depiction of the people of God.[91] For since the reference to the murderous activity of the beast occurred in a brief and abrupt manner in the episode of the Two Witnesses (11:7), the account of 12:1–15:4 then serves in part to provide a detailed account of the opposition to the people of God[92]—an opposition that is noted both to have its ancestry traced to the very beginning and one that has been satanically inspired.[93] Furthermore, the intercalations focus exclusively on the people of God; whereas, this account focuses more broadly on the opposition to the people of God.

The account of 12:1–15:4 presents a unique situation in regards to its role in the structure of Revelation. Bauckham comments,

> The beginning of chapter 12 seems an uncharacteristically abrupt fresh start, devoid of literary links with anything that precedes.... There are not even the kind of literary links backwards to preceding sections of the book which John provides elsewhere at major transitions which might otherwise seem like entirely fresh beginnings.[94]

Consequently, Bauckham suggests that John deliberately constructed this section in order to generate the impression that he is making a "fresh start." Such a fresh start, "is required simply because the narrative

---

91. That is in terms of the focus on the portrait of the people of God, 12:1–14:5 builds on the thematic depiction of the people of God as found in 11:1–13. This, however, is by no means the only function of this narrative.

92. In fact, one may examine the depth of chapters 12–14 in recapitulating the events of chapter 11. This confirms Bauckham's conclusion relating to this latter account: "We can begin to see that what chapters 12–14 add to the account in 11:3–13 is primarily a much fuller exposition of the conflict between the forces of evil and the witnessing church, to which 11:7 briefly alludes," *Climax*, 285.

93. Consequently, I see no reason for adopting the conclusion of Ford who postulated a major break, and for a time, a second source, at 12:1. See: Ford, *Revelation*, 50–54. Swete, Allo, and Feuillet have all proposed a major break at 12:1 (Swete, *Apocalypse*; Allo, *l'Apocalypse*; Feuillet, *The Apocalypse*, 29–30).

94. Bauckham, *Climax*, 15.

of the woman and the dragon begins chronologically earlier than any previous part of his visionary narrative."[95]

The end of this narrative (15:2–4), however, utilizes the same technique of overlapping that served to link the seven Seals with the seven Trumpets. That is, 15:2–4, in continuation of the narrative of chapters 12–14, presents the people of God who have been victorious over the beast. Preceding this conclusion, however, is the introduction of seven angels with seven Bowls (15:1). And following it is the description of these angels as making preparations for pouring them out in 15:5–8.[96] This is also evidenced by the link forged in the references to the temple in 11:19 and 15:5–6. Thus, by means of the overlapping technique the narrative of 12:1–15:4 is linked with the presentation of the seven Bowls.[97] By means of this technique John has also linked the account of the series of seven Trumpets with the series of the seven Bowls in the same manner in which he linked the series of seven Seals with the seven Trumpets.[98] Bauckham affirms, "Thus, despite the intervention of chapters 12–14, the whole sequence of Bowls is clearly marked as a development of the seventh trumpet."[99]

Furthermore, the result is that John has connected the series of seven Trumpets with the series of seven Bowls by means of a double intercalation.[100] In this double intercalation, 10:1–11:13 both interrupts the seven Trumpets and serves as the foundation for the narrative of the Woman and her offspring and the opposition to them on the part of the Dragon and the Beasts (12:1–15:4). This results in a dual function for 11:15–19 as well. For the description of the seventh trumpet serves both as the conclusion to the

---

95. Bauckham, *Climax*, 15.

96. See: Bauckham, *Climax*, 16.

97. Contra Steinmann who contends a climax is reached in ch 11 (which ends the depiction of the triumph of Christianity against Judaism) and that 12–20 transition from the historical narrative to the apocalyptic vision (predicting the fall of Rome). Hopkins, "Historical Perspective,": 43.

98. This conclusion, thus, leads to a rejection of the chiastic structure as presented by Strand in that he sees the major dividing line in Revelation as occurring between chapters 14–15. This assessment, however, contends that the whole of 4:1–16:21 presents the core of John's revelation, and that Revelation 15:1 links with the three series of sevens in the manner presented.

99. Bauckham, *Climax*, 9.

100. Bauckham, *Climax*, 15–18.

series of seven Trumpets, as well as an intercalation between the accounts pertaining to the people of God (10:1–11:14; 12:1–15:4).

Therefore, the narrative of 12:1–15:4 serves in part to expand upon the opposition of the beast towards the people of God as presented in the intercalation of 10:1–11:13.[101] Considine affirms,

> The two passages in chapters 11 and 12–13 are parallel. The protection spoken of in the one is the preservation related in the others. The Gentile domination in chapter 11 is the same as the activity of the Beast in 12 and 13. The fate of the Witnesses in 11:3–13 is the same as the fate of those who keep the commandments of God in 12:17.[102]

Closing of the Visionary section of Revelation (17:1–22:9)

The section 17:1–22:9 is unequivocally the most complex and, consequently, the most disagreed upon section of the Apocalypse.[103] Since, however, my thesis concerns the depiction of the people of God in the account of the Two Witnesses and generally in the pre-consummation era, a thorough analysis of this section is not warranted. Overall, I affirm the evidence set forth first by Giblin,[104] and then by Bauckham,[105] that the verbal links between the final unit within the visionary section of the book (21:9–22:9) directly correlates this section with the first half of the prior

---

101. Fiorenza concludes that 10:1–15:4 forms the center of the book. This central section "is the prophetic interpretation of the political and religious situation of the book" ("Composition and Structure," 366). She further suggests that Revelation is patterned along the lines of the Greek drama in which "the climax falls near the center of the action, and the denouement comes near the end" ("Composition and Structure," 365). She adds to the strength of this conclusion the fact that the placing of the climax in the center was also the practice in Roman poetry and that "students of the literature of Israel and Judaism have found the same structural pattern" ("Composition and Structure," 365). This proposition could be accepted here, but only with modifications. In order not to divert too far from the focus of this section only tow points will be made at this juncture. First, my proposed delineations of 4:1–16:21 do not align with Fiorenza's in all facets. Secondly, I affirm the primacy of the intercalation of 10:1–11:13 in terms of its depiction of the people of God, and the subsequent function of 12:1–15:4 in terms of its role of detailing the opposition to the people of God.

102. Considine, "Two Witnesses," 386.

103. Beale lists nine different proposals in major commentaries and articles for setting forth the structure of this section. See: Beale, *Revelation*, 109.

104. Giblin, "Structural and Thematic Concerns," 489.

105. Bauckham, *Climax*, 4–5.

unit comprising 17:1–19:10.[106] Giblin, in fact, proposes that 17:1–22:9 forms three sections, which themselves form an ABA' pattern.[107] These three sections comprise 17:1–19:10, 19:11–21:8, and 21:9–22:9.

Giblin's thesis is supported by the numerous parallels within the opening (17:1–19:10) and closing (21:9–22:9) sections. First, these two sections open with virtually identical language, 'Καὶ ἦλθεν εἷς ἐκ τῶν ἑπτὰ ἀγγέλων τῶν ἐχόντων τὰς ἑπτὰ φιάλας καὶ ἐλάλησεν μετ' ἐμοῦ λέγων, Δεῦρο, δείξω σοι' (and one of the seven angels having seven bowls came and spoke with me saying, "come here, I will show you . . ." : 17:1; 21:9). Both sections then incorporate a description of John's heavenly transport: 'καὶ ἀπήνεγκέν με ἐν πνεύματι' (and he carried me away in the spirit: 17:3; 21:9). Furthermore, the conclusions to each section are likewise verbally similar. For each section closes with an affirmation of the trustworthiness of the message imparted to John: 'Οὗτοι οἱ λόγοι πιστοὶ καὶ ἀληθινοί" (these words are faithful and true: 19:9; 22:6). Also, each then contains a reference to John's attempt to worship the angel: 'ἔπεσα προσκυνῆσαι ἔμπροσθεν τῶν ποδῶν' (I fell to worship before the feet . . . : 19:10; 22:8), which is then followed by the angels rebuke, 'καὶ λέγει μοι, "Ὅρα μή"' (and he said to me, "do not do it": 19:10; 22:9) and a command, 'τῷ θεῷ προσκύνησον' (to worship God: 19:10; 22:9). That the introductions reference "one of the angels who had the seven Bowls" (17:1; 21:9) also serves to link both sections with the previous series of seven Bowls.

Thematically the accounts of 17:1–19:10 and 21:9–22:9 parallel one another in that in each account John sees a city described in terms of a woman. Thus, Bauckham suggests that the former account depicts the final judgment of evil and the latter the completion of the new creation.[108] All of this provides a solid foundation for viewing these two accounts in terms of one another. Thus, the descent of the New Jerusalem (21:9–22:9) provides the counterpart to the episode of the fall of Babylon (17:1–19:10), and both serve as dual conclusions to chapters 6–16.[109]

Consequently, the unit comprising 17:1–21:8 is rightly divided after 19:10 (17:1–19:10; 19:11–21:8). The middle unit (19:11–21:8) serves as a

106. For detailed argumentation see: Bauckham, *Climax*, 4–6.
107. Giblin, "Structural and Thematic Concerns," 490.
108. Bauckham, *Climax*, 7.
109. Bauckham, *Climax*, 4–7.

bridge between the accounts of the two opposing cities. Bauckham suggests that it details the events that intervene between the fall of Babylon and the descent of the New Jerusalem.[110] But, this section serves a number of other functions as well.

First, 19:11–21:8 also links many of the previous accounts in terms of a promise/anticipation-fulfillment. For example, those who cried out to the mountains and rocks for mercy in 6:15 receive the ultimate condemnation in 19:18. Also, the child who was snatched up in 12:5, the one 'ὃς μέλλει ποιμαίνειν πάντα τὰ ἔθνη ἐν ῥάβδῳ σιδηρᾷ' (who is to rule all nations with a rod of iron), returns to administer that rule in 19:15. Other parallels include the treading of 'τὴν ληνὸν τοῦ οἴνου' (wine press) in 14:20 and 19:15. The gathering of the kings of the earth for the battle against God and Christ on the great day of "God Almighty" in 16:14, 16 and 19:15, 19 are also parallel accounts. Regarding this divine title, Bauckham keenly observes that "τοῦ θεοῦ τοῦ παντοκράτορος" (God, the Almighty) appears only in 16:14 and 19:15. He notes,

> The full title "the Lord God Almighty," John's equivalent of the Old Testament's Yahweh Sabaoth, occurs in that full form just seven times (1:8; 4:8; 11:17; 15:3; 16:7; 19:6; 21:22), while the shorter form 'ὁ θεὸς ὁ παντοκράτορος' (God, the Almighty) occurs twice (16:14; 19:15). Thus, these two occurrences themselves perform a literary function, helping to link 16:12–16 to 19:11–21, in which battle the former presages takes place."[111]

Furthermore, the description of Christ in 19:11–16 contains a number of allusions that parallel the description of Christ in 1:12–20. Thus, 19:11–20:15 link with previous sections in that the enemies of God are destroyed in reverse order of their introduction (Death and Hades; Dragon; Beast and False Prophet; Babylon). Finally, the threat of 11:18 is carried out in chapters 19 and 20.

Consequently, the bridge unit of 19:11–21:8 serves a capacity well beyond that of merely intervening in the accounts of the two cities. For if the account of the destruction of Babylon serves as the final description of the judgment of evil, then 19:11–21:8 serves to enhance this description by adding the destructions of the Beast, the False Prophet, and the Dragon, and, in essence, incorporates the whole of the Apocalypse into

---

110. Bauckham, *Climax*, 5.
111. Bauckham, *Climax*, 33.

the description of the final judgment. This bridge section, however, clearly serves to introduce the account of the New Jerusalem as well. For the account of the New Jerusalem (21:9–22:9) begins with the exhortation "Δεῦρο, δείξω σοι τὴν νύμφην" (come, I will show you the bride: 21:9), which serves to indicate that a more complete description of the Bride of 21:2 follows.

CONCLUSION

This chapter has attempted to lay the foundation for a more detailed examination of John's portrait of the people of God in the pre-consummation portion of Revelation. As a result of this analysis of the structure of Revelation it is has become apparent that no simplistic effort to delineate the overall structure of Revelation will suffice. Though John eases an assessment of the overall flow of the narrative by the employment of verbatim repetition, he also complicates it by the insertion of two intercalations and by overlapping various sections.

This inquiry suggests that John's extended depictions of the people of God in the pre-consummation visionary section of the Apocalypse appear essentially in three narratives: 7:1–17 (the 144,000 and the Great Multitude); 11:1–13 (the Two Witnesses); and 12:1–14:5 (the Woman and the Dragon, the Beasts, and the 144,000), and it is to these accounts that we now turn in our investigation of John's depiction of the people of God.[112] This will then be followed by an examination into the depiction of the people of God in the seven letters (2:1–3:22).

---

112. In addition to these extended narratives pertaining to the people of God, there are isolated, brief, and somewhat parenthetical references to the people of God throughout the Apocalypse. Since, however, these add nothing to the overall depiction of the people of God, they are excluded from this examination.

6

7:1–17 and John's Portrait of the People of God in Light of the Four Themes Present in the Account of the Two Witnesses

THE QUESTION ARISES AT this juncture as to how the depiction of the Two Witnesses accords with the people of God throughout the Apocalypse. This chapter aims to compare the portrait of the Two Witnesses with John's portrait of the people of God in the accounts of the 144,000 (7:1–8) and the Great Multitude (7:9–17). This chapter will not attempt to provide a thorough exegesis of this passage. Instead, this account will be viewed in order to discern the presence, or lack thereof, of the four themes that appeared in the account of the Two Witnesses.

THE DIVINE PROTECTION OF THE 144,000

Though the sealing of the 144,000 from each of the tribes of Israel has fostered a great number of interpretations, I intend to confirm first that they are the people of God, who are afforded divine protection.[1] That

---

1. Attempts to identify the 144,000 are usually classified in accord with whether or not they are exclusively ethnic Israelites (a faithful remnant) or a spiritual Israel (the Church; though this view may include Jewish and Gentile Christians, or even OT and NT saints): note: Further distinctions may exist among these groups especially as to whether or not the designation 144,000 is meant literally or symbolically.

Ethnic Israelites: Allo, *L'Apocalypse*, 93; Corsini, *The Apocalypse*, 158–60; Feuillet, "Les 144,000 Israelites,": 191–224; Harrington, *Apocalypse*, 129; Kraft, *Offenbarung*, 126–28; Rowland, *The Open Heaven*, 91; Seiss, *Apocalypse*, 1.160–69; Thomas, *Revelation*, 1–7, 473–82; Walvoord, *Revelation*, 140–41; Zahn, *Introduction*, 368.

Spiritual Israel: Aune, *Revelation*, 2.443; Bauckham, *Climax*, 215–29; Beale, *Revelation*,

God protects the 144,000 derives from the stated purpose for their being sealed: namely, according to 7:3, the people of God are afforded protection from the plagues of chapter 6.[2] Ezekiel 9 is likely the background for this sealing.[3] For Ezekiel employs the notion of a mark on the foreheads of the faithful Israelites in order to protect them from harm; while the unfaithful are slain.

This passage, thus, provides the most explicit declaration of the divine protection accorded the people of God. The protection derived from the sealing reappears in 9:4 where the locusts: 'καὶ ἐρρέθη αὐταῖς ἵνα μὴ ἀδικήσουσιν τὸν χόρτον τῆς γῆς οὐδὲ πᾶν χλωρὸν οὐδὲ πᾶν δένδρον, εἰ μὴ τοὺς ἀνθρώπους οἵτινες οὐκ ἔχουσι τὴν σφραγῖδα τοῦ θεοῦ ἐπὶ τῶν μετώπων' (and they were told that they should not harm the grass of the earth, nor any green plant, nor any tree, but only those who do not have the seal of God upon their foreheads).

THE 144,000 AS WITNESSES?

The evidence for the contention that the people of God in 7:1–17 are depicted as witnesses is certainly much less defined. Though the suggestion that the 144,000 serve as witnesses is widely accepted among commentators, there is admittedly no explicit textual indicators for such a conclu-

---

409–15; Beckwith, *Apocalypse*, 535; Beagley, *The 'Sitz im Leben' of the Apocalypse*, 47; Beasley-Murray, *Revelation*, 140–41; Boring, *Revelation*, 129–32; Caird, *Revelation*, 94–98; Charles, *Revelation*, 1.200; Giblin, *Revelation*, 91–92; Harrington, *Revelation*, 98–101; Hendriksen, *Conquerors*, 129; Morris, *Revelation*, 111–12; Mounce, *Revelation*, 157–58; Smalley, *Revelation*, 182.

2. It is important to note that the narrative of 7:1–3 occurs temporally prior to the unleashing of the events entailed in the six seals. For, as Beale asserts, "Vv 1–3 must be referring to a time immediately preceding the plagues of 6,1–8. . . . If the time of 7:1–3 did not directly precede that of 6:1–8, there would be an irreconcilable contradiction between ch. 6 and 7:1–3, since it is clear in ch. 6 that the first six seals harm the earth and its inhabitants, while in the beginning of ch. 7 the earth and its inhabitants are portrayed as not yet harmed" (Beale, *Revelation*, 408).

3. See: Allo, *L'Apocalypse*, 108; Aune, *Revelation*, 2.440, 2.456–59; Beale, *Revelation*, 409–10; Beasley, *Church's Enemies*, 47; Boring, *Revelation*, 128; Bousset, *Offenbarung*, 281; Caird, *Revelation*, 96–97; Collins, *Apocalypse*, 51–52; Fiorenza, *Revelation*, 66; Harrington, *Apocalypse*, 129–30; Hengstenberg, *Revelation*, 1.292–94; Hughes, *Revelation*, 93; Keener, *Revelation*, 235; Kraft, *Offenbarung*, 126; Lohmeyer, *Offenbarung*, 66; Michaels, *Revelation*, 112; Morris, *Revelation*, 111; Mounce, *Revelation*, 157; Stefanovic, *Revelation*, 255; Thomas, *Revelation*, 64; Thompson, *Revelation*, 107; Wilcock, *Heaven Opened*, 79. There is, however, a significant difference between Ezekiel 9 and Revelation 7; namely, that those sealed in Revelation appear to suffer harm.

sion. That they serve as witnesses may be justified only by means of the accumulation of implicit features and by an appeal to the portrayal of the people of God in the whole of the Apocalypse.

Among those who affirm that the 144,000 represent witnesses or evangelists, most fail to provide any textual argumentation for this assertion. Walvoord, for example, puts forward the suggestion that the 144,000 are ethnic Israelites who are converted in order to bear witness for the gospel during the tribulation period.[4] In his commentary, however, he does not mention any exegetical evidence for this assertion. Beale's inference perhaps merits some attention. He asserts that the presence of Christ's name on their foreheads confirms their role as witnesses and enables them to persevere and confess his name. He concludes, "Hence, the seal empowers the 144,000 to perform the witnessing role intended for true Israel."[5] Beale's supposition is strengthened by the identification of the seal with the role of the indwelling of the Holy Spirit.

Bauckham, perhaps, argues more convincingly that the 144,000 constitute an army for the purpose of a holy war.[6] In his assessment, they prove victorious not by actually waging war with arms. Instead, they are victorious in the same way that Christ was victorious—that is, Christ's armies truly are: 'οὗτοι οἱ ἀκολουθοῦντες τῷ ἀρνίῳ ὅπου ἂν ὑπάγῃ' (these are the ones who follow the Lamb wherever He goes; 14:4). Bauckham postulates that "following the Lamb wherever he goes means imitating both his truthfulness, as the 'faithful witness' . . . and the sacrificial death to which this led."[7]

The evidence may gain further support by an examination of the relationship to suffering and witness. It has already been noted that suffering and martyrdom are directly associated with the activity of witnessing throughout Revelation. Thus, by this inductive process one may find a measure of support for the contention that the 144,000 are witnesses.

---

4. As a pretribulational premillenialist, Walvoord believes that the church will be raptured to Heaven at the beginning of the final seven years that precede Christ's return. Around that time, 144,000 Jews are converted in order to be witnesses during the church's absence. See: Walvoord, *Revelation*, 140.

5. Beale, *Revelation*, 411.

6. Bauckham, *Climax*, 217–237. See also, Boring who adds, "'Thousand' also has a military connotation, a division of the army. The 'thousands of Israel' is used of Israel's army and has the same ring to it as 'the battalions of Israel'" (*Revelation*, 131).

7. Bauckham, *Climax*, 232.

Nonetheless, that the people of God serve as witnesses may be affirmed only in light of the accumulation of implicit suggestions and not by means of any explicit textual indication. Thus, the postulation that the people of God are portrayed as witnesses based on 7:1–17 alone is admittedly suspect.

THE GREAT MULTITUDE AND SUFFERING PERSECUTION

That the people of God are depicted as suffering persecution, even to the point of death, is more easily arrived at in the account of 7:1–17. The clearest indication that the people of God suffer persecution and/or martyrdom here resides in the angelic declaration that the Great Multitude comprises: 'Οὗτοί εἰσιν οἱ ἐρχόμενοι ἐκ τῆς θλίψεως τῆς μεγάλης' (these are the ones who are coming out of the great tribulation; 7:14).

The expression, 'τῆς θλίψεως τῆς μεγάλης' (the great tribulation) may reference the tribulation of Dan 12:1.[8] The Danielic context incorporates a time of persecution and suffering among the people of God.[9] This appears warranted in that the use of 'θλίψις' (tribulation) elsewhere in Revelation corresponds to the context of persecution.[10] A comparison of Matt 24:21, and the only other use of 'θλίψις' (tribulation) with the adjective 'μεγάλη' (great) in the NT, confirms this conclusion. For, in Matthew's account, the expression occurs in the context of widespread and unparalleled distress. Thus, Caird concludes concerning the Great Multitude, "It is not their salvation that the martyrs are celebrating, but their triumphal passage through persecution."[11]

Furthermore, there is reason to associate the many who are dressed in white robes ('ἐλεύκαναν': lit. made white; or pure) in Rev 7:14 with the martyrs of 6:9–11. Though not definitive, it appears warranted to associate this robed multitude with the martyrs under the altar in 6:11, since both groups are similarly clothed in white robes. Though such robes may connote purity—as with the clothes in 3:18 and 19:8—it seems best to associate them with martyrdom in 7:14 for several reasons.

---

8. See: Aune, *Revelation*, 2.471; Beale, *Revelation*, 433; Collins, *Apocalypse*, 51–52; Harrington, *Apocalypse*, 132; Hughes, *Revelation*, 93; Keener, *Revelation*, 244; Kraft, *Offenbarung*, 130; Lohmeyer, *Offenbarung*, 69; Mounce, *Revelation*, 164; Stefanovic, *Revelation*, 265; Thompson, *Revelation*, 110.

9. Cf. Dan 11:30–39, 44; 12:10.

10. Cf. 1:9; 2:9, 10, 22.

11. Caird, *Revelation*, 100. See also, Charles, *Revelation*, 209–14.

First, the literary parallels between 7:14 and 6:11 are stronger than those between 7:14 and 3:18 and 19:8. For both 6:11 and 7:14 refer to the clothes as 'στολὴ' (robe); whereas, the clothing in 3:18 is 'ἱμάτιον' (garment), and in 19:8 it is 'βύσσινος' (fine linen). Furthermore, 19:8 is eliminated from the discussion both as a result of its location in the narrative and from the fact that both 7:14 and 6:11 use cognate terms for white,[12] while 19:8 uses an expression for purity.[13] Thus, even though 'λευκός' appears in 3:18, it appears that 6:11 provides the most explicit verbal parallel for the white robes in 7:14.

Morris, however, dissents from this position. He claims, "Against this, there is no indication in the narrative such as we get elsewhere, *e.g.* the reference to those 'slain because of their testimony for Jesus' (6:9)."[14] Morris, however, fails to account for the association of the Great Multitudes' white robes (7:14) with that of the martyrs under the altar in 6:9–11.[15] It appears that, by this verbal association with an earlier passage, John, at least implicitly, associates the Great Multitude with the martyrs under the altar.[16] This suggests that the white garments of 7:14 portray the Great Multitude are martyrs.

In addition, there is some evidence that behind both 6:9–11 and 7:9–17 reside allusions to Daniel 7. In his remarks on the death and resurrection of the Two Witnesses in Revelation 11, Beale notes:

> Dan. 7:21 is a prophecy of a final kingdom on earth that will persecute and defeat God's people. Afterward, the persecutors themselves will be judged and the saints will inherit the kingdom of the world (so Dan. 7:22–27). In particular, Dan. 7:22 says that God 'gave judgment to the saints,' which is a suitable anticipated, prophetic answer to the saints' prayer for judgment of the oppressors in Rev. 6:10–11. John sees this prophecy as fulfilled in the world's persecution of the church at the end of history.[17]

12. 7:14 uses the verbal form 'λευκαίνω' (make white), while 6:11 uses the cognate noun 'λευκός' (white).

13. 'λαμπρὸν καθαρόν' (bright and pure).

14. Morris, *Revelation*, 113–14.

15. See: Boring, *Revelation*, 131.

16. Therefore, Beasley-Murray overstates the situation when he claims: "It is a puzzling feature to the present writer that the majority of commentators on the Revelation in this century identify the *great multitude* with the martyrs. Of this there is not a hint" (Beasley-Murray, *Revelation*, 145).

17. Beale, *Revelation*, 588.

One may loosely associate the Great Multitude as those who have inherited the kingdom with those who have overcome such persecution and suffering. These connections, however, cannot be established with certainty in the confines of this work. Therefore, though the suggestion that the people of God's presence in heaven connotes their suffering martyrdom is appealing in light of the whole of the Apocalypse—which often portrays the people of God as martyred,—it cannot be fully justified from the immediate context of Revelation 7:9–17.

Nonetheless, Rev 7:1–17 provides some basis for the conclusion that the people of God are those who have endured persecution.

VINDICATION OF THE GREAT MULTITUDE

That the Great Multitude are vindicated according to the account of 7:1–17 derives in part from their presence in heaven before the throne of God. This receives support from the fact that those before the throne are identified as: 'Οὗτοί εἰσιν οἱ ἐρχόμενοι ἐκ τῆς θλίψεως τῆς μεγάλης' (these are the ones who are coming out of the great tribulation; 7:14). One may well contend that John's intent at this juncture of the Apocalypse is to encourage his readers with this proleptic account of their final destiny. That this entails their ultimate vindication is in the least implied.

CONCLUSION: THE FOUR THEMES AND THE PEOPLE OF GOD IN REVELATION 7

We have thus seen that the four themes, each of which were clearly present in the account of the Two Witnesses (11:1–13), are generally not as explicitly present in the intercalation of 7:1–17. In accord with the first theme, the sealing of the 144,000 affirms their divine protection. In accord with the second theme, however, the evidence is marginal as to whether they are presented as witnesses. In accord with the third theme, the reference to the people of God as having come out of the great tribulation supports the contention that they have endured suffering, persecution, and possibly martyrdom—though this theme is not as stressed as in the account of the Two Witnesses. Finally, in accord with the fourth theme, the presence of the people of God in heaven affirms that this narrative asserts their vindication.

REVELATION 7:1-17: TWO GROUPS OR ONE? THEMATIC EVIDENCE FOR THE UNITY OF THE TWO GROUPS[18]

At this point, it is worth noting that of the four themes pertaining to the people of God the evidence for the first two themes was derived primarily from the account of the 144,000 (7:1-8). Moreover, the account of the Great Multitude (7:9-17) provided the material pertaining to the last two themes. Consequently, if, as it is often suggested, the intercalation of 7:1-17 references two groups within the community of the people of God, then it appears that John does not depict the whole of the people of God in accord with the four themes. For the 144,000 are not portrayed as enduring persecution and being ultimately vindicated; and, similarly, the Great Multitude are not characterized as divinely protected or as witnesses.

I suggest, however, that a thematic approach, which examines the people of God in accord with the four themes, provides insights into our understanding of the intercalation of 7:1-17. For if we were to read the accounts of the 144,000 and the Great Multitude as a unity, then the depiction of the people of God in 7:1-17—in terms of the four themes—accords well with the portrait of the people of God in the account of the Two Witnesses (11:1-13). That is, the four themes appear in the whole of the narrative of 7:1-17 in parallel with the intercalation of 11:1-13.

Such a reading receives further support from the structural analysis of Revelation. For there we noted that the intercalation of 7:1-17 parallels the account of the Two Witnesses in both form and function. We observed that both accounts were intercalations; each occurs after the sixth item in their corresponding series of judgments; and, both address the state of the people of God amidst their corresponding judgments. Therefore, we have structural indicators that suggest that these accounts may be viewed in light of one another. And when we do so, namely when the account of 7:1-17 is read in light of the 11:1-13, we find thematic similarities between the accounts. This warrants a tentative conclusion that the 144,000 and the Great Multitude represent the same group from two differing perspectives. A comparison of the people of God throughout Revelation further suggests that the 144,000 (7:1-8) and the Great Multitude (7:9-17) represent that same group of persons.

---

18. See: Dalrymple, 'These are the Ones,' 396-406.

A COMPARATIVE LOOK AT THE IDENTITY OF THE PEOPLE OF GOD THROUGHOUT REVELATION IN ORDER TO SUPPORT THE CONTENTION THAT THE 144,000 AND THE GREAT MULTITUDE ARE THE SAME GROUP FROM TWO PERSPECTIVES

This section endeavors to examine the various means by which John identifies the people of God throughout the Apocalypse in order to support the contention that the 144,000 and the Great Multitude reference the same group. The comparative evidence in favor of viewing the 144,000 and the Great Multitude as the same group is multifaceted.[19]

The 144,000 in 7:1-8 and 14:1-5

First, I suggest that the 144,000 of 7:1-8 are the same persons as the 144,000 of 14:1-5. This results from the presence of several key verbal parallels. First, in both passages they number 144,000. In addition, in both passages, the 144,000 have a mark 'ἐπὶ τῶν μετώπων αὐτῶν' (on their foreheads: 7:3; 14:1). In the former, the mark is the 'σφραγῖδα θεοῦ ζῶντος' (the seal of the living God; 7:2). In the latter, the 144,000 are described as, 'ἔχουσαι τὸ ὄνομα αὐτοῦ καὶ τὸ ὄνομα τοῦ πατρὸς αὐτοῦ' (having His name and the name of His Father; 14:1). Thus, in both cases, we have the description of a group of 144,000, who have on their foreheads, a seal, or the name of the Lamb and the Father.

The equivalence of the seal of the living God with the name of the Lamb and the Father, thus further equating the two groups, is confirmed by contrasting it with the mark of the beast in 13:16-17.[20] There John explicitly proclaims that the mark is the name of the beast that is placed upon the foreheads of the recipients (13:17). The contrastive elements of the mark of the beast with the seal of God include the fact that both are upon the foreheads and both represent the name: either of God, or of the beast. This finds literary confirmation with John's juxtaposition of the description of the name of the beast with a description of the followers of the lamb: who have the name of the Lamb and the Father upon their foreheads.[21] Hendriksen notes,

---

19. Those who affirm this position include: Beagley, *Church's Enemies*, 47; Boring, *Revelation*, 128-32; Collins, *Apocalypse*, 52; Johnson, *Triumph*, 134.
20. Cf. Morris, *Revelation*, 110; Mounce, *Revelation*, 264.
21. Beale, *Revelation*, 716.

> The seal indicates that he belongs to Christ; worships him; breathes his spirit; thinks his thoughts after him; etc. Similarly, the mark of the beast symbolizes that the unbeliever, who persists, in his wickedness, belongs to the beast; hence, to Satan, worships the devil; breathes his spirit; etc.[22]

Thus, it is apparent why John does not mention the 144,000 of 14:1–5 as having the seal of God. Instead, by metonymy, he replaces seal with the name of the Lamb and the Father for the purpose of contrasting them with the followers of the beast. R. H. Charles concludes, "There can be no question as to the identity of the two bodies."[23] Likewise, Caird affirms, "The one hundred and forty-four thousand of the present vision [7:3–8] cannot be different from the hundred and forty-four thousand of xiv. 1."[24]

Therefore, the 144,000 of 7:1–8 and 14:1–5 should be viewed as the same group in light of the similar descriptions of them as 144,000, who have on their foreheads the seal, or name of God.

The 144,000 and the People of God Who are before the Throne in 22:1–5

A comparison of the 144,000 in both 7:1–8 & 14:1–5 with the people of God in 22:1–5 strongly suggests that the people of God in the latter passage also constitute members of the same group as the 144,000. For both the 144,000 in 7:1–8, and those in the New Jerusalem are named, 'οἱ δοῦλοι αὐτοῦ' (His servants; 22:3).[25] In conjunction with the 144,000 of 14:1–5, the people of God in the New Jerusalem are described as those who will have, 'τὸ ὄνομα αὐτοῦ ἐπὶ τῶν μετώπων αὐτῶν' (His name on their foreheads; 22:4; cp. 14:1). Thus, all three of these accounts describe the people of God as having a mark on their foreheads. Since I have already established that there are sufficient grounds for identifying the seal of God (7:1–8) with the name of God (14:1–5), there is no reason not to extend this identification to those in the New Jerusalem; thus, further equating the groups within each of these three passages.

---

22. Hendriksen, *Conquerors*, 182.
23. Charles, *Revelation*, 201.
24. Caird, *Revelation*, 94.
25. Though in 7:3 they are termed "τοὺς δούλους τοῦ θεοῦ ἡμῶν" (servants of our God).

The People of God Who are before the Throne in 22:1–5 and the Great Multitude of 7:9–17

There are several factors that suggest the identification of the people of God in 22:1–5 with the Great Multitude of 7:9–17. First, in both passages mention is made of the presence of the 'τοῦ θρόνου' (throne: 7:15; 22:3). Secondly, they are called servants engages in the worship of God (7:15; 22:3). Thirdly, the sun does not beat on them (7:16; 22:5). Fourthly, both make mention of their presence before the Lamb (7:17; 22:1). Finally, in both passages the water of life is present (7:17; 22:1).

An examination of the wider context of 21:1–22:5 with 7:9–17, exhibits further parallels. For both passages contain references that God 'σκηνώσει' (will dwell) with the faithful (7:15; 21:3), the ending of thirst (7:16; 21:6), the presence of the 'ἐπὶ ζωῆς πηγὰς ὑδάτων' (spring of living water; 7:17; 21:6), and that 'ἐξαλείψει ὁ θεὸς πᾶν δάκρυον ἐκ τῶν ὀφθαλμῶν αὐτῶν' (God will wipe every tears from their eyes; 7:17; 21:4).

Summary and Comparison with the Redeemed in 5:9

Therefore, if we identify the 144,000 of 7:1–8 with the 144,000 of 14:1–5, and also with those before the throne in 21:1–22:5, and if the people of God in 21:1–22:5 are the same as the people of God in 7:9–17, then the people of God in 7:9–17 must be the identified with the 144,000 in 7:1–8 and 14:1–5.

Furthermore, there are numerous verbal parallels relating the people of God in 14:1–5 to the Great Multitude of 7:9–17 and the redeemed of 5:9. For example, in both 14:4 and 5:9 we have a group who were purchased for God.[26] In 14:4, those purchased were "ἀπὸ τῶν ἀνθρώπων" (from among men). Revelation 5:9, however, expands this to include men, "ἐκ πάσης φυλῆς καὶ γλώσσης καὶ λαοῦ καὶ ἔθνους" (from every tribe and tongue and people and nation). The similarity in these expressions derives from a comparison with 7:9, where John notes that the great multitude was "ἐκ παντὸς ἔθνους καὶ φυλῶν καὶ λαῶν καὶ γλωσσῶν" (from every nation, tribe, people, and tongue). Commenting on 7:9, Beale suggests, "This is virtually the same phrase as in 5:9b, both being based on the formulas of Daniel 3–7."[27] Most scholars and commentators, in fact, affirm that those

---

26. Cp. "ἠγόρασας τῷ θεῷ" (you purchased for God; 5:9) and "ἠγοράσθησαν . . . τῷ θεῷ" (they were purchased for God; 14:4).

27. Beale, *Revelation*, 413.

ἐκ πάσης φυλῆς καὶ γλώσσης καὶ λαοῦ καὶ ἔθνους' (from every tribe, tongue, people, and nation) in 5:9 are the same as the great multitude in 7:9–17.[28] Since I have already contended that we should equate the great multitude of 7:9–17 with the 144,000 of 14:1–5, then the extension of the equation to those in 5:9–10 logically follows. This strongly suggests that the 144,000 were purchased from every nation, and not just Israel.[29]

Also supporting the parallels between chapters 5 and 7 is the verbal pattern of "hearing" and "seeing." On this point, Bauckham contends:

> The vision of the 144,000 and the innumerable multitude in chapter 7 forms a parallel to that of the Lion and the Lamb in chapter 5. Just as in 5:5–6, John *heard* that the Lion of the tribe of Judah and the Root of David had conquered, but *saw* the slaughtered Lamb, so in chapter 7 he *hears* the number of the sealed (7:4) but *sees* an innumerable multitude (7:9). It seems likely, therefore, that the relation between the 144,000 and the innumerable multitude is intended to be the same as that between the Lion and the Lamb.[30]

To Bauckham's understanding we might suggest that Revelation 7 not only continues the pattern of John *seeing* and then *hearing*, but that in each account the hearing section contains greater depth of detail (cf. 5:6 with 5:7–14; 14:1 with 14:2–5; 15:2 with 15:3–4; 17:1–6 with 17:7–18). Michael Wilcock comments,

> What is the relation between them [the great multitude] and the 144,000? They are one and the same. For whatever else the white-robed multitude may be, they are certainly servants of God; and if they are servants, they are sealed (verse 3); and if they are sealed, they are the 144,000 (verse 4). But how can this be—how can a limited number, all Israelites, be the same as a numberless multitude drawn from every nation? Yet again, we put ourselves in John's place. What he *heard* was a voice from heaven, declaring the results of God's census of his people.... What he *saw*, on the other hand, was that this definite total, known to God, is from the hu-

---

28. See: Aune, *Revelation*, 2.467; Bauckham, *Climax*, 27, 34, 224–226, 264, 265, 326–337; Beale, *Revelation*, 413; Mounce, *Revelation*, 162; Harrington, *Revelation*, 119; Johnson, *Triumph*, 134; Stefanovic, *Revelation*, 265; Thomas, *Revelation*, 66; Thompson, *Revelation*, 108.

29. This counters the primary objection of identifying the two groups of Revelation 7: namely, that the two groups represent diverse ethnic groups; as in: Barnhouse, *Revelation*, 142–53; Cohen, *Revelation*, 138–42; Seiss, *Apocalypse*, 1; Walvoord, *Revelation*, 139–49.

30. Bauckham, *Climax*, 215–16. Emphasis original. See also: Sweet, *Revelation*, 150.

man point of view a numberless multitude. Similarly, from God's standpoint, they are all 'Israel', his people; from our standpoint, they come from every nation under heaven.[31]

Bauckham provides a further rejoinder to those who distinguish the two groups. He suggests that the innumerability is intended to demonstrate the fulfillment of the Abrahamic promise that God would provide Abraham with an innumerable number of descendants (Cf. Gen 13:16; 15:5; 22:17; 26:4; and, "multitude of nations" Gen 17:4–6; 35:11; 48:19). This covenantal perspective provides a valuable insight in support of the position adhered to here. The reference to the 144,000 as from each of the tribes of Israel initiates the covenantal perspective. That the Great Multitude are innumerable and from every nation confirms the fulfillment of God's promise to Abraham.

CONCLUSION

The analysis of the people of God in 7:1–17 affirms that there is a correspondence between John's depiction of the people of God in this account with that of the Two Witnesses. Our thematic comparison with the account of the Two Witnesses in fact leads to the conclusion that the 144,000 of 7:1–8 are the same persons as the Great Multitude of 7:9–17, and that John portrays the people of God in each account similarly. The 144,000 and the Great Multitude may then be seen as depicting the same group from differing perspectives: one viewed from earth and the other from heaven. This conclusion was buttressed by the evidence that the 144,000 of 14:1–5 are the same group as the 144,000 of 7:1–8, which likewise constitute the same group as the Great Multitude of 7:9–17, and the inhabitants of the New Jerusalem in 22:1–5.

Therefore, the beginning of our examination into the manner in which John depicts the people of God provides some indication that the four themes in the account of the Two Witnesses recur in other depictions of the people of God.

---

31. Michael Wilcock, *Heaven Opened*, 80–81.

7

12:1—14:5 The Woman, Her Offspring, and the Four Themes

OUR THIRD EXTENDED ACCOUNT of the people of God in the pre-consummation era of Revelation is that of the Woman and her offspring (12:1–17[18])—which continues through the accounts of the Dragon, the Beasts, and the 144,000 (13:1–14:5). This chapter endeavors to determine the depiction of the people of God in this account in comparison with the people of God in the account of the Two Witnesses and the four themes pertaining to the people of God.

We must note that the narrative of the Woman and her offspring (12:1—14:5), especially as it relates to the people of God, functions in a manner distinct from that of the two intercalations (7:1–17; 10:1—11:13). For the intercalations sought to address the status of the people of God amidst the accompanying series of sevens, as well as to present a delay in the narrative of each series. We have seen that the account of the Woman and her offspring serves in part to expand the narrative of 10:1–11:13. The specific relationship of the two accounts as it relates to the people of God is that the narrative of 12:1—14:5 provides details into the nature of the 'πόλεμον' (war) against the people of God in 11:7.

What about the inclusion of 13:1—14:5 with the account of the Woman and her offspring (12:1–17[18])? Certainly, the account of the Woman and her offspring begins in 12:1 (or 11:19).[1] It appears that one

---

1. As with: Allo, *L'Apocalypse*, 174–236; Aune, *Revelation*, 660; Beale, *Revelation*, 621–800; Bauckham, *Climax*, 15–18; Bousset, *Offenbarung*, 335–383; Hendriksen, *Conquerors*, 162–188; Kraft, *Offenbarung*, 162–200; Morris, *Revelation*, 150–81; Mounce,

12:1—14:5 The Woman, Her Offspring, and the Four Themes

of the John's objectives in this narrative relates to his intent to provide an historical perspective relating to the 'πόλεμον' (war) against the people of God. John informs his readers that the 'πόλεμον' (war) is satanically inspired and that it has an historical precedence in that Satan has always been in pursuit of the people of God. It appears warranted, however, to suppose that the narrative of the Beasts (13:1[12:18]-18) and the 144,000 (14:1-5) functions in part as a continuation of the narrative of the Woman and her offspring.[2] For Rev 13 also illuminates the brief reference to war in 11:7 and delineates the nature of the war (13:7); including Satan's authorizing of the two Beasts. Chapter 14:1-5 closes the narrative by assuring the people of God of their final destiny. That this unit continues the narrative of chapter 13 is evident in part by the contrast of the 144,000 in 14:1-5 with those who received the mark of the Beast in 13:16-18.

THE DIVINE PROTECTION OF THE PEOPLE OF GOD

That the people of God in 12:1—14:5 are accorded divine protection is made fairly explicit first in that the woman, and by extension her offspring, are taken "εἰς τὴν ἔρημον" (into the desert; 12:6, 14).[3] That God

---

Revelation, 229-81; Poythress, *Returning King*, 60, 133-52; Wilcock, *Heaven Opened*, 115-38.

2. See chapter 5, in which I discussed the structure of this passage. I acknowledge that the structural indicator uniting 12:1-15:4 is present in the repetition of "Καὶ εἶδον," (and I saw) which links the sections beginning in 13:1 back to the visionary sequence begun in 12:1 (or 11:19). Thus, most commentators view this material in seven distinct units (though they do not all agree as to the precise boundaries of those units). My intent, however, is to view the thematic links within these units as they pertain to the fate of the people of God. In doing so, this analysis does not transcend any structural boundaries. For, as Aune suggests, "Between the narrative describing the sounding of the seventh trumpet (11:15-18) and the narrative of the seven bowls (15:1-16:21) are three subtexts (11:19-12:17; 12:18-13:18; 14:1-20), which are framed by these narratives. The visions that make up this section form a roughly continuous narrative of eschatological events" (*Revelation*, 2.660). Bauckham adds, "Chapters 12-14 form a series of visions reaching from the birth of Jesus Christ (12:1-5), or even from the garden of Eden (12:9) in which the conflict between the woman and the serpent began, to the parousia and the judgment (14:14-20)" (*Climax*, 284). Bauckham further argues that 12:1—14:5 comprise a section "in which John portrays the combatants in the eschatological war" (*Climax*, 229). Thus, since the narrative incorporates the people of God in 12:13 this will serve as the starting point for my analysis. Since the narrative concerning the fate of the people of God ends in 14:5, this will serve as the point of closing.

3. Though 12:6 says she 'ἔφυγεν' (fled) into the desert, 12:14 indicates that 'ἐδόθησαν... αἱ δύο πτέρυγες τοῦ ἀετοῦ τοῦ μεγάλου' (the two wings of a great eagle were given) to the

is the source of the protection afforded the woman derives from the explicit statement in 12:6 that the place was, "ἡτοιμασμένον ἀπὸ τοῦ θεοῦ" (prepared by God; 12:6); as well as the likely use of the divine passive "ἐδόθησαν" (were given) in 12:14.[4]

Though the wilderness motif may well connote either a place of tribulation or a place of refuge, the context of Rev 12 clearly favors the latter.[5] Wall notes,

> Actually the desert motif, as employed by the biblical writers, envisions two contrasting experiences. On the one hand, it is the fallen and evil place where people experience the absence of God's shalom; it is the place of tribulation and temptation. . . . On the other hand, it is the place where the resources of a good God are found, where a faithful people can experience a measure of God's shalom this side of God's final victory over the Evil One.[6]

That Rev 12:6 and 14 contextually indicate a place of God's divine protection[7] is supported by the association of desert imagery. That such imagery conveys the notion of God's divine protection for His people derives from the prevalence of Exodus language.

Exodus imagery, which pervades Revelation, in fact, provides a significant backdrop for this chapter.[8] First, there is the association of the

---

woman; and presumably her offspring (12:17).

4. That God is the actor here is derived from the consistent use of 'ἐδόθη' (he/it was given) and 'ἐδόθησαν' (they were given) as divine passives (*passivum divinum*) in Revelation (6:2, 4, 8, 11; 7:2; 8:2, 3; 9:1, 3, 5; 11:2, 3, 13; 12:14; 13:5, 7, 14, 15; 19:8; 20:4). Cf. Aune, *Revelation*, 2.394–95, 2.527–28; Beale, *Revelation*, 377.

5. The wilderness in the OT (and reproduced in the NT) was the place of judgment and wild animals. It was also a place of sin as the NT reiterates in Acts 7:39–43, 1 Cor 10:1–13, and Heb 3:7–4:7. Though the latter meaning may be implied in the use of wilderness in Rev 17:1–9, it is not likely the use in this instance. Instead, I will argue that here it conveys a place of divine provision and protection. See also, Aune, *Revelation*, 2.691; Beale, *Revelation*, 645–46; Boring, *Revelation*, 158; Caird, *Revelation*, 151–52; Fiorenza, *Revelation*, 81; Ginzberg, *Legends of the Jews*, 7.112; Hengstenberg, *Revelation*, 463–64; Hughes, *Revelation*, 137–38; Johnson, *Revelation*, 182–83; Morris, *Revelation*, 155; Mounce, *Revelation*, 234; Stefanovic, *Revelation*, 383; Thomas, *Revelation*, 104; Yeatts, *Revelation*, 222.

6. Wall, *Revelation*, 161–62.

7. Though Lindsay has asserted that the wilderness is the ancient city of Petra, and the eagle that transports the woman is the, "aircraft from the U.S. Sixth Fleet in the Mediterranean" (Lindsay, *New World*, 167), the understanding of most is that some measure of Divine protection is afforded the woman.

8. See: Aune, *Revelation*, 2.705–06; Bauckham, *Climax*, 187; Beale, *Revelation*,

12:1—14:5 The Woman, Her Offspring, and the Four Themes 101

Dragon in Rev 12 with the OT association of Pharaoh and Egypt to a Dragon.⁹ Furthermore, the use of "τρέφωσιν" (nourished; 12:6) has associations with the manna the Israelites partook of while in the wilderness. Finally, the wilderness, as a place of protection from the Dragon, reminds the reader of Israel's flight into the wilderness and escape from Egypt. Beale comments, "The woman's flight to the wilderness also recalls the end-time exodus or restoration, when Israel was expected to return in faith to the Lord and again be protected and nourished by him in the wilderness (Isa. 32:15; 35:1; 40:3; 41:18; 43:19–20; 51:3; Jer. 31:2; Ezek. 34:25)."¹⁰ Morris adds, "The wilderness is the opposite of 'the great city' which is 'Sodom and Egypt' (11:8) and which always opposes God and God's people. In the days of old God's people escaped from Egypt into the wilderness, and symbolism from Egypt is in mind throughout this chapter."¹¹ Hendriksen agrees, suggesting, "In the desert of affliction—the earthly sojourn—he has prepared a place for them and nourishes them with the manna of the Word."¹² Mounce affirms,

> For John's readers the wilderness in this context would not suggest a desert waste inhabited by evil spirits and unclean beasts, but a place of spiritual refuge. The purpose of the vision is to assure those facing martyrdom that God has prepared for them a place of spiritual refuge and will enable them to stand fast against the devil. The duration of the divine nourishment (1,260 days) corresponds to the period of persecution (cf. 11:2; 13:5). The place is one set in readiness by God himself.¹³

Furthermore, in association with this OT imagery, John notes that the woman was given "αἱ δύο πτέρυγες τοῦ ἀετοῦ τοῦ μεγάλου" (the two wings of the great eagle; 12:14). This parallels Isaiah's exhortation to the

---

643–46, 669, 670, 673, 674, 675–76; Boring, *Revelation*, 152, Caird, *Revelation*, 153; Court, *Myth and History*, 117; Fiorenza, *Revelation*, 81; Harrington, *Apocalypse*, 173; Hendriksen, *Conquerors*, 142; Hengstenberg, *Revelation*, 476–77; Hughes, *Revelation*, 141; Johnson, *Triumph*, 185; Keener, *Revelation*, 322–23; Michaels, *Revelation*, 152; Morris, *Revelation*, 159; Seiss, *Apocalypse*, 2.374, 377, 381, Stefanovic, *Revelation*, 383, 393, 394; Thomas, *Revelation*, 103, 06; Thompson, *Revelation*, 136; Wilcock, *Heaven Opened*, 117–18, 119, 121; Yeatts, *Revelation*, 222, 227, 228.

9. Cf. Ps 74:13, 14; 89:10; Isa 30:7; 51:9; Ezek 29:3; 32:2–3; Hab 3:8–15.
10. Beale, *Revelation*, 643.
11. Morris, *Revelation*, 159.
12. Hendriksen, *Conquerors*, 172.
13. Mounce, *Revelation*, 234.

people of God: that upon return from the wilderness they will, "mount up with wings like eagles" (40:31). Mounce concludes, "The woman is given the two wings of a great eagle, symbolizing divine deliverance and enablement.... In time of persecution God protects his own."[14]

Evidence that divine protection is granted to the people of God appears also in 12:16: where, "καὶ ἐβοήθησεν ἡ γῆ τῇ γυναικὶ καὶ ἤνοιξεν ἡ γῆ τὸ στόμα αὐτῆς καὶ κατέπιεν τὸν ποταμὸν ὃν ἔβαλεν ὁ δράκων ἐκ τοῦ στόματος αὐτοῦ" (And the earth helped the woman, and the earth opened its mouth and drank up the river which the Dragon poured out of his mouth). This same expression occurs in the LXX of Exod 15:12, where it is said that God caused the waters to swallow the pursuing Egyptian army. Beale claims, "In both instances, God caused the earth to open and swallow that which opposed the establishment and welfare of his people. Thus, the allusion in Revelation figuratively refers to God's protection of the church."[15] Walvoord, who most often prefers a literalistic reading of Revelation, affirms,

> It is more plausible that this passage should be understood in a symbolic way. The flood cast after Israel is the total effort of Satan to exterminate the nation, and the resistance of earth is the natural difficulty in executing such a massive program.... Whether the exact meaning of these two verses can be determined with certainty, the implication is that Satan strives with all his power to persecute and exterminate the people of Israel. By divine intervention, both natural and supernatural means are used to circumvent this program and to carry a remnant of Israel safely through their time of great tribulation.[16]

Therefore, in this narrative John reiterates the conception that the people of God enjoy divine protection. For they in the language and imagery of the Exodus account are taken to the wilderness—a place of spiritual refuge. There they are "nourished" by God. And, though subject to satanic onslaught, even the Earth will swallow up Satan's floodwaters.

---

14. Mounce, *Revelation*, 241.
15. Beale, *Revelation*, 675.
16. Walvoord, *Revelation*, 195–96.

12:1—14:5 The Woman, Her Offspring, and the Four Themes 103

THE PEOPLE OF GOD AS WITNESSES

Secondly, the people of God in the account of 12:1—14:5 are portrayed as witnesses of the gospel. The depiction of the people of God as witnesses in this narrative derives from the proclamation of 12:11: "καὶ αὐτοὶ ἐνίκησαν αὐτὸν διὰ τὸ αἷμα τοῦ ἀρνίου καὶ διὰ τὸν λόγον τῆς μαρτυρίας αὐτῶν" (And they overcame him because of the blood of the Lamb and because of the word of their testimony).[17] Trites comments on the principle conveyed in this and similar passages in the Apocalypse: "The 'conquerors' for John are the faithful witnesses who are martyred for holding the testimony borne by Jesus."[18] It is this testimony, in fact, that produces the persecution against them. Trites affirms, "On account of this confession, however, persecutions immediately come to those who obey the commandments of God and adhere to the testimony of Jesus."[19] Beale further defends this position when he notes, "The notion that their testimony is not only the basis but also the instrument by which their 'overcoming' is accomplished may be implied, since διὰ with the accusative to indicate the basis of something is very close to the idea of means, as in 13:14."[20]

Therefore, in light of John's continued association of the persecution toward the people of God and their witnessing activity, it is not surprising that the people of God are again portrayed as witnesses. For, as we will now examine, the stress of this account pertains to the suffering of the people of God, which as has been noted is strongly correlated to the faithful proclamation of the testimony of Jesus.

THE PEOPLE OF GOD AS SUFFERING PERSECUTION

That the Two Witnesses are persecuted is explicitly present in the account of 11:1–13. As stated in the opening to this chapter, it is this theme that the narrative of 12:1—14:5 now seeks to expand. In fact, within this

---

17. There is some discussion over the nature of the genitive "αὐτῶν" (their). Though some commentators prefer to see this as an objective genitive, most prefer the subjective genitive. The subjective genitive makes the most sense in light of the emphasis throughout Revelation on witnessing concerning the gospel of Christ (Even John's own imprisonment was for the "testimony of Jesus" 1:9). Thus, most of the major English translations read, "of their testimony" (ASV; ESV; KJV; NAB; NAS; NIV; NKJ; NLT; NRS; RSV).

18. Trites, *Concept of Witness*, 160.

19. Trites, *Concept of Witness*, 159.

20. Beale, *Revelation*, 663–64.

section the vigorous and continuous persecution of the people of God intensifies to an extent that the Beast is said, "νικῆσαι" (to conquer; 13:7) the people of God. This account, in fact, provides greater details relating to the nature of the opposition to the people of God, and provides the historical perspective for this conflict.

The persecution against the people of God in this section appears first in 12:13. There the Dragon is said to have 'ἐδίωξεν' (pursued) the woman and later her offspring as well (12:17). This verb is variously rendered "pursued"[21] or "persecuted."[22] In either case, however, the substance of the text connotes Satanic persecution. For, even if rendered "pursued", the obvious motivation for the 'pursuing' of God's people would be for the purpose of "persecuting" them.[23]

Also, conveying persecution is the fact that the serpent "ἔβαλεν ... ἐκ τοῦ στόματος αὐτοῦ ὀπίσω τῆς γυναικὸς ὕδωρ ὡς ποταμόν" (poured ... water like a river out of his mouth after the woman; 12:15). That 'τοῦ στόματος' (mouth) indicates words-teaching—in this case false—is evident from the parallels in 9:17–18 and 16:13–14.[24] That 'τοῦ στόματος' (mouth) may also connote persecution stems from the contrast with the sword in Christ's mouth.[25] Caird, in fact, postulates that this imagery conveys Satan's "slanderous attacks."[26] This conclusion receives justification from the purpose clause that concludes 12:15. For there it is stated that the serpent spewed this river, 'ἵνα αὐτὴν ποταμοφόρητον ποιήσῃ' (in order to cause her to be carried away by the flood).

The use of flood imagery further accents Satan's attempts to harm the people of God. Referencing the attempt of the Dragon to pour out water after the woman, Thomas notes, "It is, of course, the same attempt that was made in the Exodus from Egypt, but Satan's plan backfired when the flood waters of the Red Sea came in deluge and judgment upon the Egyptians and not the Israelites."[27] Beale concludes from this imagery, "Therefore, OT and Jewish use of the flood waters metaphor and the use

---

21. ESV; NIV; RSV; NEB; JB.
22. NAS; KJV; BDAG.
23. Beale, *Revelation*, 668.
24. Johnson, *Triumph*, 185.
25. Cf. 1:16; 19:15; cp. also 2 Thess 2:8.
26. Caird, *Revelation*, 159.
27. Thomas, *Revelation*, 106.

12:1—14:5 The Woman, Her Offspring, and the Four Themes 105

of mouth metaphors in the Apocalypse indicate that the image of the flood proceeding from the serpent's mouth portrays his attempt to destroy the church by deception and false teaching."[28]

The persecution of the people of God further intensifies in the narrative of 12:17. The failure of the floodwaters as well as the earlier efforts to harm the woman's child (12:4) results in the Dragon being "ὠργίσθη" (enraged) at the woman. Consequently, the Dragon went off 'ποιῆσαι πόλεμον μετὰ τῶν λοιπῶν τοῦ σπέρματος αὐτῆς' (to make war with the rest of her offspring; 12:17).

The height of the persecution masterminded by the Dragon climaxes in the details of this war as narrated in 13:1–10.[29] There Satan enlists the aid of the Beast out of the sea. He empowers this Beast (13:2), who subsequently intensifies the 'πόλεμον' (war) against the saints (13:7).[30] In almost unprecedented language, the narrative continues by noting that the Beast "ἐδόθη" (was given; 13:7; divine passive) the ability, 'νικῆσαι αὐτούς' (to conquer them).[31] Verse 15 adds that those who fail to worship the Beast are killed. Surely this represents the height of cosmic opposition to the people of God.

---

28. Beale, *Revelation*, 673.

29. Beagley suggests, "the practical implementation of this attack [of 12:17] seems to be described symbolically in the following chapter [13]" (*Enemies*, 72–73).

30. The repetition of "ποιῆσαι πόλεμον" (to make war) supports in part the conception that 13:1–10 expands on the account of 12:13–17[18].

31. This rendering is the same as that of the ESV. The NAS renders this verb 'overcome.' Though this seemingly contradicts Christ's claim in Matt 16:18, a possible resolution for this discrepancy resides in the account of the Two Witnesses of chapter 11. If the narrative of chapter 13 recapitulates in any manner the events surrounding the two witnesses, then one may surmise that just as the Two Witnesses were killed (and depending on one's view as to the identity of the Two Witnesses) and they appeared defeated, yet, they were ultimately vindicated. As Beale contends,

"Christ's work is now the dominate interpretive lens through which one understands OT expectations. In Rev. 11:1–2 the temple of the church is patterned after the cross of Christ, who is the true temple. Like Christ, the church will suffer and will appear to be defeated. Nevertheless, through it all, God's presence will abide with the church's members, protect them from any contamination leading to eternal death, and guarantee them ultimate victory. That believers throughout the entire Christian age are in view, rather than only those of the first century or those living at the end of history, is suggested by the observation that 11:1ff. patterns the Christian community after the suffering of Christ, a pattern characteristic of all saints throughout the inter-advent age" (*Revelation*, 561).

The Persecution of the People of God in Rev 13:5-7

The relationship between the accounts of the defeat of the people of God in 11:7 and 13:5-7 provides further insights into nature of John's depiction of the people of God in the pre-consummation era. An analysis of the relationship between the depiction of the people of God in 11:1-13 and 13:5-7 strengthens two of the arguments presented in this work. Namely, that 13:5-7 provides another instance of the people of God being addressed in terms of temple imagery. Also, that the beast wages war against the entire people of God in 13:5-7 supports the postulation that the Two Witnesses are representative of the entire people of God.

It has been noted that one of the functions of John's account of the defeat of the people of God at the hands of the beast in 13:5-7 is to recapitulate and expand on the previously brief description of the beast's murder of the Two Witnesses in 11:7.[32] The strong thematic relationship between these two passages strengthens this contention as well.

The beast's war against 'τοὺς ἐν τῷ οὐρανῷ σκηνοῦντας' (those who dwell in heaven; 13:5-7) is strongly reminiscent of the beast's war against the Two Witnesses (11:7). For there are numerous verbal and thematic parallels that relate the description of the attack of the beast in both passages. First, in both accounts John notes that it is the 'θηρίον' (beast; 11:7; 13:1) who wages war against them. Also, in both narratives the beast is described as 'ἀναβαῖνον' (coming up; 11:7; 13:1) and is said to 'ποιῆσαι πόλεμον' (to make war; 11:7; 13:7)[33] against the people of God. Furthermore, in each the result of the war is that the beast 'νικήσει' (will conquer: 11:7; to conquer: 13:7)[34] the people of God. These consistent linguistic parallels serve as strong indicators that these accounts depict the same event.[35]

---

32. Johnson labels this 'anticipation.' He suggests, "A structural feature that at first seems disconcerting but in the long run proves illuminating is the element of anticipation. Symbolic figures and events that are to be disclosed in greater detail later in the book are often introduced briefly at an earlier point" (*Triumph*, 42-43).

33. In each passage the same verbal combination is present in the Greek: the verb is a form of 'ποιεω,' and the noun a form of 'πόλεμος.'

34. Again the verbal parallel is retained by the use of the same verb 'νικαω.'

35. That the verbal links between the account of 11:7 and 13:5-7 are not verbatim may be accounted for by Bauckham's thesis (see chapter 2) that John avoids verbatim repetition in parallels accounts because he intends to use such as a verbal key for identifying vital structural elements. Nonetheless, the linguistic parallels between the accounts of 11:7 and 13:5-7, though not verbatim, are strong indicators that they are to be viewed

That the two accounts parallel one another is also evidenced by the fact that the recipients of the beast's murderous activities in both 11:7 and 13:7 relate to the same individuals. In John's description of the attack on the people of God by the beast in Rev 13:5-7, the beast is said to blaspheme God, His Name, and His 'τὴν σκηνὴν' (tabernacle; 13:6); which is further defined as 'τοὺς ἐν τῷ οὐρανῷ σκηνοῦντας' (those who dwell/tabernacle in heaven; 13:6). The verse reads:

13:6a: καὶ ἤνοιξεν τὸ στόμα αὐτοῦ εἰς βλασφημίας πρὸς τὸν θεὸν
13:6b: βλασφημῆσαι τὸ ὄνομα αὐτοῦ καὶ τὴν σκηνὴν αὐτοῦ,
13:6c: τοὺς ἐν τῷ οὐρανῷ σκηνοῦντας

Based on the syntactical and contextual considerations in 13:6, it appears that the best reading of the verse is that 6a provides the focus (i.e., God) for the beast's blasphemous actions. That is, the beast is said to blaspheme God. Verse 6b then functions appositionally to 6a and provides complementary details as to what constitutes blaspheming God: i.e., the beast blasphemes both God's name and His dwelling place (6b). This second clause (6b) then becomes the basis for the appositional clause in 6c.[36] That is, 6c serves to specify what is entailed by both "God's name" and "His dwelling place." Therefore, 'τοὺς ἐν τῷ οὐρανῷ σκηνοῦντας' (those who dwell in heaven) are the object of the beast's blasphemies.[37]

This reading of Rev 13:6 is supported by several features. First, the change from the noun 'βλασφημίας' (blaspheme) in 6a to the verbal cognate 'βλασφημῆσαι' (to blaspheme) in 6b suggests that 6b functions epexegetically to 6a.[38] Other considerations include the overall structure of the sentence and the immediate context. For in 6b the presence of 'καὶ' (and) between two articular nouns, both of which are followed by the genitive

---

in light of one another.

36. 6c is epexegetical to 6b: just as 6b is to 6a. See Aune, *Revelation*, 2.717

37. This understanding of Rev 13:6 is facilitated by the translations found in the NAS and the ESV ("It opened its mouth to utter blasphemies against God, blaspheming his name and his dwelling, that is, those who dwell in heaven"), as well as that of some commentators: e.g., Aune suggests, "'to blaspheme,' is used epexegetically in order to specify precisely how the beast blasphemed God: 'that is, to blaspheme his name and dwelling'" (*Revelation*, 2.717).

38. Had John repeated the noun 'βλασφημίας' (blaspemy) one may well have concluded that the beast would be blaspheming two things: i.e., God and something else. Instead, the alteration of the clause (from εἰς and accusative, plus a preposition and object; to an infinitive and object) serves to indicate a transition in the function of the latter clause(s).

personal pronoun ('αὐτοῦ'; his), suggests that this καὶ (and) functions as a simple connective. Thus, had John also desired to join 6b to 6a as a simple connective—i.e., in the sense of adding to the list of things that the beast blasphemes—we would have expected him to employ a similar use of καὶ (and) as he did following 6a. That there are no καὶ's (and's) connecting 6a and 6b confirms that 6b does not add to the list of items that the beast blasphemes, but that the latter clause provides an explanatory function.[39]

Furthermore, the account in 13:5–7 describes the people of God in terms of temple imagery. For in 6b John notes that the beast will blaspheme 'τὴν σκηνὴν αὐτοῦ' (His tabernacle),[40] which 6c then defines as, 'τοὺς ἐν τῷ οὐρανῷ σκηνοῦντας' (those who dwell in heaven). Therefore, the people of God, those who dwell in heaven, are identified as 'τὴν σκηνὴν αὐτοῦ' (his tabernacle). That the designation 'τοὺς ἐν τῷ οὐρανῷ σκηνοῦντας' (those who dwell in heaven) applies to earthly saints is evidenced by John's use of this title as an intended contrast to the wicked.

Though it is true, as many commentators have noted, that the designation 'τοὺς ἐν τῷ οὐρανῷ σκηνοῦντας' (those who dwell in heaven) properly applies to the true spiritual status of the people of God.[41] That is, though they dwell on earth, they are spiritually inhabitants of heaven. In fact, it appears that John's designation of them as residents in heaven serves primarily to contrast them with the repeated reference to the wicked under the rubric, 'οἱ κατοικοῦντες ἐπὶ τῆς γῆς' (those who dwell upon the earth).[42] This title for the wicked appeared earlier in 3:10 and 6:10 where they are referenced as the objects of the 'ὥρας τοῦ πειρασμοῦ' (hour of testing) and the recipients of God's vengeance for the shed blood of the people of God.[43]

That the people of God are referenced as heaven dwellers in contrast to the earth dwelling wicked receives further confirmation from the parallel with the account of the Two Witnesses. For in both passages John describes the beast's attack against the people of God, resulting in their apparent defeat, and concludes it with the response of "those who dwell on the earth"

---

39. This understanding of 13:6 is reflected in virtually every major English translation. The NJB's rendering, though not an exception to the understanding advocated here, is admittedly ambiguous.

40. The ESV and NAB

41. Cf Eph 2:6.

42. See: Stefanovic, *Revelation*, 407.

43. Cf. also, 8:13; 11:10 (2x); 13:8, 12, 14 (2x); 17:2, 8.

(11:10 "sending gifts"; 13:8 "worshipping the beast"). We should note that in the latter account the earth dwellers are said to consist of 'οὗ οὐ γέγραπται τὸ ὄνομα αὐτοῦ ἐν τῷ βιβλίῳ τῆς ζωῆς' (those whose names are not written in the book of life; 13:8). This title excludes the people of God and forms the basis for John's attempt to reference the people of God by the use of another title. The title, 'τοὺς ἐν τῷ οὐρανῷ σκηνοῦντας' (those who dwell in heaven), provides a fitting and contrastive designation for the people of God. For John, those who reside on the earth have given their allegiance to the beast. Therefore, those marked with the 'σφραγῖδα θεοῦ ζῶντος' (seal of the living God; 7:2) reside in heaven.

That the people of God are the focus of the beast's efforts in 13:5–7 also stems from the following considerations. First, the beast's blaspheming attack on the Name of God (13:6) is likely directed at the people of God since it is they who 'ἔχουσαι τὸ ὄνομα αὐτοῦ καὶ τὸ ὄνομα τοῦ πατρὸς αὐτοῦ γεγραμμένον ἐπὶ τῶν μετώπων αὐτῶν' (having His Name and the name of His Father written upon their foreheads (14:1).[44] Secondly, 13:7, which expands on the account of the beast's war, mentions only the people of God when it says that the beast was given, 'ποιῆσαι πόλεμον μετὰ τῶν ἁγίων καὶ νικῆσαι αὐτούς' (to make war with the saints and to conquer them). Thirdly, the parallels in the account of the Two Witnesses (11:1–13) and the war of the beast (13:5–7) confirm that the people of God are the recipients of the beasts attack just as the Two Witnesses were in chapter 11.

One may, however, wish to suggest that 13:6 does not provide a legitimate parallel to 11:1–2 since John employs two different designations for the "temple." For he uses 'σκηνή' (tabernacle) in 13:6, and 'ναός' (temple) in 11:1. This argument, however, does not mitigate the contention made here. What I have argued is that both passages apply heavenly tabernacle language to the people of God. Furthermore, if this point were pressed we would see that John uses both "σκηνή" (tabernacle) and "ναός" (temple) in Rev 21:3 and 21:22 to relate God's presence among His people. Therefore, one may well suggest that the difference could have

---

44. This appears to apply the principle of Matt 25:31–46 that whatever was done to one of God's children was done to God. Admittedly, the context of Matt 25:31–46 relates to acts of charity and kindness toward the people of God. Revelation, however, appears to reverse the principle applying it in a negative context. That a negative application is permissible derives from the blessings/curses associated with the Abrahamic covenant (Gen 12:3).

resulted from a stylistic variation. Beale, in fact, concludes, "The equation of the saints with the heavenly tabernacle is virtually the same identification made in 11:1-2, where true believers living on earth were equated with the invisible, indestructible sanctuary of God."[45]

Finally, that the persecution of the people of God in 13:5-7 parallels the murder of the Two Witnesses receives further confirmation from the employment of the Danielic time period. The 'μῆνας τεσσεράκοντα [καὶ] δύο' (forty-two months) in 13:5, is certainly the same forty-two months in 11:2. I have already established that 11:3-13 amplifies 11:1-2 and that the murder of the Two Witnesses (11:7) expands on the trampling of the holy city. That the beast's attack on the people of God in 13:5-7 occurs during the same three and one-half years as the trampling of the holy city suggests that it recapitulates the murder of the Two Witnesses.

Therefore, the persecution against the people of God serves as the primary feature in John's presentation of the people of God in 12:1—14:5. John informs his readers that the mastermind of the persecution against the people of God is none other than the one he had just introduced as "ὁ ὄφις ὁ ἀρχαῖος, ὁ καλούμενος Διάβολος καὶ ὁ Σατανᾶς" (the ancient serpent, who is called the devil and Satan; 12:9) and that such persecutions have always been present. This 'πόλεμον' (war) against the people of God will continue until the Beast has obtained an apparent defeat of the entire people of God community.

THE VINDICATION OF THE PEOPLE OF GOD

The fourth focus relates to the vindication of the people of God. The vindication of the people of God does not appear within this unit until 14:1-5. This is not unexpected, however, in that the emphasis in these chapters falls upon the present 'πόλεμον' (war) between the Dragon and the people of God. Throughout chapters 12 and 13 John continuously reminds his readers of God's sovereign control of history, of the defeat of the devil, and of their need to persevere during Satan's desperate attempts to thwart the progress of the gospel. Beale affirms, "The greater part of chs. 12-13 concerned the persecution of believers by forces of unbelief led by Satan and his two beastly allies. . . . Now ch. 14, together with 15:2-4, shows the final reward of the persecuted faithful."[46] By contrasting the people of

---

45. Beale, *Revelation*, 697.
46. Beale, *Revelation*, 730-31.

God who have the seal of God (14:1), with those who have the mark of the beast (13:16-18), John articulates the eternal fate of the people of God (14:1-5) in opposition to the apparent temporal prosperity of the wicked.

Therefore, just as the description of the 144,000 of chapter 7 ends with the great multitude in heaven, and the episode of the two witnesses in chapter 11 climaxes with their vindication, so also here the depiction of the war between the Dragon and the woman and her offspring, ends with the vindication of the people of God.

The triumph of the people of God in heaven constitutes an essential component of John's account. John portrays Christ as triumphant. He likewise views his followers as sharers in that triumph. John, therefore, after describing what appears to be the ultimate defeat of the people of God in 13:7, quickly reassures them of the true and final result of the 'πόλεμον' with the Dragon and the Lamb.[47] The result: it is the people of God who are described as: 'οὗτοι οἱ ἀκολουθοῦντες τῷ ἀρνίῳ ὅπου ἂν ὑπάγῃ' (these are the ones who follow the Lamb wherever He goes" (14:4).

CONCLUSION

In regard to the depiction of the people of God, the narrative of 12:1—14:5 continues the narrative of 11:1-13 and expands on the account of the Two Witnesses by primarily detailing the nature of the opposition to the people of God. For John, the people of God have always been persecuted in large part because they bear witness. John, furthermore, informs his readers that it has always been and continues to be the Dragon who has masterminded and sponsored the efforts to eradicate the people of God. John, however, continues to assure them that they, like the Israelites before them, enjoy God's sovereign protection—life in the wilderness. Finally, it is the people of God, though apparently defeated, who will 'ἀκολουθοῦντες τῷ ἀρνίῳ ὅπου ἂν ὑπάγῃ' (follow the Lamb wherever he goes).

Therefore, though this section focuses on developing the theme of the opposition to the people of God, the four themes indeed are present within the section of 12:1—14:5. The reiteration of these themes provides further justification that each of the four themes serve as a foundation for understanding of John's characterization of the people of God and his hortatory intent.

---

47. Cp. 17:14.

8

The Seven Letters, the People of God, and the Four Themes

THUS FAR THIS WORK has been primarily concerned with identifying the portrait of the people of God in the pre-consummation visionary section of Revelation. It behooves us now to compare the results of this investigation with the depiction of the people of God in the seven letters of Rev 2:1–3:22. Since, as I have argued, John's depiction of the people of God reflects a hortatory intent of exhorting them to persevere in faithful witnessing amidst persecution, the question arises as to how this corresponds with his depiction of the people of God in the seven letters.

THE DIVINE PROTECTION OF THE PEOPLE OF GOD

The assurance of the divine protection of the people of God forms the background of the seven letters. Though only the letter to Philadelphia (3:7–13) contains an explicit affirmation of God's protection upon the people of God, it will be demonstrated that the divine protecting of the people of God forms the undergirds each of the letters.

That the people of God are sovereignly protected is evidenced first by the depiction of Christ as the sovereign Lord of creation who is: 'ὁ κρατῶν τοὺς ἑπτὰ ἀστέρας ἐν τῇ δεξιᾷ αὐτοῦ, ὁ περιπατῶν ἐν μέσῳ τῶν ἑπτὰ λυχνιῶν τῶν χρυσῶν' (the one who holds the seven stars in his right hand, the one who walks among the seven golden lampstands; 2:1; cf 1:16). This description of Christ in the introduction to the letter to Ephesus sets forth God's sovereign administration over the affairs of the churches. Smalley affirms that what is meant here is that Jesus, "controls and protects the churches."[1] Now I do not intend to suppose that Christ as the sovereign Lord who watches over the people of God is the primary theme associated with this description of Christ. In fact, this aspect of Christ may well be secondary to the conception of Christ as the judge who is keenly aware of the conduct of the Ephesian church.[2] Nonetheless, the implication that God administers His sovereign control over the affairs of the churches forms an important backdrop to each of the seven letters.

The most explicit affirmation of the divine protection of the people of God comes in the letter to Philadelphia. Here Christ assures the church that 'κἀγώ σε τηρήσω ἐκ τῆς ὥρας τοῦ πειρασμοῦ' (I will keep you from the hour of testing; 3:10). Though some have argued that Rev 3:10 has in mind a secret 'rapturing' of the church—a taking of them out of the midst of tribulation[3]—the consensus affirms that Christ exhorts the people of God to maintain their witness with the assurance of God's sovereign protection. This appears justified in light of the only other occurrence of 'ἐκ' (out of/from) with 'τηρέω' (I will keep) in John 17:15. There the phrase certainly stresses a "keeping" or "protecting" of the people of God.[4]

THE PEOPLE OF GOD AS WITNESSES

That the seven letters depict the people of God as primarily engaged in witnessing evidences itself most clearly in the use of 'λυχνίας' (lampstands) to symbolize the churches. It has already been established that the use of lampstand imagery connotes the witness bearing function of the people of God. Thus, though the seven letters contain no explicit reference to the witness bearing activity of the people of God, the lampstand imagery serves to establish the association of the churches in their role as witnesses. Consequently, one may suppose that the churches' function as bearing witness is assumed and that their faithfulness, or lack thereof, in each of the letters is predicated on their maintaining their witness. Several examples serve to illustrate this point.

---

1. Smalley, *Revelation*, 60; see also, Morris, *Revelation*, 59.
2. See Beale, *Revelation*, 229; Smalley, *Revelation*, 60
3. See: Thomas, *Revelation 1–7*, 287–88; Walvoord, *Revelation*, 87.
4. For a detailed study of Rev 3:10 in this regard see: Robert H. Gundry, *The Church and the Tribulation*, (Grand Rapids: Zondervan, 1973), 54–61.

First, in the letter to Ephesus the church is chastised because 'τὴν ἀγάπην σου τὴν πρώτην ἀφῆκες' (you abandoned your first love; 2:4). Beale contends that this rebuke results from the fact that, "they no longer expressed their former zealous love for Jesus *by witnessing to him in the world*."[5] The association of 'ἡ ἀγάπη' (love) with 'μαρτύριον' (witness) in Matt 24:12–14 supports Beale's assertion.

Also, that the letters have an underlying assumption that the people of God are called as witnesses gains support by the reference to Antipas (2:13) in the letter to Pergamum; who is identified by the appositional phrase 'ὁ μάρτυς μου ὁ πιστός μου' (my faithful witness). Also, this designation immediately follows on the word of encouragement to the church of Pergamum for 'κρατεῖς τὸ ὄνομά μου' (you hold fast my Name; 2:13). Furthermore, the title 'ὁ μάρτυς, ὁ πιστός' (the faithful witness) belongs to Christ in 1:5.

Finally, the letter to Thyatira also hints at the church's role of witness. For they are commended for their, 'τὰ ἔργα καὶ τὴν ἀγάπην καὶ τὴν πίστιν καὶ τὴν ὑπομονήν' (works, love, faith, and endurance). Beale comments that these, "are works of persevering witness to the outside world. That this is specifically meant is discernible from the fact that when 'love,' 'faith,' and 'endurance,' especially 'endurance and faith,' appear elsewhere in the book they almost always refer to persevering witness."[6] Again Beale's assertion merits attention in light of the overall depiction of the people of God as those who bear witness in Revelation.

THE PEOPLE OF GOD AS SUFFERING PERSECUTION

That the people of God in the seven letters are enduring persecution stands virtually uncontested among modern commentators. For John has already introduced himself to his readers as a 'συγκοινωνὸς ἐν τῇ θλίψει καὶ βασιλείᾳ καὶ ὑπομονῇ ἐν Ἰησοῦ' (partner in the tribulation and kingdom and patient endurance in Jesus; 1:9). In addition to the general assumption of persecution and suffering that resides along the surface of the Apocalypse, there are two particular indications within the seven letters that these churches are enduring persecution and even martyrdom.

First, the church in Smyrna receives praise for having been faithful during tribulation and a warning that further difficulties await them.

---

5. Beale, *Revelation*, 230. Emphasis original.
6. Beale, *Revelation*, 260.

Thus, the angel exhorts them: 'μηδὲν φοβοῦ ἃ μέλλεις πάσχειν' (do not fear what you are about to suffer; 2:10). This suffering, the angel explains, includes imprisonment and, perhaps, even death. The church at Pergamum receives a similar warning: where, even though there is no indication of impending death, we are informed that the martyrdom of Antipas has already occurred (2:13).

Secondly, the encouragement of Christ to the Philadelphians that 'τηρήσω' (I will keep) them from the hour of testing (3:10) suggests that the people of God experience suffering and persecution.[7] Though this suffering affects, 'ἐπὶ τῆς οἰκουμένης ὅλης πειράσαι τοὺς κατοικοῦντας ἐπὶ τῆς γῆς' (on the whole world, to test those who dwell on the earth), this does not serve to indicate that the people of God are exempt from suffering.[8] For the Apocalypse maintains a constant interrelationship between the divine wrath upon the wicked and the suffering of the people of God. This tension often takes the form of a direct cause-effect relationship.[9]

Also, since, as we have argued, the suffering of the people of God in the Apocalypse correlates directly with the proclamation of the gospel by the people of God—that is, the people of God suffer because they proclaim—then one may surmise that the evidence for the suffering of the people of God also supports the contention for the previous theme that they function as witness-bearers.

THE VINDICATION OF THE PEOPLE OF GOD

The vindication of the people of God also serves as a backdrop to the letters to the seven churches. For each letter ends with a promise to "Ο νικῶν" (The one who overcomes; 2:11, 26; 3:5, 12, 21; though the dative is employed in 2:7, 17). In the Apocalypse, the one who over-

---

7. I have already contended that such *keeping* is a preservation through tribulation and not an exemption from suffering.

8. The designations 'the whole-world' and 'those who dwell on the earth' appear to specify the unrighteous as the objects of this testing. Though the use of 'οἰκουμένη' references all persons, the final clause in 3:10 appears to specify the unrighteous. For the designation 'τοὺς κατοικοῦντας ἐπὶ τῆς γῆς' serves as a technical designation for those who do not side with God (appearing eight other times; cf 6:10; 8:13; 11:10 [2x]; 13:8, 14 [2x]; 17:8; cf variant form in 13:12; 14:6; 17:2). Rev 13:8 unequivocally identifies the 'earth-dwellers' with 'οὐ γέγραπται τὸ ὄνομα αὐτοῦ ἐν τῷ βιβλίῳ τῆς ζωῆς' (those whose names have not been written in the book of life).

9. Cf 16:6, and the causal use of 'ὅτι,' where the divine wrath upon the wicked is a result of the wicked's treatment of the people of God. See also, 6:9–11; 8:3–5.

comes is the one who endures faithfully to the end. Only later does the Apocalypse make clear that the vindicated are indeed "Ο νικῶν' (the one who overcomes). The significance of the use of "Ο νικῶν' (the one who overcomes) in the seven letters manifests itself in 3:21. This last occurrence equates the overcoming of the people of God with the overcoming of Christ: 'ὡς κἀγὼ ἐνίκησα' (as I overcame; 3:21). This, along with the presence of "Ο νικῶν' (the one who overcomes) in the New Jerusalem (21:7), assures the reader that it is these who are the true victors. The reiteration of this phrase to each of the seven churches serves to indicate the significance of "overcoming."

ADDITIONAL THEMES PERTAINING TO THE PEOPLE OF GOD IN THE SEVEN LETTERS

Though each of the four themes pertaining to the depiction of the people of God appear in the seven letters, the seven letters also evidence other themes that were essentially absent from the visionary section of the Apocalypse. For example, the seven letters constantly warn the people of God against falling away and compromise (2:4–6, 14–16, 20–23; 3:2–3, 15–19). Does this militate against the contention of this work that the four themes pertaining to the people of God comprise the essence of John's portrayal of the people of God?

The presence of auxiliary themes in the seven letters does not militate against the thesis that the four themes provide the primary features characterizing the people of God. For one, the body of this work has demonstrated that the four themes serve as the matrix for John's depiction of the people of God in the pre-consummation visionary section of the Apocalypse. Also, the presence of each of the four themes in regards to the people of God in the seven letters serves to confirm the importance of these themes throughout the Apocalypse.

Finally, that the seven letters are generically distinct from the visionary section, which begins in 4:1, provides an explanation for the disjunction between the depiction of the people of God in the seven letters and the people of God in the visionary section.

That the letters are written to and focus primarily upon particular churches with real issues—both positive and negative—provides the explanation for John's more explicit directives to the churches.[10] John

---

10. This includes the mentioning of Antipas by name (cf 2:13). This does not deny

addresses real churches that had compromised the ideals set forth later in the Apocalypse. The visionary section, however, primarily addresses the Church universal and, thus, presents more general, idealist principles. This accounts, in part, for the differences between the portrait of the people of God in the seven letters and the people of God in the visionary section. That these differences do not conflict with one another may be accounted for on the basis that the seven letters are concerned with the people of God in relation to peculiar circumstances. That is, some within these churches had succumbed to temptations and fears that hindered their witness.

CONCLUSION

Consequently, the depiction of the people of God in the seven letters accords with presentation of the people of God in terms of the four themes. God's sovereign protection of the people of God reflects more of who He is, than the resultant state of the people of God. The absence of an explicit command to the churches (i.e., lampstands) to bear witness, derives more from the fact that this is what lampstands do. For it borders on unnecessary redundancy to command lampstands to shine.[11] Furthermore, to associate that fact of the churches suffering with their bearing witness also seems unnecessary. For assuredly they knew this relationship. Finally, the use of some form of 'νικάω' in each of the seven letters serves to emphasize that they will be the ultimate victors (cf 3:22).

Most importantly, for the sake of this work, is the presence of each of the four themes pertaining to the people of God. The only discrepancy between John's portrait of the people of God in the seven letters with the people of God in the visionary section relates to the fact that the seven letters address particular people with peculiar issues and consequently other features that transcend the four themes appear.

---

that, as with many of the NT epistles, the writer is aware of a wider audience: hence, John concludes each of the seven letters with, "Ὁ ἔχων οὖς ἀκουσάτω τί τὸ πνεῦμα λέγει ταῖς ἐκκλησίαις" (let him who has an ear hear what the Spirit says to the churches; 2:7, 11, 17, 29; 3:6, 13, 22). The point here is that the primary focus of the letters is on the particular churches and their circumstances.

11. It would be equally unnecessary to exhort a king to rule, or a teacher to teach. One may see a letter addressed to a teacher encouraging them to teach well, or to teach more often.

9

The Christological Significance of John's Portrait of the People of God

CHRIST IS THE CENTER of the Apocalypse. Or, perhaps, it may be better stated—Christ is the Apocalypse. As Minear notes, "When one asks where, in the first eight verses, the focus of John's interest fell, he can be fairly sure of the answer: on the work of Jesus Christ. . . . Whether we think of this document as a book, as a letter, or as a series of visions, Jesus Christ remains the central figure."[1] In this chapter, I intend to determine the correspondence between John's portrait of the people of God with his Christological conceptions. For, in the words of C. B. Caird, in Revelation, "each Christian is called to an *imitatio Christi*, a holding fast to the testimony of Jesus. Each is called to be a Conqueror, repeating in his own life the archetypal victory of Christ."[2] Pattemore affirms, "Revelation's ecclesiology is crucially dependent on its christology."[3]

The role of Christology in Revelation will be examined in accord with three of the four themes that I have set forth in relation to the people of God. For it appears that that the portrait of Christ not only accords with John's overall portrait of the people of God, but that Christ forms the model for which they are called to emulate.[4] There is, however,

1. Minear, *New Earth*, 11.
2. *Revelation*, 297.
3. Pattemore, *The People of*, 216.
4. This chapter, therefore, is not so much a chapter on Christology in Revelation—a topic that would encompass more than one dissertation in itself—but how the portrait of the people of God in Revelation is reflective of John's christology.

The Christological Significance of John's Portrait of the People of God

one caveat in this examination into the role of Christology in John's portrayal of the people of God: namely, that the first of the four themes, the divine protection afforded the people of God, is never mentioned in relation to Christ.[5] The lack of such, however, does not militate against my thesis. For its absence may be accounted for on the basis of the fact that Revelation stresses Christ in terms of His glorified state, which has no need of such protection.[6]

JESUS IS 'THE FAITHFUL WITNESS'

I have contended that the call of the people of God to witness relates one of the primary hortatory purposes of Revelation. It is significant, therefore, to note that John places at the forefront of his presentation of Christ, His faithfulness as a witness.[7] This is evident in the designation of Christ as 'ὁ μάρτυς, ὁ πιστός' (the faithful witness) in 1:5.[8] That John's

---

5. There is at least one potential parallel in this regard between the Two Witnesses and Christ. That is, that they are both portrayed as having words (fire and a sword) that proceed from their mouths. I do not suppose, however, that the sword that proceeds from Christ's mouth in any way represents His divine protection or even His prophetic ministry, and, consequently, there is no real thematic parallel.

Also, it is the reality of persecution and the tribulations that confront the people of God that has led to John's comforting reminder that they enjoy God's sovereign protection over their souls just as God protected Christ. For John's introductory description of Christ lists Him as: 'ὁ μάρτυς, ὁ πιστός' (the faithful witness; 1:5). This is immediately followed by the title, 'ὁ πρωτότοκος τῶν νεκρῶν' (the firstborn of the dead; 1:5). Admittedly, however, one cannot press this feature to the level of a theme pertaining to John's portrait of Christ.

6. The absence of the divine protection of Christ is what we may have expected in terms of the hortatory nature of the Apocalypse. After all, I have contended that John wants his readers to emulate Christ as a witness, who faced persecution, and was ultimately vindicated. For John to exhort them to faithfully persevere—as Christ did—with the knowledge that they enjoy God's sovereign protection, would appear to be a natural step. Yet, even though assuring them that Christ also was divinely protected would have further maintained the parallel between the roles of the people of God and Christ, it is by no means necessary for John to draw on such a tradition.

7. It would perhaps be justified for us to examine the concept of witnessing and persecution at the same time. For, undoubtedly, the relationship between Christ's bearing witness and His death is inseparable.

8. Though both the NA27 and UBS4 have a comma separating 'ὁ μάρτυς' (witness) and 'ὁ πιστός' (faithful), I affirm, along with nearly every modern English translation, that they should be read as one. This follows from the use of the same title in 2:13, in which case neither of the Greek texts insert a comma. Furthermore, taking these two as a single predicate results in the application of three titles to Christ in 1:5 (cf. Aune,

hortatory concern was to exhort his readers to follow Christ in the call to evangelism is evident from the fact that the people of God are to emulate Jesus and that the designation 'ὁ μάρτυς, ὁ πιστός' (the faithful witness) constitutes the first description of Christ in Revelation. Minear, in fact, concludes that Jesus, "was therefore introduced as the confirming witness *par excellence.*"[9]

That Jesus is an exemplar of faithful witnessing for the people of God to emulate derives confirmation from the application of the identical title ('ὁ μάρτυς μου ὁ πιστός μου'; my faithful witness; 2:13) to Antipas.[10] The designation of Antipas by means of the same title that was applied to Christ appears to connote Antipas as one who testified in the manner of Christ. Thus, Court concludes, "Because of the parallel title there is some recognition of the fact that the crucified Lord is the model of the Christian witness."[11] The reader, of course, does not have far to go to see the implications of such a notion.

The use of 'ὁ μάρτυς, ὁ πιστός' (the faithful witness) for Christ in 3:14, prefaced with ('ὁ ἀμήν; the amen) further associates Christ with one who testifies faithfully.[12] For there Christ as the faithful witness is further complemented with the adjective, 'καὶ ἀληθινός' (and true). Minear correctly notes that "the association with *the Amen* with *the True* implies the absolute credibility and reliability of the person."[13] Thus, Bauckham observes,

> Jesus himself is the faithful witness (1:5; 3:14) because he maintained his witness even to the point of death, beyond which it was vindicated as true witness in his resurrection. In this way, he won a victory over all evil, which, in 5:6–14, was already depicted as leading to the universal worship of God and the Lamb. But the way in which his victory takes effect in bringing the nations to repentance and faith is through his followers' participation in his

---

Revelation, 1.25). The use of three titles is common in Revelation (cf 1:4, 8, 9, 17; 2:2, 3, 5; 4:9, 11; 8:7; 10:6; 17:8).

9. Minear, *New Earth*, 12.

10. The only difference in the two titles is superficial: for, 2:13, being the words of Christ himself, adds the pronoun 'μου' (my).

11. Court, *Myth and History*, 90.

12. Though Aune suggests that the use of this title in 3:14 references the witness of the exalted Christ (*Revelation*, 1.37–38). Smalley affirms that Jesus is the witness both in 'history and beyond it' (*Revelation*, 34).

13. Minear, *New Earth*, 12.

The Christological Significance of John's Portrait of the People of God

victory. When they too maintain their witness even to death and are seen to be vindicated as true witnesses, then their witness participates in the power of his witness to convert the nations.[14]

Finally, that Christ is the exemplar of the people of God who serves as a witness is evident by the parallel imagery applied to both Christ and the church. Kline observes that the use of the lampstand imagery, taken from Zechariah, has a Christological undergirding. He notes,

> In Revelation 11 (esp. v. 4), the most explicit reference to Zechariah's fifth vision, the menorah symbolism is applied to the two prophet figures representing the church. An extensive parallel between the nature and historical course of the mission of Christ and the prophet-menorah community directs attention to the way the church is being formed in the Lord's menorah image.[15]

CHRIST AS SUFFERING PERSECUTION

As with the portrait of the people of God, the conception of persecution in relation to Christ is intimately connected with His role as the witness. In fact, it may well be stated that Revelation's depiction of the people of God in correlation with Christ provides the primary background for the persecution of the church.[16] Three points serve to support the assertion that Christ's suffering and death are paradigmatic for the people of God.

First, there is the promise contained in the exhortation in the closing of the letter addressed to the church of Laodicea. There John references the promise that, "Ὁ νικῶν" (the one who overcomes) will be granted the right 'καθίσαι μετ' ἐμοῦ ἐν τῷ θρόνῳ μου, ὡς κἀγὼ ἐνίκησα καὶ ἐκάθισα μετὰ τοῦ πατρός μου ἐν τῷ θρόνῳ αὐτοῦ' (to sit with Me on My throne, as I also overcame and sat down with My Father on His throne; 3:21). From this Fiorenza concludes, "The eschatological fate of Christian prophets and witnesses is very much like that of their Lord."[17] Boring similarly notes, "Jesus was the prototypical martyr (1:5; 3:14; 22:20). Language about Jesus (and his martyrdom) is used interchangeably with language about Christians (and their martyrdom)."[18]

---

14. Bauckham, *Climax*, 280–81.
15. Kline, *Glory in our Midst*, 145.
16. Cp. John 15:18–20.
17. Fiorenza, *Revelation*, 78.
18. Boring, *Revelation*, 145.

Second, the association of the suffering of the people of God with that of Christ is also connoted in 1:9 where John references himself as a fellow-partaker 'ἐν τῇ θλίψει καὶ βασιλείᾳ καὶ ὑπομονῇ ἐν Ἰησοῦ' (in the tribulation, kingdom, and patient endurance in Jesus). The singular use of the article to introduce the three datives serves to link them as a unity in some sense. The significance for our interests relates to the fact that this three-fold designation of the people of God parallels the three-fold description of Christ in 1:5. Furthermore, these three datives are all linked by the concluding prepositional phrase 'ἐν Ἰησοῦ' (in Christ). Thus, the people of God share in the suffering by their association with Christ. Minear states, regarding this verse: "To the prophet this agony was a genuine continuation of Jesus' own passion. We would, in fact, be justified in translating the phrase as 'full partners in Jesus' passion.'"[19]

Third, a look into the account of the Two Witnesses confirms several parallels between the suffering of the people of God and that of Christ. First, there is the association of the place of the murder of the Two Witnesses (11:8) with the crucifixion of Christ. Furthermore, John notes that the bodies of the Two Witnesses were allowed to remain unburied for three and one-half days (11:9). Aune notes that, "The statement that the two prophets were lying dead in the public square for *three and one-half* days suggests a partial parallel to the three-day period between the death and resurrection of Jesus."[20] We noted already that one may object to the association of the death of the Two Witnesses with that of Christ because of the alteration of the three days associated with Christ's burial and resurrection to three and one-half days. In chapter 2, it was noted that John's preference for three and one-half (cf 11:3; 12:6, 14; 13:5)—especially as it relates to the Danielic era of suffering—and the possible association with the three and one-half years of Jesus' ministry may provide an explanation for his use of three and one-half here. The fluidity of the imagery of the apocalypse, however, still allows for an association of the death of the Two Witnesses and three days and three nights of Christ's entombment. Bauckham contends,

> The parallel continues with the resurrection and ascension of the witnesses after three and a half days (11:9, 11). John has converted the 'third day' of the Gospel tradition into 'three and a half days,'

---

19. Minear, *New Earth*, 23.
20. Aune, *Revelation*, 2.587.

just as the tradition he followed with regard to Elijah's drought converted the 'third year' of 1 Kings 18:1 into 'three and a half years'. The fate of the witnesses is given an apocalyptic period appropriate to the allusion to Daniel 7:21 in 11:7, but the Danielic allusion is interpreted by reference to the history of Jesus which provides the model for his faithful followers.[21]

Fourth, John stresses throughout the Apocalypse the atoning significance of Jesus' death. Thus, in 5:9 the Lamb is worthy to open the scroll, 'ὅτι ἐσφάγης καὶ ἠγόρασας τῷ θεῷ ἐν τῷ αἵματί σου ἐκ πάσης φυλῆς καὶ γλώσσης καὶ λαοῦ καὶ ἔθνους' (because you purchased for God by your blood *people* from every tribe, tongue, people, and nation). This is also evident in the account of the Great Multitude whose robes have been made white 'ἐν τῷ αἵματι τοῦ ἀρνίου' (by means of the blood of the lamb; 7:14).

Finally, the overall depiction of the suffering of the people of God is reminiscent of the suffering of Jesus in the fact that the Witnesses die and ascend to heaven.[22] As Caird succinctly states, "Like him they have their Easter Day."[23] The correspondence of these features in the narrative of the Two Witnesses to the death and resurrection of Christ supports Beale's conclusion:

> That believers throughout the entire Christian age are in view, rather than only those of the first century or those living at the end of the history, is suggested by the observation that 11:1ff. patterns the Christian community after the suffering of Christ, a pattern characteristic of all saints throughout the inter-advent age.[24]

VINDICATION AND JESUS

Certainly the vindication of the people of God and the affirmation of the blessed hope that awaits them provides one of the major sources of comfort to the people of God who are afflicted. It is only natural, however, that those who are so exhorted desire further evidence of the assurance of such encouragement: hence, the beauty of the Apocalypse. For John assures his

---

21. Cf. Bauckham, *Climax*, 280.
22. See: Court, *Myth and History*, 99.
23. Caird, *Revelation*, 138.
24. Beale, *Revelation*, 561.

readers that Christ, The Faithful Witness, is also the 'ὁ πρωτότοκος τῶν νεκρῶν' (the firstborn of the dead; 1:5). As Minear notes,

> As Christ had validated his testimony to God by joining the company of the dead, so God had validated Christ's testimony by raising him and making him the first of many dead men to be raised, pledging through him his intention to vindicate all who 'washed their robes in the blood of the Lamb.'[25]

The vindication of Christ pervades the Apocalypse. In the opening depiction of Christ, John notes that He is, 'ὁ ζῶν, καὶ ἐγενόμην νεκρὸς καὶ ἰδοὺ ζῶν εἰμι εἰς τοὺς αἰῶνας τῶν αἰώνων' (the living One, and I am the One who was dead and behold is living forever and ever; 1:18). Later, in the account of the Woman and the Dragon John notes that though the Dragon wanted to 'καταφάγῃ' (devour; 12:4) her child, instead, 'ἡρπάσθη τὸ τέκνον αὐτῆς πρὸς τὸν θεὸν καὶ πρὸς τὸν θρόνον αὐτοῦ' (her child was snatched up to God and to His throne; 12:5). This snacthing up to God relates to the vindication of the child.[26]

The identification of Christ as vindicated recurs throughout the seven letters of chs 2–3. Thus, in the opening of the letter to Smyrna Jesus is, 'ὁ πρῶτος καὶ ὁ ἔσχατος, ὃς ἐγένετο νεκρὸς καὶ ἔζησεν' (the First and the Last, who was dead and came to life; 2:8). That this designation serves as the paradigm for the people of God is evident in that the letter to Smyrna closes with the encouragement to the people of God that, 'ὁ νικῶν οὐ μὴ ἀδικηθῇ ἐκ τοῦ θανάτου τοῦ δευτέρου' (the one who overcomes will not be hurt by the second death; 2:11).

This note of encouragement resides alongside the exhortation of 3:21 that 'ὁ νικῶν δώσω αὐτῷ καθίσαι μετ' ἐμοῦ ἐν τῷ θρόνῳ μου, ὡς κἀγὼ ἐνίκησα καὶ ἐκάθισα μετὰ τοῦ πατρός μου ἐν τῷ θρόνῳ αὐτοῦ' (the one who overcomes I will give to him to sit with Me on My throne, as I also overcame and sat down with My Father on His throne). Thus, Hendriksen concludes, "*He* is victorious; as a result, so are *we*, even when we seem to be hopelessly defeated."[27]

---

25. Minear, *New Earth*, 12.

26. Though John does not build on the parallel between the resurrection/vindication of the people of God and Christ, Paul does use the same verb for the people of God in 1 Thess 4:17.

27. Hendriksen, *Conquerors*, 8.

CONCLUSION

Thus, it is apparent that the depiction of the people of God in Revelation correlates with John's Christology. John appears to have predicated his conception of the people of God primarily in accord with his conception of the person and work of Christ. Kline, in fact, while commenting on the Two Witnesses of Rev 11, asserts, "As their career unfolds in verses 3-12, the reader cannot miss the similarity of its pattern to that of Jesus' ministry. A time of proclamation and signs, issuing in staunch opposition and the violent death of the witnesses in the great city, 'where also our Lord was crucified' (so verse 8 adds, making the parallelism explicit), is followed by the resurrection of the martyrs and their ascension in a cloud."[28] Thus, the people of God are to be witnesses as Christ was the faithful witness. They are to overcome in suffering and perhaps death as Christ overcame. And, they will be resurrected and vindicated as was Christ resurrected and vindicated.

Thus, aside from the lack of reference to the divine protection of Christ, with each of the remaining three themes John bases his depiction of the role and function of the people of God upon the person and work of Christ. The message to the churches rings clear: Jesus was the faithful witness, which led inexorably to His death and His resurrection: thus, so shall you do likewise!

---

28. Kline, *Images of the Spirit*, 90–91.

10

The People of God in Daniel and the OT Apocalypses, and the Apocalypses of the Second Temple

I HAVE THUS FAR argued that John's portrait of the people of God in Revelation accords with four themes and that these themes are largely derived from John's Christology. In this chapter, attention is turned to compare and contrast John's conception of the people of God with that of Jewish apocalyptic literature of the Second Temple (ST) period. Thus, we will examine the people of God both in the apocalyptic portions of the OT[1] and in later Jewish apocalyptic writings[2] in order to ascertain the relationship between this body of literature and John's depiction of the people of God.[3] The question under investigation essentially relates to

1. Primarily, the apocalyptic portions of Ezekiel, Daniel, and Zechariah are in view.

2. Since this examination endeavors to determine if John's conceptions pertaining to the people of God were already 'in the air,' or whether his perception of the people of God was unique to himself, parallels or contrasts with the whole body of ST literature may well be noted. In fact, some of the points of comparison and/or contrast may even occur within literature that post-dates both Revelation and the ST. Though such works are not necessarily the focus of this inquiry, as a point of comparison/contrast occasional references to them may occur throughout this chapter. However, since the apocalyptic writings of the OT and among the ST literature provide the most natural starting place as a point of comparison with Revelation, these works are primarily in view.

3. For discussions pertaining to the genre 'apocalypse' see: J. J. Collins, *The Apocalyptic Imagination* (Grand Rapids: Eerdmans, 1998); J. J. Collins, "Genre, Ideology and Social Movements in Jewish Apocalypticism," in *Mysteries and Revelations* (ed. John J. Collins and James H. Charlesworth; Sheffield: Sheffield, 1991); J. J. Collins, "Introduction: Towards the Morphology of a Genre," *Semeia* 14 (1979): 1–20; J. J. Collins, "The Jewish

whether or not John was unique in his portrayal of the people of God, or did he conform to standard apocalyptic depictions?

JOHN'S USE OF DANIEL IN HIS PORTRAIT OF THE PEOPLE OF GOD

An examination of John's portrait of the people of God suggests that John employed Danielic motifs and refashioned them in light of his own perceptions of the people of God. Specifically, it appears that John has employed Danielic imagery and language as the basis for his account of the Two Witnesses—and in particular the measuring of the Temple in 11:1-2. Since Daniel is widely recognized as the paradigmatic work for much of the apocalyptic literature of the ST period and even the eschatological discourses in the Synoptics and Paul,[4] it is not surprising that John's portrait of the people of God corresponds most closely with that of Daniel.[5]

Apocalypses," *Semeia* 14 (1979): 21-51. Paul Hanson, *The Dawn of the Apocalyptic* (Philadelphia: Fortress, 1979); Robert Funk, ed., *Apocalypticism* (New York: Herder and Herder, 1969); David Hellholm, ed., *Apocalypticism in the Mediterranean World and the Near East* (Tubingen: J. C. B. Mohr, 1983).

For a discussion of genre and Revelation see: Aune, "The Apocalypse of John and the Problem of Genre," *Semeia* 36 (1986): 66-91; J. J. Collins, *Daniel: with an Introduction to Apocalyptic Literature* (Grand Rapids: Eerdmans, 1984), 6-19.

On the genre of Revelation see: Aune, *Revelation*, lxx-xc; Beale, *Revelation*, 37-43; George E. Ladd, "Why not Prophetic-Apocalyptic?" *JBL* 76 (1957): 192-200; Bruce Malina, *On the Genre and Message of Revelation: Star Visions and Sky Journeys* (Peabody, Ma.: Hendrickson, 1995); F. D. Mazzaferri, *The Genre of the Book of Revelation From a Source-Critical Perspective* (Berlin: de Gruyter, 1989); Michaels, *Revelation*, 14; Morris, *Revelation*, 22-25.

4. This is no more apparent than in *Ezra* 12.11-12, which explicitly cites Daniel: "The eagle which you saw coming up from the sea is the fourth kingdom which appeared in a vision to your brother Daniel. But it was not explained to him as I now explain or have explained it to you." Lars Hartman, in fact, has persuasively demonstrated the use of Daniel in the eschatological discourses of the synoptic gospels (*Prophecy Interpreted: The Formation of Some Jewish Apocalyptic Texts and of the Eschatological Discourse of Mark 13 Par.* [Coniectanea Biblica, NTS 1; Lund: Gleerup, 1966], 145-77).

5. Beale, in fact, suggests that Daniel provided a *Vorbild* for much of the Jewish literature of the ST period as well as Revelation (*The Use of Daniel in Jewish Apocalyptic Literature and in the Revelation of John* [Lanham: University Press of America, 1984], 313-20). Aune, in his section on source criticism and Rev 11:3-13, suggests that John has actually reworked a Palestinian text dated prior to A.D. 70 (*Revelation*, 588). Though the evidence for this is in question, this type of assertion lies beyond the purview of our interests. The question for our investigation here concerns whether or not the themes that John has utilized in his depiction of the people of God are paralleled in ST apocalyptic works. That is, was John depicting the people of God in accord with the traditional

John's use of Daniel, primarily relates to the sufferings foretold by Daniel, though reference to the divine preservation of the people of God and their subsequent vindication are also present. One significant change, however, appears to have been introduced by John. Namely, that Daniel seemingly depicts the defeat of the entire community of the people of God, while John suggests that though all of the people of God are persecuted only some will suffer martyrdom. In regard to John's use of Daniel, however, it appears that most scholars have not completely recognized the subtle manner in which John reshapes these Danielic themes. For, it is precisely through John's reuse of Daniel, and the slight changes that he introduces, that one grasps more fully the dimension of John's portrait of the people of God. Specifically, John has adapted and modified Daniel's portrayal of the war and defeat of the people of God in Dan 8:10–14 and conformed it so that it accords with his own conception of the people of God.

John's Use of Daniel 7 in Revelation 11–14

That John is reading Daniel is first evidenced by the proliferation of Danielic themes and imagery throughout Rev 11–14—especially John's account of the beast (Rev 11:7; 13:1–7). Though the abundant use of Dan 7 does not relate directly to John's portrait of the people of God, it serves to establish the basis upon which a comparison between the people of God in Daniel, and in particular Dan 8:11–14, may be made with the people of God in Rev 11:1–13.

John's dependence on Daniel 7 derives first from his account of the Beast from the sea, which demonstrates dependence on the four beasts of Dan 7. The relationship between Dan 7 and Rev 13, in fact, is readily apparent from a comparison of Daniel's four beasts (Dan 7) with the beast of Rev 13:1–8. Most commentators agree that the beast of Rev 13 is best viewed as a composite of the four beasts of Dan 7.[6] J. J. Collins affirms that, "In Revelation 13 the single beast that rises from the sea combines salient characteristics of each of the four beasts in Daniel 7."[7]

---

understanding of the role and function of the people of God, or did John have a unique understanding of the role and function of the people of God?

6. Cf. Beale, *Revelation*, 683–703; Hendriksen, *Conquerors*, 146; Morris, *Revelation*, 161; Mounce, *Revelation*, 245.

7. J. J. Collins, *Daniel*, (Minneapolis: Fortress, 1993), 107.

Thus, John's beast is said to have, 'κέρατα δέκα καὶ κεφαλὰς ἑπτὰ καὶ ἐπὶ τῶν κεράτων αὐτοῦ δέκα διαδήματα' (ten horns and seven heads and upon his horns ten diadems; 13:2). This conforms to the combined features of the four beasts of Daniel (cp Dan 7:3-7, 20, 24 LXX).[8] The seven heads total the number of heads of Daniel's four beasts and the ten horns and ten diadems recall Daniel's fourth beast.[9] Also, John's beast has animal like features: "τὸ θηρίον ... ἦν ὅμοιον παρδάλει καὶ οἱ πόδες αὐτοῦ ὡς ἄρκου καὶ τὸ στόμα αὐτοῦ ὡς στόμα λέοντος' (the beast was like a leopard and his feet were like a bear and his mouth was like a lion; 13:2).[10] These correspond with Daniel's first three beasts, which are depicted in accord with the creatures that John has assimilated in his beast (cf Dan 7:4-6 LXX).[11] These parallels, in fact, are so striking that one may reasonably surmise that the four beasts of Dan 7 have formed the tapestry from which John has woven his account of the beast. Beale goes so far as to propose that Rev 13:1-7 "are a creative reworking of Dan 7:1-7."[12]

Furthermore, the suggestion that John's account of the beast (Rev 11:7; 13:1-7)[13] draws upon the imagery of the Daniel's four beasts appears justified in light of the fact that John has also imported into his depiction of the beast in Rev 13 contextual features derived from Dan 7. This is evidenced first in that the beast in Rev 13 comes up 'ἐκ τῆς θαλάσσης' (out of the sea; 13:1).[14] In Daniel, all four of the beasts are similarly depicted

---

8. Mounce, though affirming that the beast of Rev 13 is a composite of the four beasts of Dan 7, dissents from the position that the seven heads of the beast in Rev 13 are a composite of the total number of heads of Daniel's four beasts—preferring instead to associate the 'seven' heads with its symbolic significance (*Revelation*, 245-46). Though Mounce, perhaps, is correct in accentuating the significance of the number 'seven,' I see no reason for not also associating the seven heads with the combined number of heads of Daniel's four beasts.

9. Mounce, *Revelation*, 245

10. See: Hendriksen, *Conquerors*, 145;

11. Though the feminine 'λέαινα' occurs in 7:4.

12. Beale, *Revelation*, 683.

13. That the beast in Rev 11:7 is the same beast as that of 13:1-7 has been defended in the structural analysis of chapter 2; where I argued that the function of 13:1f was to elucidate the nature of the opposition to the Two Witnesses, which was only briefly alluded to in 11:7. This identification is virtually unanimous among commentators. See: Caird, *Revelation*, 161.

14. For the correspondence of the 'sea' in Revelation and Daniel see: Caird, *Revelation*, 137.

as coming up 'ἐκ τῆς θαλάσσης' (7:3: LXX).¹⁵ This account of the beasts coming up from the sea is paralleled in *4 Ezra* 11.1. *Fourth Ezra* 11-12, however, also closely parallel Dan 7 and are clearly dependent upon it. In fact, the interpretation of the fifth vision to Ezra specifically associates this vision with Dan 7.

Secondly, the beast in Rev 13 has, 'στόμα λαλοῦν μεγάλα καὶ βλασφημίας' (a mouth speaking great things and blasphemies; 13:5). The object of these blasphemies is then identified as God Himself ('εἰς βλασφημίας πρὸς τὸν θεόν': in blasphemies against God; 13:6). This is strongly reminiscent of the depiction of the little horn in Dan 7:8, 11, 20. In fact, the same combination of 'στόμα λαλοῦν μεγάλα' occurs in the LXX of Dan 7:8 and 20.

Thirdly, the account of the beast in Rev 13 parallels Dan 7 in that the object of the blasphemies in both passages is God. That the little horn in Daniel blasphemes God derives from the interpretation provided in Dan 7:25, where it is said that he will 'λόγους πρὸς τὸν ὕψιστον λαλήσει' (he will speak words against the Most High).¹⁶ Fourthly, the contextual parallels between Dan 7 and Rev 13 also appear in that the war against the saints¹⁷ in Dan 7:21 and Rev 13:7 are referenced in almost identical terms. For Dan 7:21 reads: 'ἐποίει πόλεμον μετὰ τῶν ἁγίων καὶ ἴσχυσεν πρὸς αὐτούς' (he was making war against the saints and was strong against them),¹⁸ while Rev 13:7 states: 'ποιῆσαι πόλεμον μετὰ τῶν ἁγίων καὶ νικῆσαι αὐτούς' (to make war against the saints and to conquer them). Beale, in fact, concludes that the beast's war against the people of God in Revelation "can be considered a reflection of the horn's warring against the saints in Daniel 7."¹⁹

Fifthly, Beale suggests that since the Dragon imagery in Rev 12:3-4 derives from Dan 7-8, it is reasonable to suppose that the same imagery

---

15. It is not certain what Greek version of Daniel John may have had available to him. For sometimes John is more in line with the LXX and other times he corresponds with Theodotion. See: Beale, *Use of Daniel*, 235.

16. See: Collins, *Daniel*, 108; Mounce, *Revelation*, 249.

17. A long battle has brewed over the identification of the '!yvi_yDIq;-~[' (lit. 'holy ones') in Dan 7. The immediate intent of Dan 7, however, is beyond our focus. In terms of the focus on Revelation in the present work, it is widely agreed that John has read Dan 7 as a reference to human persons. See: Vern S. Poythress, "The Holy Ones of the Most High and Daniel vii," *VT* 26 (1976): 208-13.

18. LXX Theodotion.

19. Beale, *Use of Daniel*, 231.

is being employed in the depiction of the beast in Rev 13. He notes, "The dragon in Revelation 12 was seen as the ultimate force behind the earthly kingdoms of the world. And here the same Danielic imagery of horns and heads applied to the dragon is applied to a second beast, one arising from the sea, to depict the dragon's minion."[20]

Finally, the authorization clause '... ἐδόθη αὐτῷ' (was given to him; 13:5) derives from Dan 7:6. Beale, in fact, notes that, "Not only is much of the allusion taken word-for-word from the Danielic texts, but the three elements of a blaspheming mouth, an authorization clause ... and a decreed period of time during the end time are unique to Daniel in the OT."[21] Caird further observes that the conception of God granting to whom He desires derives from Dan 4:17, 25, 32.[22] Thus, it is apparent that John has depicted his beast in terms applicable to the four beasts of Dan 7 and he has done so with a background that incorporates a number of features from Dan 7.

John's dependence on Dan 7, however, is also evident from the consistent allusions to Dan 7:14. Beale affirms that John's "language has not only been molded in general by that of Daniel, but a specific affinity with Daniel 7:14 is apparent."[23] He lists three examples in Rev 13:7–8 where Dan 7:14 appears to serve as the primary background.[24] First, there is the granting of sovereign authority ('ἐδόθη αὐτῷ ἐξουσία'; Rev 13:7; Dan 7:14). Secondly, this authority is over all on the earth who will offer worship (Rev 13:7b-8; Dan 7:14). Thirdly, Beale notes that in both passages all of this unfolds in accord with a book (Rev 13:8; Dan 7:10). These affinities, of course, relate to John's use of irony, for the authority and worship in Dan 7:14 is offered to the heavenly son of man; whereas, in Rev 13 they are given to the beast. Beale notes, "The beast's authority and worship is then but an ironic taunting prelude to the coming victory of the Son of man."[25]

That John likewise has Dan 7 in view in the account of the Two Witnesses (11:1–13) is evident from several factors. First, Rev 11 also

---

20. Beale, *Revelation*, 683–84.
21. Beale, *Revelation*, 695.
22. Caird, *Revelation*, 253.
23. Beale, *Use of Daniel*, 235; *Revelation*, 699–700.
24. Beale, *Use of Daniel*, 235–36.
25. Beale, *Revelation*, 700.

alludes to themes present in Dan 7. This is evident in Revelation's explicit use of the Danielic time period, which first occurs in Dan 7:25 (11:2 and 11:3).[26] That the brief depiction of the beast in Rev 11:7 accords with these depictions further confirms the identification of the beast in Rev 11 with that of Rev 13.[27] Finally, the beast that makes war against the Two Witnesses in Rev 11:7 is identical to the beast in Rev 13:1-7. Therefore, it stands to reason that it has the same associations with the four beasts of Dan 7.

John's Use of Daniel 8 in Rev 11:1–2

Of particular importance for this investigation into John's portrait of the people of God in relation to Daniel is the use of Dan 8:10–14 in Rev 11-12.[28] In fact, I suggest that Dan 8:10-14 provides one of the primary backgrounds for the imagery of Rev 11:1-2.[29] In regard to Rev 11:2, Fekkes, in his work on the use of Isaiah in Revelation, concedes, "If a specific source is to be sought, Dan. 8.10–14 . . . offers more by way of correspondence in language and context than Isa 63.18, especially since both Daniel 8 and Revelation 11 limit the trampling to a set period of time."[30]

As most commentators have observed, Dan 8 is closely related to the details of the vision of Dan 7.[31] Hartmann, in fact, notes that Dan 2, 7, 8, and 11 "were closely associated with each other," to the extent that it would be "unnatural" for later expositions not to associate these

---

26. See chapter 2 for the discussion on the importance of the three and one-half years of Daniel in Rev 11. Cf. Tremper Longman III, *Daniel* (NIVAC; Grand Rapids: Zondervan, 1999), 201.

27. Rev 11:7 states, 'ποιήσει μετ' αὐτῶν πόλεμον καὶ νικήσει αὐτοὺς' (he will make war with them and conquer them). See chapter 2 for a discussion of the relationship between Rev 11:7 and 13:1-7.

28. See also: Beagle, *Apocalypse*, 77; Collins, *Apocalypse*, 90.

29. Only Bauckham develops this link in the manner in which it is noted here (*Climax*, 267-73); However, see also, Beale, *Revelation*, 570; Ford, *Revelation*, 170; Mounce, *Revelation*, 215; Smalley, *Revelation*, 274.

30. J. Fekkes, *Isaiah and the Prophetic Traditions in the Book of Revelation* (JSNTSS 93; Sheffield: Sheffield University Press, 1994), 175-76.

31. Longman suggests that "the connection of Daniel 8 with chapter 7 is obvious" (*Daniel*, 201); See also, Collins, *Daniel*, 328; Sinclair B. Ferguson, *Daniel*, (CCS 19; Waco, Tex.: Word, 1988), 167; John E. Goldingay, *Daniel* (WBC 30; Dallas, Tex.: Word, 1989), 201, 06, 08; Louis F. Hartman, *The Book of Daniel* (Garden City, N.Y.: Doubleday, 1978), 223, 30; Karl F. Keil, *The Book of the Prophet Daniel* (Edinburgh: T & T Clark, 1884), 284; E. J. Young, *The Prophecy of Daniel* (Grand Rapids: Eerdmans, 1949), 165.

passages.³² Since, as it is has been argued throughout this work, Rev 12–14 serve in part to expand on the nature of the opposition to the people of God that was briefly described in Rev 11:7, and, since Dan 7 forms the primary background for John's depiction of the beasts in Rev 13, it is not surprising that Dan 8 provides a significant background for Rev 11:1–2.

It deserves mention, however, that the presence of Dan 8 is not limited to Rev 11:1–2. For the theme regarding the beast's blasphemies against God in Rev 13:6 derives from Dan 8:11–14.³³ Collins, in fact, concludes that "the elaboration of the motif in Rev 13:6 can be explained as a paraphrasing of Dan 8:10–14; compare 8:25."³⁴ Collins further notes other parallels between Dan 8 and Rev 13:³⁵ First, both Dan 8:10 and Rev 13:6 present an attack on heavenly beings. Both Dan 8 and Rev 13 depict a rebellion against God (Dan 8:11; Rev 13:6) and the Temple (Dan 8:11; Rev 13:6). And both Daniel and Revelation provide a context for the duration of these events (Dan 8:14; Rev 13:5b). To this we may note that John's use of 'ποιέω' (make) in 13:5, 7 as a generalized term for the beast's persecuting activities parallels Dan 8:12, 24. Beale, furthermore, suggests that the imagery associated with the horn of Dan 8 and the tyrant of Dan 11:30 "have been combined in Rev 13:4 in the same way that all four beasts of Daniel 7 have been combined into the one beast of Rev 13:1–2."³⁶ Finally, the presence of 'ὁ τόπος' (place; Dan 8:11 LXX) likely accounts for John's use of the same term in designating the 'place' of refuge granted to the woman in Rev 12:6, 14. Beale, in fact, argues that Dan 8:10–14 is in view in Rev 13:6 based on the use of this passage in Rev 12.³⁷

That John, in Rev 11:1–2 as well as 12:1–14:5, utilizes Dan 8:10–14 is also evidenced by the thematic parallels among them. Most significantly for this research both Dan 8:10–14 and Rev 11:1–2 depict the people of God in terms of temple imagery. For Dan 8:13 depicts the trampling of the 'holy place and the host' in terms similar to Rev 11. Interestingly, in the interpretation of the vision in Dan 8, which occurs in Dan 8:15–26,

---

32. Hartmann, *Prophecy Interpreted*, 146.
33. See: Beale, *Revelation*, 697; Morris, *Revelation*, 142–43; Mounce, *Revelation*, 215;
34. Collins, *Daniel*, 108.
35. See: Collins, *Daniel*, 108.
36. Beale, *Revelation*, 696.
37. Beale, *Revelation*, 697.

mention is made of only the destruction of the 'holy people' (8:24).³⁸ Keil and Delitzsch note, "The words of the angel, ver. 24, show that by the stars we are to understand the people of the saints, the people of God."³⁹ This corresponds with John's consistent use of temple imagery as referencing the people of God. Beale notes the parallels and suggests that, "The equation of the saints with the heavenly tabernacle is virtually the same identification made in 11:1-2, where true believers living on earth were equated with the invisible, indestructible sanctuary of God."⁴⁰

One difference, however, appears to distinguish the text of Dan 8 from that of Rev 11:1-2. Daniel seemingly implies that all of the people of God will suffer at the hands of the little horn. In fact, the imagery of Dan 8:11-13 connotes that those who 'συμπατηθήσεται' (will be trampled under foot; 8:13; LXX [Theod]: 'καταπάτημα'; LXX)⁴¹ encompasses the entire Temple as well as all of the host. The interpretation of the vision of Dan 8 also affirms that 'φθερεῖ ... δῆμον ἁγίων' (he will destroy . . . the holy people; 8:24). Daniel, therefore, in asserting the power of the little horn seemingly depicts a victory over all of the people of God.

Admittedly, one may conclude that John has followed this tradition when he depicts the victory of the beast over the people of God (11:7; 13:7). For with regard to the Two Witnesses in Rev 11:7 the beast 'ποιήσει μετ' αὐτῶν πόλεμον καὶ νικήσει αὐτοὺς καὶ ἀποκτενεῖ αὐτούς' (will make war with them and overcome them and kill them). Since I have asserted that the Two Witnesses represent the entire covenant community, the beast's defeat of the Two Witnesses may well be said to encompass the entire covenant community. To this one may add the similar thought in Rev 13:7, where the beast was given authority to make 'πόλεμον μετὰ τῶν ἁγίων καὶ νικῆσαι αὐτούς' (war with the saints and to overcome them). Thus, John appears to follow the tradition of Dan 8 in depicting

---

38. Goldingay proposes that the references to the Temple may have been meant by Daniel to reference people. He notes, "references to the earthly sanctuary in vv 11-12 could suggest that the heavenly army is the Jewish people, or the priesthood in particular, viewed as of heavenly significance because of their relationship with the God of heaven" (*Daniel*, 209).

39. Keil and Delitzsch, *Daniel*, 296.

40. Beale, *Revelation*, 697.

41. Bauckham has surmised that John has both Dan 8:13 and Zech 12:3 in mind here due to the use of the same word in both texts—though he assumes that a particular reading of Zech 12 was present to whoever translated the LXX (*Climax*, 270-71).

the entirety of the people of God as suffering martyrdom at the hands of a foreign oppressor.

Now a number of points could be raised to contend that John does not depict the entirety of the people of God as suffering defeat at the hands of the beast—including the presence of irony and the fact that 13:10 hints that not all will suffer martyrdom. The issue at this juncture, however, relates to John's use of Dan 8 in the account of the measuring and trampling of the Temple in 11:1–2. For here John does not depict the entirety of the people of God as suffering defeat via martyrdom. This is evidenced by the fact that though the "Temple" is measured it is said that, 'πατήσουσιν' (they will trample; 11:2) the outer courts.[42] It should be noted, however, that John may well have intended that on the one hand his readers should see in these accounts the defeat of the entire community, while at the same time they knew full well that the victory of the beast would not ultimately result in the death of every one of the people of God.

Of primary importance here is the fact that John appears to have read Dan 8 in accord with his overall understanding of the role of the people of God in Revelation. For the reference to trampling derives specifically from Dan 8:13. In Daniel, however, the '"trampling" (Dan 8:13) applies to the holy place and the host. For John, however, the '"trampling" is limited to the outer courts. This fits with John's narrative in that he follows the command to measure the Temple (11:1), which indicates the divine protection of it, with the command that the outer courts were to be left unmeasured (11:2). This, John is told in language that parallels Dan 8:13, is 'ὅτι' (because)[43] the nations 'πατήσουσιν' (will trample)[44] it for forty-two months.

Bauckham, in fact, argues that John employs the "curious use of ἔκβαλε" (cast out; Rev 11:2) in an effort to interpret Dan 8:11.[45] He contends that the use of ἔκβαλε ('cast out') would not have been appropriate in relation to the temple itself; hence, John understands Daniel's prophecy as referring "to the court of the temple."[46] Thus, Bauckham suggests that John read the prophecy of Daniel in slightly different terms than what

---

42. This, of course, becomes explicit in the murder of the Two Witnesses (11:7).
43. This is the causal use of ὅτι.
44. This verb is the cognate of the compound 'καταπάτημα' used in Dan 8:13.
45. Bauckham, *Climax*, 270.
46. Bauckham, *Climax*, 270.

appears from the explicit indicators of Dan 8. He contends that John's "interpretation of Daniel 8:11–13 stresses what is no more than implicit in his reading of Daniel: that the sanctuary, with its altar and the priests who worship in it, is preserved from defilement and trampling by the nations."[47]

According to Bauckham, John has made this distinction in order to emphasize that though Daniel has prophesied that the little horn will indeed attack God's people, nonetheless, God will protect them. He concludes,

> He [Daniel] is distinguishing the inner, hidden reality of the church as a kingdom of priests (cf. 5:10) who worship God in his presence from the outward experience of the church as it is exposed to persecution by the kingdom of the nations. The church will be kept safe in its hidden spiritual reality, while suffering persecution and martyrdom.[48]

From this we understand that John interprets Daniel's prophecy about the attack on the Temple and the host of heaven solely in terms of the people of God, which Daniel appears to do as well (cf Dan 8:24), but then proceeds to distinguish between the Temple that is measured for protection and the outer court that will be trampled on by the nations. Thus, John conforms his reading of Daniel to his conception of the people of God. That is, he utilizes and applies Dan 8:10–14, but transforms the notion of the temple being trampled to the trampling of the outer court.

It appears that this aligns with John's hortatory concerns for his readers. Thus, while affirming that the eschatological era in which the cosmic battle against God's saints—often described as a profanation of God's temple as in Dan 8—John maintained his concern for his readers by clarifying for them that not all of them were to suffer martyrdom. Thus, they are to maintain their testimony in light of the surety of God's provision for their souls.

THE PEOPLE OF GOD IN THE ST APOCALYPTIC LITERATURE[49]

How does John's conception of the people of God compare with other ST apocalypses? John's depiction of the people of God closely parallels the ST

---

47. Bauckham, *Climax*, 272.
48. Bauckham, *Climax*, 272.
49. This section will include, when pertinent, discussions pertaining to the OT apoc-

apocalypses with regard to the suffering of the people of God. However, the themes of divine protection and the vindication of the people of God, though present in some of the ST apocalypses, are consistently more prominent in Revelation. But, it is in regards to the portrayal of the people of God as witnesses, a thought that is essentially absent in the ST literature, that distinguishes Revelation from the ST apocalypses.[50]

It deserves mention that the thematic analysis of the Jewish apocalypses and eschatological texts by Hartmann has only modest similarities to the present investigation.[51] For his focus, though including the people of God/elect, expands well beyond these themes. Hartmann lists five general themes that characterize these works: A) Background of evil times and catastrophes B) Divine Intervention C) Passing of judgment D) Fate of sinners E) Time of salvation and the blessed state of the elect. He contends that these themes are prevalent in the OT as well. He cites, for example, Exod 1–15, Dan 7:23–27 and Isa 59:1–21. Hartmann's analysis, however, relates to themes that are generally present throughout this literature and, therefore, do not specifically address the people of God. Consequently, there is little correspondence between his research and the present work.

What follows is an analysis of the ST apocalypses, with occasional references to the OT and secondary literature in regards to each of the four themes that I have argued form the matrix for the depiction of the people of God in Revelation. Each theme will be examined in order to ascertain the level of continuity/discontinuity with Revelation.

---

alypses: especially Ezekiel and Zechariah. Primarily, however, the objective here is to compare John's perception of the people of God with that of the ST apocalypses. Since we have detailed John's relationship with Daniel and, thereby, his use of the OT in his portrait of the people of God, the focus now turns to the non-canonical literature in order to ascertain how and in what manner they follow suit (or, perhaps, John follows suit!).

50. It is doubtful, therefore, that John has depended on any of the ST non-canonical apocalypses for his portrait of the people of God. For aside from the dependence on Daniel that we have established, there are little commonalities between John's account of the people of God and any of the ST apocalypses. Of course, the suggestion that John was aware of various non-canonical 'traditions' is reasonable. Bauckham, in fact, has argued for John's use of non-canonical sources in his employment of the Neronic traditions in Rev 13 and 17; as well as with other isolated traditions (*Climax*, 38–91, 423–31).

51. See: Hartman, *Prophecy Interpreted*, 23–49.

The Divine Protection of the People of God

The imagery behind the theme of divine protection, as with most of the imagery in Revelation, clearly derives from the OT. I have suggested that the primary indication for the divine protection of the people of God in the account of the Two Witnesses is conveyed by the command to measure the temple (Rev 11:1). Such language resonates most significantly with the language and themes of the OT: as evidenced by the fact that "'measuring" in the OT finds ample attestation as a metaphorical device for divine protection. Thus, John asserts that the people of God are divinely protected by employing imagery derived from the OT. John, however, presents this theme with far more stress than is evident in literature of the ST period. For this theme, though occasionally present in some ST writings (e.g., *4 Ezra* 2.28–30; *Apoc Ab.* 29.17; *2 Bar.* 29.2; 32.1; 40.2; 71.1) is either absent or not present with the same force as in Revelation.

In regards to the use of "'measuring" in the OT, it is apparent that this theme is most prominently found in Ezek 40–48,[52] which Beale suggests provides the most direct background for Rev 11:1–2.[53] Zechariah 1–2 also serves as a background for the measuring of the Temple of God in Rev 11:1–2.[54] In Zechariah, after first affirming that the Temple will be rebuilt, it is then declared that, "a measuring line will be stretched over Jerusalem" (1:16). Then in Zech 2:2, the purpose of this measuring is said to be, "to measure Jerusalem, to see how wide it is and how long it is." The use of measuring in Zech 1–2, therefore, carries the notion of the divine provision for the rebuilding of the Temple and the city with the result that the Temple expands beyond the boundaries of the entire city. Thus, in the words of Hendriksen, "On the basis of the immediate context, the parallel expression ([Rev] 21:15), and the Old Testament background (Ezk. 40:5; 42:20; Zc. 2:1), we arrive at the conclusion that measuring the sanctuary means to set it apart from that which is profane; in order that, thus

---

52. The context of Ezekiel, in fact, displays a number of parallels with Revelation 11. The most notable is the association of the measuring with that of an ideal temple. The measuring in Ezekiel, however, has even closer parallels with the measuring of Rev 21:15. See: Bornkamm, "Komposition," 132–49; Harrington, *Apocalypse*, 151.

53. Cf Beale, *Temple*, 315–320. See also: Barnhouse, *Revelation*, 193; Stefanovic, *Revelation*, 339.

54. Aune contends that the measuring of Rev 11 more directly alludes to Zech 2:1–5 than to Ezek 40:3–42:20 (*Revelation*, 2.604). See also: Barnhouse, *Revelation*, 194.

separated, it may be perfectly safe and protected from all harm."[55] This notion of divine protection is precisely what I have argued is conveyed in Rev 11:1–2.

But, whereas, for John this theme provides a vital background, it is rarely introduced in the ST works under discussion. The greatest parallel with John's conception of the present divine protection of the people of God may well be found in *4 Ezra*. There it is noted that, "The nations shall envy you but they shall not be able to do anything against you, says the Lord. My hands will cover you, that your sons may not see Gehenna. Rejoice, O mother, with your sons, because I will deliver you, says the Lord" (*4 Ezra* 2.28–30). This exhortation provides the most explicit parallel to the conception of the divine protection that is afforded the people of God in Revelation. Even in *4 Ezra* it is somewhat overshadowed by the fact that the main body of the work (chs 3–14) consistently questions the justice of God in light of the present circumstances of the people of God. In fact, this affirmation of the divine protection of the people of God may even be discarded if the assertion of Metzger is valid that chs 1–2 of *4 Ezra* are a Christian insertion.[56]

Another text that parallels John's presentation of the people of God as divinely protected is found in *Apoc Ab.* 29.17, where it reads, "And then from your seed will be left the people of God men in their number, protected by me, who strive in the glory of my name toward the place prepared beforehand for them." Even here, however, the parallel is only partial. For the *Apoc. Ab.* references the protection afforded the Israelites during the plagues upon Egypt. Such a protection was from physical harm. Revelation, however, appears to place an emphasis on spiritual protection.[57]

---

55. Hendriksen, *Conquerors*, 126.

56. Bruce Metzger, "The Fourth Book of Ezra," In *OT Pseudepigrapha* (ed. J. H. Charlesworth; London: Darton, Longman & Todd, 1983), 1.517. Metzger's proposition may even account for the discrepancy between ch 2 and chs 3–14 on this issue.

57. Though, one may contend that exemption from physical harm is conveyed in Rev 9:4. This, however, is disputed on that count that the people of God are excluded from the deception of the dragon and his minions. The demonic nature of the locusts, thus, may be understood in terms of the lying and deceptive activities of Satan and its' consequences. For further discussion, see: Aune, *Revelation*, 2.530 Beale, *Revelation*, 495–96; Smalley, *Revelation*, 228–29.

The clearest parallels with this Johannine theme are found in 2 *Baruch*.⁵⁸ In this work, the author notes several times that the people of God will be afforded divine protection. For example, in 2 *Bar.* 29.2 it reads, "For at that time I shall only protect those found in this land at that time." Later, in 2 *Bar.* 32.1, the author notes, "He shall protect you in the time in which the Mighty One shall shake the entire creation." Similar expressions are found in 2 *Bar.* 40.2; 71.1. There is, however, one real distinction in the presentation of this theme in both Revelation and 2 *Baruch*. Namely, that in 2 *Baruch* God's preservation is closely associated with the abiding faithfulness of the people in relation to the covenant. For example, 2 *Bar.* 46.5–6 states, "But only prepare your heart so that you obey the Law. . . . If you do this, those good tidings will come to you of which I spoke to you earlier."⁵⁹ Murphy, in fact, notes that the author stresses the fact that "relationship to the covenant is the deciding factor."⁶⁰ This association is affirmed by the large number of conditional sentences in 2 *Baruch*, which associate covenant keeping with divine protection and sovereign blessing.⁶¹ Thus, disaster—as in the destruction of the Temple in Baruch—results from the sins of the people.

This Deuteronomic perspective evolves in the apocalypses and literature of ST Judaism in general to the point that the promises regarding restoration become eschatologically fulfilled.⁶² Thus, though the consequences of sin are presently experienced, the reward for the people of God must wait until the eschaton. In Revelation, however, persecution and suffering are more directly tied to the inevitability that results from the opposition of their eschatological adversary as played out in the cosmic war throughout history. This is not to suggest that Revelation contains no suffering of the people of God as a result of their sins. Such a notion,

---

58. Though 2 *Bar* was likely penned after the destruction of the Temple in A.D. 70, it is valuable for our concerns in that it was written independently of Revelation. Thus, themes present in both works may be compared and evaluated in order to discern whether or not John was employing traditional imagery or not.

59. 2 *Bar.* 46:5–6; 77:3–10.

60. Murphy, *Structure and Meaning*, 21

61. E.g., 32.1; 44.7; 46.5, 6; 75.7, 8; 77.6, 16; 78.6, 7; 84.3, 6; 85.4.

62. A. F. J. Klijn suggests that the promises of divine protection in 2 *Baruch* are directly tied to the protection of the land in the eschatological era ("2 Baruch," In *OT Pseudepigrapha* (ed. J. H. Charlesworth; London: Darton, Longman & Todd, 1983), 1.618).

however, is primarily contained in the addresses to the seven churches.[63] Throughout the pre-consummation visionary section of Revelation the people of God are portrayed as victors who proclaim the gospel, suffer as a result of it, and are shown to be victorious in their resurrection.

Thus, outside of the fact that John employs OT imagery in order to convey the conception that the people of God are divinely protected, there is relatively little correspondence between John's conception of the people of God as divinely protected and the portrayal of the people of God in the apocalypses of the ST period. Commonly, these ST works accent the viewpoint that history is divinely guided. This often conveys the message to the people of God that they are to take comfort in the fact that eventually—often sooner rather than later—God will consummate history and provide them with their rewards.[64] This literature, however, regularly denies the notion that the world offers any good for the people of God. In the apocalypses, the present world, in typical dualistic fashion, affords only suffering and despair, while the heavenly kingdom offers hope and relief.

For John, however, God is not only in control of where history is going, but He is also in control of the present circumstances to the extent that the fate of every member of the kingdom of God is divinely secured.[65] I do not intend to suggest, however, that Revelation differs in its outlook of the world as being opposed to God. For Revelation concurs with the apocalypses that the world is place of 'θλῖψις' (tribulation; cf 1:9; 2:9, 10, 22; 7:14) for the people of God. In fact, the solemn admonition remains: 'εἴ τις εἰς αἰχμαλωσίαν, εἰς αἰχμαλωσίαν ὑπάγει· εἴ τις ἐν μαχαίρῃ ἀποκτανθῆναι αὐτὸν ἐν μαχαίρῃ ἀποκτανθῆναι' (if anyone is to be taken into captivity, into captivity he will go; if anyone is to be killed by the sword, by the sword he will be killed; 13:10). Thus, though on the one hand John agrees with the ST apocalypses that the present world offers tribulation and suffering, on the other hand, he provides a more posi-

---

63. Cf. Cf. 2:5, 14, 16, 22–23; 3:3, 16.

64. That the apocalypses were hortatory in nature is often overlooked. In his commentary on Second Baruch, Murphy notes, "The real point of the book is to be found in the exhortation of the people," (*The Structure and Meaning of Second Baruch* [Atlanta, Ga.: Scholars Press, 1985], 124). Earlier Murphy argued that the structure of Second Baruch reveals the hortatory nature of the work (*Structure and Meaning*; See especially p 9).

65. Thus, the force of the divine passives in Revelation. See especially: Aune, *Revelation*, 2.394–95; 2.527–28; Beale, *Revelation*, 377, 695.

tive picture of the present circumstances of the people of God. The Two Witnesses, for example, are portrayed as effectively proclaiming the gospel and unable to suffer harm until their testimony is finished (11:5–7).

For John, however, the present is also the beginning of the victorious battle, which will end with the ultimate victory of Christ at His return. Therefore, John portrays the people of God as soldiers prepared for battle. The victory, however, was secured at the cross.[66] The present effects of this victory include the fact that the Dragon has been thrown down (12:9). For the people of God, then, Christ's victory guarantees their victory. This, in fact, may well be the force of the proleptic affirmation in 7:14–17. It is the conception of the people of God as presently victorious and protected that seemingly has a place of greater stress in John as compared to the ST apocalypses; and may well account for the more positive depiction of the present circumstances of the people of God.

Therefore, though the conception of the people of God as divinely protected appears sporadically in some of the ST apocalypses, it does not enjoy the same stress as it does in Revelation. John, thus, appears more concerned with exhorting his readers to persevere in faithful witnessing, despite the opposition they may presently encounter, since God is sovereignly protecting them. The historical apocalypses, however, are more concerned to accent God's sovereign control of history. For them there is essentially no victory in the present age.

What may account for the uniqueness of John's stress on the present circumstances of the people of God? Perhaps, it was John's Christological perspective. It is nonetheless surprising that Judaism's stress on the covenant did not lead the ST apocalypses into the same conclusion. Most likely this was the result of the consistently horrific plight of the Jewish people to whom the apocalypses were addressed. After years of suffering with no relief in sight, the apocalypses began to look to the consummation as the era of relief and hope. In essence, then, the proclamation of *4 Ezra*, though in accord with Revelation, stands out as an exception and is not characteristic of the general viewpoint presented in this literature.

---

66. Cf Rev 5. Though elsewhere John may well present a greater stress on the resurrection or even the ascension (Rev 12).

The People of God as Witnesses

Undoubtedly, John's focus on witnessing greatly distinguishes Revelation's portrait of the people of God from that of the literature of ST Judaism. We have seen that witnessing serves as one of the primary features of the people of God in Revelation. Such a designation is evident in the use of the lampstand imagery both in application to the seven churches (Rev 2–3) and the Two Witnesses (11:4). We have also demonstrated that John's call to witness is intimately connected with the resultant persecution and suffering of the people of God. The call to witness to the nations, however, is absent in the apocalypses of the ST period.[67]

In the ST apocalypses, witnessing is limited in terms of the people's relationship to God through covenant keeping and as a witness to one another. For example, in *2 Bar.* 17.4, Moses, by bringing the Law to Israel, was a light to them: "He brought the Law to the descendants of Jacob and he lighted a lamp to the generation of Israel." The apocalypses in contrast tend to either pronounce judgment upon the unbeliever, or to focus on their own faithfulness to the covenant.[68] For John, the coming of Christ, 'τὸ φῶς τὸ ἀληθινόν' (the true light: John 1:9), results in the commissioning of the people of God to imitate Christ. It is this call to persevere in faithful witnessing, which results in persecution, that sets Revelation apart from the apocalypses of the ST period.

The People of God as Suffering Persecution

The greatest correspondence between Revelation's portrait of the people of God and the apocalypses of ST Judaism relates to the depiction of the people of God as suffering persecution. For it is virtually a universal characteristic of this literature that the people of God suffer during this lifetime.[69] F. J. Murphy, in fact, comments with regard to the theme of persecution and suffering in *2 Baruch*, that the language of suffering "is a topos of the wisdom literature."[70] In regards to John's portrait of the

---

67. Certainly the conception of being a light to the nations was present in the OT (cf Isa 49:6).

68. The latter is the exhortation of 2 Baruch. Cp *2 Bar.* 52:6–7

69. Passages that stress the suffering of the people of God in this present world include: *1 En.* 108.8–9; *Jub.* 23.23–31; *2 Bar.* 15.8; 25.3–4; 26.1–27.11; *Sib. Or.* 601–05; *As. Mos.* 8.1–5; and, *4 Ezra* 11.42.

70. Murphy, *Structure and Meaning*, 16.

people of God as suffering and enduring persecution, however, a significant distinction appears with that of the apocalypses of the ST period. Namely, that the literature of ST period often associates the sufferings of the people of God in terms of their failure to keep the covenant. This contrasts with Revelation, where, as noted above, the suffering of the people of God in Revelation is not connected with their sins, but with their faithful proclamation of the gospel.[71]

In terms of the correspondence between Revelation and the ST theme of suffering, it is apparent that John employs ST imagery into his portrait of the suffering of the people of God. First, there is the depiction of the people of God as coming out of tribulation. John notes that the people of God are, 'οὗτοί εἰσιν οἱ ἐρχόμενοι ἐκ τῆς θλίψεως τῆς μεγάλης' (these are the ones who are coming out of the great tribulation; 7:14). This corresponds primarily with the Danielic portrait of the people of God as both enduring persecution and suffering.[72] The Danielic context incorporates a time of persecution and suffering among the people of God.[73] Beale affirms, "That Daniel is in mind is also apparent from the fact that the phrase 'great tribulation' occurs in the NT outside Revelation only in Matt. 24:21, where it is part of a fuller and more explicit reference to Dan. 12:1."[74] In Daniel 11–12, the people of God are clearly depicted in terms of encountering a violent opposition.[75] This era of tribulation is to be unparalleled in history (Dan 12:1). This notion of the Divine protection of the people of God amidst this unparalleled distress is also present in 1 QM 1.8–11. There it is prophesied that God will protect the Israelites as they pass through this period.

---

71. Though to some extent there is a distinction here between the impending judgment on some of the seven churches in chs 2–3 for their failure to witness and keep the covenant and the people of God in the visionary section of Revelation.

72. See: Aune, *Revelation*, 2.471; Beale, *Revelation*, 218–19, 292, 405, 432–35, 635, 650–52, 661, 1037; Collins, *Apocalypse*, 51–52; Harrington, *Apocalypse*, 132; Hughes, *Revelation*, 93; Keener, *Revelation*, 244; Kraft, *Offenbarung*, 130; Lohmeyer, *Offenbarung*, 69; Mounce, *Revelation*, 164; Stefanovic, *Revelation*, 265; Thompson, *Revelation*, 110.

73. Cf. Dan 11:30–39, 44; 12:10.

74. Beale, *Revelation*, 433.

75. Whether Daniel's readers would have viewed the account from 11:36ff as referencing a 2nd century B.C. fulfillment or as a purely eschatological reference is not pertinent here.

Secondly, the prayer of the saints under the altar in Rev 6:9–11,[76] which alludes to the suffering of the people of God,[77] parallels several OT passages. The cry of the people of God, often expressed by the interjection, "Ἔως πότε," is, in fact, prevalent in the OT[78] and in the apocalyptic literature of ST Judaism.[79] Commonly, these pleas entail an appeal for justice more than vengeance.[80] This cry, in fact, is directly paralleled by Zech 1:12, where the stress is certainly not one of vengeance. Bauckham, in fact, suggests that, "it became a question asked by apocalyptic writers about the time which must pass until the decisive, eschatological intervention of God."[81] It appears likely, however, that both John and the apocalypses of ST Judaism derived their traditions from the OT.

Overall, the abundance of the references to the suffering of the people of God in both the apocalypses of ST Judaism and Revelation may be accounted for on the basis of the settings in which they were penned.[82] The depiction of them as suffering was essentially the fate of the people of God for which God was in control. The primary distinction between John and the ST literature relates to the reason for the suffering. For John, the suffering of the people of God is a direct corollary to their faithful witnessing in covenant fulfillment and not the result of their failure to keep the covenant.

---

76. Revelation 6:9–11 serves a vital role in the narrative of Revelation. God's effort to answer this prayer serves a pivotal function in the narrative structure of much of Revelation. Thus, for example, the answer to their prayer serves as the theme in the overlapping section of 8:3–5; which serves to close the narrative of the seven Seals, while also serving as the introduction to the seven Trumpets.

77. Smalley notes, "The Church, in its persecuted state, comes into view" (*Revelation*, 156).

78. Cp Ps 6:3; 13:1–2; 74:10; 79:5; 80:4; 89:46; 90:13; 94:3; Jer 12:4; Dan 8:13; 12:6; Hab 1:2.

79. (cf. *1 En.* 47.1–4, *4 Ezra* 4.35–37, and *2 Bar.* 23.4–5). Bauckham compares and contrasts these accounts and their possible relation to Rev 6:9–11; though he does not address the relationship with Zech 1:12 (*Climax*, 48–56).

80. There is indeed a cry for vengeance imbedded in the plea, but the plea is certainly more than this. There is ample evidence that the Old Testament legal background provides a greater stress in regards to the obtaining of justice (cp Ps 74:10; 79:5; Zech 1:12).

81. Bauckham, *Climax*, 51.

82. Even if these cannot be ascertained with certainty, the fact that they were written to communities who were enduring, had recently endured, or, perhaps, were imminently about to endure persecution and suffering, is sufficient for our purposes.

The Vindication of the People of God

It is not surprising to find a correspondence between Revelation and the apocalypses of ST Judaism regarding the fourth theme of vindication.[83] For the very nature of this literature and the apparent circumstances in which they were penned provides the setting for which the promise of a future of peace and restoration forms the basis of exhortation. The depiction of the people of God in the ST apocalypses parallels John's depiction of the people of God as those who are victorious over their enemies as a result of their enduring suffering. As Aune notes, "It is through the endurance of suffering that the Jewish martyrs conquer their adversaries."[84] Consequently, the parallels are significant.

A notable feature of the vindication of the people of God in the ST apocalypses is that they are predominately futuristic. Thus, in referencing the future resurrection *1 En.* 51.2 notes, "And he shall choose the righteous and the holy ones from among the dead (the risen dead), for the day when they shall be selected and saved has arrived."[85] *1 Enoch* in fact closes with the assurance of the future vindication for people of God and goes to the extent of defining the people of God as those who:

> love God [and] have loved neither gold nor silver, nor all the good things which are in the world, but have given over their bodies to suffering—who from the time of their very being have not longed after earthly food, and who regard themselves as a (mere) passing breath. And they have observed this matter, the Lord having put them through much testing. . . . For they were all found loving God more than the fire of their eternal souls; and . . . they were being trodden upon by evil people, experiencing abuse and insult by them. . . . So now I shall summon their spirits. . . . I shall bring them out into the bright light, those who have loved my holy name, and seat them each one by one upon the throne of his honor (108.8–12).

---

83. In addition to the passages cited below, the vindication of the people of God may also be found in the following ST apocalyptic texts: *1 Enoch* 5.7; 10.17; 25.6; 39.6; 58.3; 91.10, 13; 92.3–4; 95.3; 100.5; 103.3; *2 Bar.* 51.8–16; 73.1–3; 82.1–2; *4 Ezra* 2.33–41, 45; *As. Mos.* 10:2–10; Dan 7:13–14; 12:1–2.

84. Aune, *Revelation*, 1.76. Cp 4 Macc 1:11.

85. Cp *1 En.* 91:10.

Throughout the apocalypses there is also a close relationship between the future vindication of the people of God and the destruction of the wicked. Thus, the passage in *1 Enoch* just cited continues:

> Then they shall see those who were born in darkness being taken into darkness, while the righteous ones shall be resplendent. (The sinners) shall cry aloud, and they shall see the righteous ones being resplendent; they shall go to the place which was prescribed for them concerning the days and the seasons (108.14–15).

Similarly *1 En.* 100.4–5 asserts,

> And the Most High will arise on that day of judgment in order to execute a great judgment upon all the sinners. He will set a guard of holy angels over all the righteous and holy ones, and they shall keep them as the apple of the eye until all evil and sin are brought to an end. From that time on the righteous ones shall sleep a restful sleep, and there shall be none to make them afraid.

The hortatory implications of the vindication of the people of God are clear: Be patient. God is in control. This is evidenced in the exhortation of *1 En.* 96.1, 3: "Be hopeful, you righteous ones, for the sinners shall soon perish from before your presence. You shall soon have authority upon them, such (authority) as you may wish (to have). . . . But you, who have experienced pain, fear not, for there shall be a healing medicine for you, a bright light shall enlighten you, and a voice of rest you shall hear from heaven." Thus the author of *4 Ezra* exhorts his readers, "Do not be anxious, for when the day of tribulation and anguish comes, others shall weep and be sorrowful, but you shall rejoice and have abundance" (2.27).[86] This provides the author with a natural platform to encourage the people of God amidst their present tribulations. Thus, Hartmann summarizes the hortatory implications by noting: "With a good deal of intensity the texts often describe the fate that will befall the sinful adversaries. Even though some resentment may underlie these passages, we should, on the one hand, be aware that the punishment of sinners has an organic place in these authors' fundamental view of God and the world and, on the other hand, bear in mind the function of consoling and admonishing."[87]

Therefore, by means of this assurance the authors possess an effective means of encouraging their readers to confront the present crisis with

---

86. Cp *2 Bar.* 73.1–3; 82.1–2.
87. Hartman, *Prophecy Interpreted*, 45.

strength and a tenacity to remain faithful. Murphy notes, "The practical result of this discussion which is desired by the author of 2B [2 *Baruch*] is that the readers turn their attention away from the sadness of the present time, and away from any longing for revenge, and towards the life of the world to come."[88]

This theme of the vindication of the people of God occurs not only throughout the apocalypses but also in the ST writings in general. Murphy notes, "In the book of Wisdom, the immortality of the righteous is used as a solution to the problem of the persecution of the good person by the wicked in this life. In describing this situation, Wisdom uses apocalyptic imagery in claiming that there is a future vindication for the righteous."[89]

One of the consistent features of the ST apocalypses relates to the stress on covenant faithfulness as a prerequisite for vindication. For example, in *4 Ezra* 7.88–98, the author notes,

> Now this is the order of those who have kept the ways of the Most High, when they shall be separated from their mortal body. . . . They laboriously served the Most High, and withstood danger every hour, that they might keep the Law of the Lawgiver perfectly. Therefore, this is the teaching concerning them: First of all, they shall see with great joy the glory of him who receives them. . . . While they were alive they kept the Law. . . . They understand the rest which they now enjoy. . . . They rejoice that they have now escaped what is mortal, and shall inherit what is to come. . . . They shall rejoice with boldness, and shall be confident without confusion, and shall be glad without fear, for they hasten to behold the face of him whom they served in life.

Similarly, *2 Bar.* 44.7 reads, "When you endure and persevere in his fear and do not forget his Law, the time again will take a turn for the better for you."[90] In fact, the wicked are often defined as those who "were contemptuous of his Law."[91]

Though it would be fair to say that the vindication of the people of God in Revelation is connected with covenant loyalty, nonetheless John affirms this while maintaining a subtle clarification. For John stresses that the evidence of covenant loyalty is the faithful witnessing of the people

---

88. Murphy, *Structure and Meaning*, 39.
89. Murphy, *Structure and Meaning*, 39.
90. The context of this statement favors an eschatological reversal of fortunes.
91. *4 Ezra* 8.58. Cf., also, *2 Bar.* 51.4.

of God. Thus, Rev 12:11 states, 'καὶ αὐτοὶ ἐνίκησαν αὐτὸν διὰ τὸ αἷμα τοῦ ἀρνίου καὶ διὰ τὸν λόγον τῆς μαρτυρίας αὐτῶν καὶ οὐκ ἠγάπησαν τὴν ψυχὴν αὐτῶν ἄχρι θανάτου' (and they themselves overcame him on account of the blood of the lamb, and on account of the word of their testimony, and because[92] they did not love their life even to death).

Therefore, the theme of the vindication of the people of God pervades the ST apocalypses and the Revelation of John. Throughout this literature the people of God are exhorted to persevere in faithful witnessing with the knowledge that they will be proven the ultimate victors.

One last thought deserves mention as it relates to the identity of the people of God in the ST apocalypses. I argued in chapter 6 that a thematic examination of the people of God in the account of the 144,000 and the Great Multitude suggests that John viewed these groups as one. That is, the 144,000 and the Great Multitude are in fact the same group from two perspectives: one earthly and the other the vindicated and heavenly. In examining the ST apocalypses it appears that a significant parallel occurs in that the identity of those who are vindicated similarly form a vast innumerable multitude. Thus, *1 En.* 39.6 reads, "And the righteous and the elect ones shall be without number before him forever and ever." And in *1 En.* 40.1 it states, "And after that, I saw a hundred thousand times a hundred thousand, ten million times ten million. An innumerable and uncountable (multitude) who stand before the glory of the Lord of the Spirits." An even more explicit parallel with Rev 7:9 occurs in *4 Ezra* 2.42 where it says, "I, Ezra, saw on Mount Zion a great multitude, which I could not number, and they were all praising the Lord with songs."[93] Thus, it appears that the ST apocalypses similarly envisioned the vindicated as comprising an innumerable multitude, which closely parallels John's assertion in Rev 7.

CONCLUSION

Therefore, we see that John has at times drawn upon the rich imagery of the OT apocalypses and the apocalypses of ST Judaism for his depiction of the people of God. At times, it appears that John even interprets

---

92. That the καὶ here is casual is acknowledged by Aune (*Revelation*, 2.655).

93. This argument does not hinge on the use of *4 Ezra*, which, as was noted above, Metzger has suggested is a later Christian insertion. If it indeed represents a latter Christian insertion this would only serve as evidence that early Christian writers viewed the Great Multitude as the fulfillment of God's covenant promises to Israel.

parts of Daniel Christologically and applies the imagery of the beast's war as pertaining to the war against the people of God. Furthermore, there are several thematic parallels between John and these writings mostly in regards to the common plight of suffering that either impacted or threatened the communities to whom these works were penned.

In regard to the four themes we have seen that for John the theme of divine protection derives from the OT apocalypses, especially Ezekiel, Daniel, and Zechariah, and a few scattered references among the ST apocalypses. This theme, however, is more prominent in Revelation than in the literature of the ST period. John's focus and stress on the witnessing activity of the people of God in Revelation is distinct from that found in the ST apocalypses. In the latter, witnessing was construed more in terms of one's covenant relationship to God and to others within the covenant community, rather than as a witness to the world. John's conception of the suffering and enduring of persecution of the people of God, however, is strongly reminiscent of the OT apocalypses; and, in fact, appears to build specifically on Daniel 8:10–14. In regards to the theme of vindication, both Revelation and the ST apocalypses relay the final victory that awaits the people of God. Therefore, John's portrait of the people of God conforms well to the depiction of the people of God in the ST apocalypses. The uniqueness of John's presentation of the people of God appears most significantly in relation to his Christological emphases.

This investigation into the apocalypses of the OT and the ST period has further strengthened the contention that Revelation contains a high level of imagery. Such imagery permeates the apocalypses and John's correspondences with them provide a measure of support for reading Revelation in a similar light. Most significantly, is John's use of the temple imagery of Dan 8:11–14 in light of the protection and suffering of the people of God in Rev 11:1–2 and Rev 13:6–7. For we have seen that John understands the "'trampling" of the "holy place" and the "host" to refer to the people of God. This provides significant support for the thesis presented throughout this work that the Temple in Rev 11:1–2 references people.

Conclusion

THIS RESEARCH HAS ENDEAVORED to provide insights into John's portrayal of the people of God in the pre-consummation era of Revelation by examining the nature of the depiction of the people of God in the account of the Two Witnesses. I have contended that John consistently portrays the people of God in accord with four themes that likely arose from John's pastoral concerns. Thus, assuming that a knowledge of the ecclesiological setting of John's readers is beyond our grasp, we have nonetheless discerned a vital purpose for which John has penned his work. The results of this analysis suggest that John desired to encourage his readers to persevere in faithful witnessing, in the face of impending persecution and possibly death, with the knowledge that they were under God's divine protection, and that in the end it will be they who are vindicated.

The implications of this research are that future study of Revelation should take into consideration these thematic issues. For, though I do not intend to suppose that this analysis has comprehensively exhausted the study of John's depiction of the people of God in pre-consummation section of Revelation, I, nonetheless, hope to have provided a matrix in which future research into John's conception of the people of God may operate. For our comparison with other pre-consummation accounts of the people of God suggests that John depicts the people of God consistently throughout the pre-consummation era of the Apocalypse.

I have also contended that John's depiction of the people of God derives from his Christological conceptions. For it is readily apparent that John predicates his conception of the people of God on the person and work of Christ. Thus, the people of God are to be witnesses as Christ was the faithful witness. They are to overcome in suffering and perhaps death just as Christ overcame. And, they will be resurrected and vindicated as was Christ resurrected and vindicated. Again, therefore, the message to the churches rings clear: the people of God are to emulate Christ by persevering as faithful witnesses who will prove the ultimate victors.

Finally, we have seen that John has been heavily influenced by apocalyptic portions of the OT, and in particular Daniel 7–8, for his depiction of the people of God. Revelation also displays affinities with the apocalypses of ST Judaism. I have contended, however, that these parallels mostly reflect the common plight of suffering that threatened the particular communities.

The distinctions between John and this body of literature primarily relate to John's Christology and the apocalypses' stress on the covenant. For the apocalypses of the ST era, faithfulness to the covenant meant divine protection and vindication, while failure to maintain the covenant meant persecution and suffering. For John, however, each of these themes are motivated by his understanding of the church's role as witnesses in light of the finished work of Christ.

In conclusion, Revelation tells a wonderful story. The Lion/Lamb has come and persevered in faithful witness, thus, so shall we! In all, our efforts remain humbled by the somber affirmation of God's call upon our lives to persevere in faithful witnessing. A call that indeed focuses on Christ!

Bibliography

Alford, Henry *The Greek Text* IV. Cambridge: Deighton, 1866.
Allo, Ernest Bernard. *L'Apocalypse*. Paris: J. Gabalda, 1933.
Arnold, Cinton E. *Three Crucial Questions About Spiritual Warfare*. Grand Rapids: Baker, 1997.
Aune, David E. *Revelation*. 3 vols. Word Biblical Commentaries 52a-c. Nashville, Tenn.: Thomas Nelson Publishers, 1998.
Aune, David E. "Intertextuality and the Genre of the Apocalypse." *SBL Seminar Papers* (1991): 142–60.
Aune, David E. *The New Testament in its Literary Environment*. Philadelphia: Westminster, 1987.
Aune, David E. "The Apocalypse of John and the Problem of Genre." *Semeia* 36 (1986): 66–91.
Aune, David E. *Prophecy in Early Christianity and the Ancient Mediterranean World*. Grand Rapids: Eerdmans, 1983.
Bachmann, Michael. 'Ausmessung von Tempel und Stadt: Apk 11,1f und 21,15ff auf dem Hintergrund des Buches Ezechiel.' Pages 61–83 in *Das Ezechielbuch in der Johannesoffenbarung*. Edited by M. Bachmann, T. Hieke, and M. Karrer. Neukirchener: Neukirchen-Vluyn, 2006.
Bachmann, Michael. "Himmlisch: der 'Temple Gottes von Apk 11.1.'" *New Testament Studies* 40 (1994): 474–80.
Bandstra, A. J. "'A Kingship of Priests': Inaugurated Eschatology in the Apocalypse." *Calvin Theological Journal* 27 (1992): 10–25.
Barker, Margeret. "The Servant in the Book of Revelation." *Heythrop Journal* 36 (1995): 494–511.
Barker, Margaret. *The Revelation of Jesus Christ*. Edinburgh: T & T Clark, 2000.
Barnhouse, Donald Grey. *Revelation*. Grand Rapids: Zondervan, 1973.
Barr, D. L. "The Apocalypse as a Symbolic Transformation of the World: A Literary Analysis." *Interpretation* 38 (1984): 39–50.
Barrois, G. A. *Jesus Christ and the Temple*. Crestwood, N.Y.: St Vladimir's Seminary Press, 1993.
Bauckham, Richard. *The Climax of Prophecy: Studies on the Book of Revelation*. Edinburgh: T. & T. Clark, 1993a.
Bauckham, Richard J. *The Theology of the Book of Revelation*. Cambridge: Cambridge University Press, 1993b.

Bauckham, Richard J. "The list of the Tribes in Revelation 7 Again." *Journal for the Study of the New Testament* 42 (1991): 99–115.

Bauckham, Richard J. "The Apocalypses in the New Pseudepigrapha." *Journal for the Study of the New Testament* 26 (1986): 97–117.

Bauckham, Richard J. "The Two Fig Tree Parables in the Apocalypse of Peter." *Journal of Biblical Literature* 10 (1985): 269–87.

Bauckham, Richard J. "The Role of the Spirit in the Apocalypse." *The Evangelical Quarterly* 52 (1980): 66–83.

Bauckham, Richard J. "The Rise of Apocalyptic." *Themelios* 3/2 (1978): 10–23.

Bauer, Walter, Frederick W. Danker, William F. Arndt, and F. Wilbur Gingrich. *A Greek-English Lexicon of the New Testament and Other Early Christian Literature*. 3rd ed., Chicago: Chicago University Press, 2000.

Beagley, Alan James. *The 'Sitz im Leben' of the Apocalypse with Particular Reference to the Role of the Church's Enemies*. Berlin: de Gruyter, 1987.

Beale, Gregory K. "The Final Vision of the Apocalypse and its Implications for a Biblical Theology of the Temple." In *Heaven on Earth*. Edited by S. Gathercole and T. D. Alexander. Carlisle: Paternoster, 2004.

Beale, Gregory K. *The Temple and the Church's Mission: A Biblical Theology of the Dwelling Place of God*. New Studies in Biblical Theology. Downer's Grove, Ill.: InterVarsity Press, 2004.

Beale, Gregory K. *The Book of Revelation: A Commentary on the Greek Text*. New International Greek Testament Commentary. Grand Rapids, Mi.: Eerdmans; Carlisle: Paternoster Press, 1999.

Beale, Gregory K. *John's Use of the Old Testament in Revelation*. Sheffield: Sheffield Academic, 1998.

Beale, Gregory K. *The Use of Daniel in Jewish Apocalyptic Literature and in the Revelation of John*. Lanham: University Press of America, 1984.

Beale, Gregory K. "The Influence of Daniel Upon the Structure and Theology of John's Apocalypse." *Journal of the Evangelical Theological Society* 27 (1984): 413–23.

Beasley-Murray, George Raymond. *Revelation*. NCB. Greenwood, S.C.: Attic Press, 1974.

Beasley-Murray, George R. *Highlights of the Book of Revelation*. Nashville, Tenn.: Broadman Press, 1972.

Beck, D. M. "The Christology of the Apocalypse of John." Pages 253–77 in *New Testament Studies: Critical Essays in New Testament Interpretation and Special Reference to the Meaning and Worth of Jesus*. Edited by E. P. Booth. New York: Abingdon-Cokesbury Press, 1942.

Beckwith, Isbon Thaddeus. *The Apocalypse of John: Studies in Introduction, with a Critical and Exegetical Commentary*. New York: Macmillan, 1919. Grand Rapids: Baker, 1967.

Best, Ernst. *Following Jesus: Discipleship in the Gospel of Mark*. Journal for the Study of the New Testament Supplement, Vol 4. Sheffield: JSOT, 1981.

Black, David Alan and David S. Dockery, eds. *Interpreting the New Testament: Essays on Methods and Issues*. Nashville, Tenn.: Broadman and Holman, 2001.

Black, Matthew. "The 'Two Witnesses' of Rev. 11:3f. in Jewish and Christian Apocalyptic Tradition." Pages 227–37 In *Donum Gentilicium*. Edited by E. Bammel, C. K. Barrett, and W. D. Davies. Oxford: Clarendon Press, 1978.

Blomberg, Craig L. "New Testament Genre Criticism for the 1990s." *Themelios* 15/2 (1990): 40–49.

Boccaccini, Gabrielle. "Daniel and the Dream Visions: The Genre of Apocalyptic and Apocalyptic Tradition." Pages 126–60 in *Middle Judaism: Jewish Thought, 300 b.c.e. to 200 b.c.e.* Minneapolis: Fortress, 1991.

Boer, M. C. de. *The Defeat of Death.* Journal for the Study of the New Testament Supplement, Vol 22. Sheffield: JSOT, 1988.

Boesak, Allan A. *Comfort and Protest: Reflections on the Apocalypse of John of Patmos.* Philadelphia: Westminster Press, 1987.

Boring, M. Eugene. "Narrative Christology in the Apocalypse." *Catholic Biblical Quarterly* 54 (1992): 702–23.

Boring, M. Eugene. *Revelation.* Interpretation. Louisville, Ky.: John Knox, 1989.

Boring, M. Eugene. "The Theology of Revelation: 'The Lord Our God the Almighty Reigns.'" *Interpretation* 40 (1986): 257–69.

Bornkamm, Gunther. "Die Komposition der apokalyptischen Vision in der Offenbarung Johannis." *ZNW* 36 (1937): 132–49.

Bousset, Wilhelm. *Die Offenbarung Johannis.* Gottingen: Vandenhoeck & Ruprecht, 1906.

Breck, John B. *The Shape of Biblical Language: Chiasmus in the Scriptures.* Crestwood, N.J.: St. Vladimir's Seminary Press, 1994.

Briggs, Robert A. *Jewish Temple Imagery in the Book of Revelation.* Studies in Biblical Literature 10. New York: Peter Lang, 1999.

Brooks, Richard. *The Lamb is All the Glory.* Welwyn: Evangelical Press, 1986.

Broshi, Magen. "The Gigantic Dimensions of the Visionary Temple in the Temple Scroll." *Biblical Archaeological Review* 13.6 (1987): 36–37.

Broshi, Magen. "Estimating the Population of Ancient Jerusalem." *Biblical Archaeologist Review* 4 (1978): 10–15.

Brown, David. *The Apocalypse: Its Structure and Primary Predictions.* London: Hodder & Stoughton, 1891.

Bruce, Frederick F. "The Spirit in the Apocalypse." Pages 333–44 in *Christ and Spirit in the New Testament: in Honor of Charles Francis Digby Moule.* Edited by B. Lindars and S. S. Smalley. Cambridge: Cambridge University Press, 1973.

Caird, George Bradford. *A Commentary on the Revelation of St. John the Divine.* Black's New Testament Commentary. Peabody, Mass.: Hendrickson, 1999.

Carson, Don A., Douglas Moo, and Leon Morris. *An Introduction to the New Testament.* Grand Rapids: Zondervan, 1992.

Casey, Jay Smith. *Exodus Typology in the Book of Revelation.* Ann Arbor, Mich.: University Microfilms International, 1982.

Charles, Robert Henry, ed. *The Apocrypha and Pseudepigrapha of the Old Testament.* Vol 2. Oxford: Clarendon Press, 1983.

Charles, Robert Henry. *A Critical and Exegetical Commentary on the Revelation of St. John with Introduction. Notes and Indices.* 2 vols. International Critical Commentary. Edinburgh: Clark, 1920.

Charlesworth, James H. ed. *The Old Testament Pseudepigrapha.* Vol 2. London: Darton, Longman & Todd, 1985.

Charlesworth, James H. ed. *The Old Testament Pseudepigrapha.* Vol 1. London: Darton, Longman & Todd, 1983.

Chilton, David. *The Days of Vengeance: An Exposition of the Book of Revelation.* Ft. Worth, Tex.: Dominion, 1986.

Clements, Ronald E. *God and Temple.* Philadelphia: Fortress, 1965.

Clifford, R. J. "The Temple and the Holy Mountain." Pages 112–15 in *The Temple in Antiquity*. Edited by T. G. Madsen. RSMS 9. Salt Lake City: Brigham Young University Press, 1984.

Clowney, Edmund P. "The Final Temple." *Westminster Theological Journal* 35 (1972): 156–89.

Cohen, Gary G. *Understanding Revelation*. Chicago: Moody, 1978.

Colclasure, Chuck. *The Overcomers: The Unveiling of Hope, Comfort, and Encouragement in the Book of Revelation*. Nashville, Tenn.: Thomas Nelson, 1981.

Collins, Adela Yarbro. "Reading the Book of Revelation in the Twentieth Century." *Interpretation* 40 (1986): 229–46.

Collins, Adela Yarbro. *Crisis and Catharsis: The Power of the Apocalypse*. Philadelphia: Westminster, 1984.

Collins, Adela Yarbro. "Persecution and Vengeance in the Book of Revelation." Pages 729–49 in *Apocalypticism in the Mediterranean World and the Near East: Proceedings of the International Colloquim on Apocalypticism: Uppsala, August 12-17, 1979*. Edited by David Hellholm. Tubingen: Mohr, 1983.

Collins, Adela Yarbro. *The Apocalypse*. New Testament Message 22. Wilmington, Del.: Michael Glazier Inc., 1979.

Collins, Adela Yarbro. "The History of Religions Approach to Apocalypticism and the 'Angel of the Waters' (Rev 16:4–7)." *Catholic Biblical Quarterly* 39 (1977): 367–81.

Collins, Adela Yarbro. *The Combat Myth in the Book of Revelation*. Missoula, Mont.: Scholars, 1976.

Collins, John J. *The Encyclopedia of Apocalypticism*. Volume 1: "The Origins of Apocalypticism in Judaism and Christianity." New York: Continuum, 1999.

Collins, John J. *The Apocalyptic Imagination*. Grand Rapids: Eerdmans, 1998.

Collins, John J. *Daniel*. Minneapolis: Fortress, 1993.

Collins, John J. "Genre, Ideology and Social Movements in Jewish Apocalypticism." Pages 11–32 in *Mysteries and Revelations*. Edited by John J. Collins and James H. Charlesworth. Sheffield: Sheffield University Press, 1991.

Collins, John J. "Daniel and His Social World." *Interpretation* 39 (1985): 131–43.

Collins, John J. *Daniel: with an Introduction to Apocalyptic Literature*. Grand Rapids: Eerdmans, 1984.

Collins, John J. "Apocalyptic Genre and Mythic Allusions in Daniel." *Journal for the Study of the Old Testament* 21 (1981): 83–100.

Collins, John J. *Daniel; First Maccabees; Second Maccabees; With an Excursus on the Apocalyptic Genre*. Wilmington, Del.: Michael Glazier, 1981.

Collins, John J. "Introduction: Towards the Morphology of a Genre." *Semeia* 14 (1979): 1–20.

Collins, John J. "The Jewish Apocalypses." *Semeia* 14 (1979): 21–51.

Collins, John J., ed. "Apocalypse: The Morphology of a Genre." *Semeia* 14 (1979).

Collins, John J. "The Mythology of Holy War in Daniel and the Qumran War Scroll: A Point of Transition in Jewish Apocalyptic." *Vetus Testamentum*. 25 (1975): 596–612.

Collins, John J. "The Son of Man and the Saints of the Most High in the Book of Daniel." *Journal of Biblical Literature* 93 (1974): 50–66.

Considine, Joseph S. "The Two Witnesses: Apoc. 11:3-13." *Catholic Biblical Quarterly* 8 (1946): 377–92.

Corsini, Eugenio. *The Apocalypse*. Wilmington, Del.: Glazier, 1983.

Court, John M. *Myth and History in the Book of Revelation*. Atlanta: John Knox, 1979.

Dalrymple, Rob. "The Use of kai, in Revelation 11,1 and the Implications for the Identification of the Temple, the Altar, and the Worshippers." *Biblica* 87 (2006): 387–94.
Dalrymple, Rob. "These are the Ones ... (Rev 7)." *Biblica* 86 (2005): 396–406.
Daniel, John and Gloria. *The Apocalypse in the Light of the Temple.* Jerusalem: Beit Yochanan, 2003.
Dehandschutter, Boudewijn. "The Meaning of Witness in the Apocalypse." Pages 283–88 in *L'Apocalypse Johannique et L'Apocalypse dans le Nouveau Testament.* Edited by J. Lambrecht. Bibliotheca Ephemeridum Theologicarum Lovaniensium 53. Gembloux: Duculot/Leuven: University Press, 1980.
Deissler, A. "Der 'Menschensohn' und 'das Volk der Heiligen des Hochsten in Dan 7." Pages 81–91. In *Jesus und der Menschenson.* Edited by R. Pesch and R. Schnackenburg. Frieburg: Herder, 1975.
Dequeker, L. "The 'Saints of the Most High' in Qumran and Daniel." *Oudtestamentische Studien* 18 (1973): 108–87.
deSilva, David A. "A Comparison Between the Three-Leveled World of the Old Testament Temple Building Narratives and the Three-Leveled World of the House Building Motif in the Ugaritic Texts KTU 1.3 and 1.4." Pages 11–23 in *Ugarit and the Bible.* Edited by G. J. Brooke, A. H. W. Curites, and J. F. Healey. Munster: Ugarit-Verlag, 1994.
deSilva, David A. "The Social Setting of the Revelation to John: Conflicts within, Fears without." *Westminster Theological Journal* 54 (1992) 273–302.
Donaldson, Terence L. "Proselytes or 'Righteous Gentiles?' The Status of Gentiles in Eschatological Pilgrimage Patterns of Thought." *Journal for the Study of the Pseudepigrapha* 7 (1990): 3–27.
Dumbrell, William J. *The End of the Beginning: Revelation 21-22 and the Old Testament.* Grand Rapids: Baker, 1985.
Dunn, James D. G. *Jesus and the Spirit.* London: SCM Press, 1975.
Dupont-Sommer, Andre. *The Essene Writings From Qumran.* Oxford: Blackwell, 1961.
Edersheim, Alfred. *The Temple.* Peabody, Mass.: Hendrickson, 1994.
Eichrodt, Walther. *Ezekiel.* Philadelphia: Westminster, 1970.
Ellingworth, Paul. *Commentary on Hebrews.* New International Greek Testament Commentary. Grand Rapids: Eerdmans, 1993.
Ellul, Jacques. *Apocalypse: The Book of Revelation.* New York: Seabury, 1977.
Ezell, Douglas. *Revelations on Revelation: New Sounds from Old Symbols.* Waco: Word, 1977.
Farrer, Austin. *The Revelation of St. John the Divine.* Oxford: Clarendon, 1964.
Fekkes, Jan. "Isaiah and Prophetic Traditions in the Book of Revelation: Visionary Antecedents and Their Development." Pages 130–33 in the *Journal for the Study of the New Testament* 93. Sheffield: JSOT Press, 1994.
Feuillet, Andre. "Les 144,000 Israelites marques d'un sceau." *Novum Testamentum* 9 (1967): 191–224.
Feuillet, Andre. *The Apocalypse.* New York: Alba House, 1965.
Feuillet, Andre. "Essai D'interpretation du chapitre 11 de L'Apocalypse." *New Testament Studies* 4 (Ap 1958): 183–200.
Ferguson, Sinclair B. *Daniel.* Communicator's Commentary Series 19. Waco, Tex.: Word, 1988.

Fiorenza, Elisabeth Schussler. *Revelation: Vision of a Just World*. Proclamation Commentaries. Minneapolis: Fortress, 1991.

Fiorenza, Elisabeth Schussler. *The Book of Revelation: Justice and Judgment*. Philadelphia: Fortress, 1985.

Fiorenza, Elisabeth Schussler. "Composition and Structure of the Book of Revelation." *Catholic Biblical Quarterly* 39 (1977): 344–66.

Fiorenza, Elizabeth Schussler. "The Eschatology and Composition of the Apocalypse." *Catholic Biblical Quarterly* 33 (1968): 537–69.

Fishbane, Michael. *Text and Texture*. New York: Schoken, 1979.

Ford, J. Massyngberde. *Revelation*. Anchor Bible 33. Garden City, N.Y.: Doubleday, 1975.

France, Richard T. *Jesus and the Old Testament*. Grand Rapids: Baker, 1971.

Funk, Robert W., ed. *Apocalypticism*. New York: Herder and Herder, 1969.

Garcia Martinez F. "The 'New Jerusalem' and the Future Temple of the Manuscripts from Qumran." Pages 180–213 in *Qumran and Apocalyptic Studies on the Aramaic Texts from Qumran*. Leiden: Brill, 1994.

Gartner, Bertil. *The Temple and the Community in Qumran and the New Testament*. SNTS 1. Cambridge: Cambridge University Press, 1965.

Gentry, Kenneth L., Jr. *Before Jerusalem Fell: Dating the Book of Revelation*. Fort Worth, Tex.: Dominion, 1989.

Giblin, Charles Homer. "Recapitulation and the Literary Coherence of John's Apocalypse." *Catholic Biblical Quarterly* 56 (1994): 81–96.

Giblin, Charles Homer. *The Book of Revelation: The Open Book of Prophecy*. Good News Studies 34. Collegeville, Minn.: Liturgical Press, 1991.

Giblin, Charles Homer. "Revelation 11.1-13: Its Form, Function, and Contextual Integration." *New Testament Studies* 30 (1984): 433–59.

Giblin, Charles Homer. "Structural and Thematic Correlations in the Theology of Revelation 16-22." *Biblica* 55 (1974): 487–504.

Ginzberg, Louis. *The Legends of the Jews*. 7 Vols.: Baltimore: Johns Hopkins University Press, 1966.

Glickman, S. Craig. *Knowing Christ*. Chicago: Moody, 1980.

Goldingay, John E. *Daniel*. Word Biblical Commentary 30. Dallas, Tex.: Word, 1989.

Goldsworthy, Graeme. *The Gospel in Revelation*. Carlisle, Cumbria, U.K.: Paternoster Press, 1994.

Goldsworthy, Graeme. *According to Plan*. Leicester: InterVarsity Press, 1991.

Goldsworthy, Graeme. *The Lamb and the Lion: The Gospel in Revelation*. Nashville, Tenn.: Thomas Nelson, 1985.

Gottwald, Norman K. "Holy War." Pages 942–44 In *The Interpreter's Dictionary of the Bible Supplement*. Edited by K. R. Crim. Nashville, Tenn.: Abingdon, 1976.

Goulder, Michael D. "The Apocalypse as an Annual Cycle of Prophecies." *New Testament Studies* 27 (1981): 342–67.

Greenberg, Moshe. *Ezekiel 21-37*. Anchor Bible 22a. New York: Doubleday, 1997.

Gundry, Robert. H. "The New Jerusalem: People as Place, not Place for People." *Novum Testamentum* 29 (1987): 254–64.

Gundry, Robert H. *The Church and the Tribulation*. Grand Rapids: Zondervan, 1973.

Guthrie, Donald. *The Relevance of John's Apocalypse*. Grand Rapids: Eerdmans; Exeter: Paternoster, 1987.

Hall, Mark Seaborn. "The Hook Interlocking Structure of Revelation: The Most Important Verses in the Book and How They may Unify its Structure." *Novum Testamentum* 44 (2002): 278-96.
Hanson, Paul D. *The Dawn of the Apocalyptic*. Philadelphia: Fortress, 1979.
Haran, M. "Temple and Community in Ancient Israel." Pages 17-25 in *Temple and Society*. Winona Lake, Ind.: Eisenbrauns, 1988.
Haran, Menahem. *Temples and Temple Service in Ancient Israel*. Oxford: Clarendon, 1978.
Harrington, Wilfred J. *Revelation*. Sacra Pagina Series 16. Collegeville, Minn.: Liturgical Press, 1993.
Harrington, Wilfrid J. *The Apocalypse of St. John*. London: Geoffrey Chapman, 1969.
Hartman, Lars. *Prophecy Interpreted: The Formation of Some Jewish Apocalyptic Texts and of the Eschatological Discourse of Mark 13 Par*. Coniectanea Biblica, New Testament Series 1; Lund: Gleerup, 1966.
Hartman, Lars. "Survey of the Problem of Apocalyptic Genre." In *Apocalypticism in the Mediterranean World and the Near East*. Ed. David Hellholm. Tubingen: J. C. B. Mohr, 1983.
Hartman, Louis Francis. *The Book of Daniel*. Garden City, N.Y.: Doubleday, 1978.
Hayward, C. T. Robert. *The Jewish Temple*. London/New York: Routledge, 1996.
Hellholm, David. "The Problem of Apocalyptic Genre and the Apocalypse of John." *Semeia* 14 (1986): 1-46.
Hellholm, David, ed. *Apocalypticism in the Mediterranean World and the Near East*. Tubingen: J. C. B. Mohr, 1983.
Hendriksen, William. *More than Conquerors: An Interpretation of the Book of Revelation*. Grand Rapids: Baker, 1961.
Hengstenberg, Ernst Wilhelm. *The Revelation of St. John, Expounded for Those Who Search the Scriptures*. 2 vols. Reprint. Cherry Hill, N.J.: Mack, 1972.
Hengstenberg, Ernst William. *The Two Witnesses: Two Olive Trees and/or Prophets of Revelation Eleven*. Reprint: Elmira, Ont.: Menno Sauder, 1971.
Hennecke, Edgar. *New Testament Apocrypha*. Vol. II. London: SCM, 1965.
Hill, D. "On the Evidence for the Creative Role of Christian Prophets." *New Testament Studies* 20 (1974): 262-74.
Hill, D. "Prophecy and Prophets in the Revelation of St John." *New Testament Studies* 18 (1972): 401-18.
Hill, D. "The Two Witnesses (Ap 11,3)." *Expositor* 22 (1921): 311-18.
Hirsch, Eric D. Jr. *The Aims of Interpretation*. Chicago: University of Chicago Press, 1976.
Hirsch, Eric D. *Validity in Interpretation*. New Haven, Conn.: Yale University Press, 1967.
Hoeksema, Herman. *Behold, He Cometh! An Exposition of the Book of Revelation*. Grand Rapids: Reformed Free Publishing Association, 1969.
Holwerda, David E. "The Church and the Little Scroll (Revelation 10, 11)." *Calvin Theological Journal* 34 (1999): 148-61.
Hopkins, Martin. "Historical Perspective of Apocalypse 1-11." *Catholic Biblical Quarterly* 27 (1965): 42-47.
Hoskier, H. C. *Concerning the Text of the Apocalypse* I-II. London: Wuaitch, 1929.
Hughes, Philip Edgcumbe. *The Book of Revelation: A Commentary*. Grand Rapids: Eerdmans, 1990.
Jauhiainen, Marko. "The Measuring of the Sanctuary Reconsidered." *Biblica* 83 (2002): 507-26.

Jenkins, Ferrell. *The Old Testament in the Book of Revelation*. Marion, Ind.: Cogdill Foundation Publications, 1972.
Johnson, Alan F. "Revelation." Pages 397–604 in *Expositor's Bible Commentary* XII. Grand Rapids: Zondervan, 1981.
Johnson, Dennis E. *Triumph of the Lamb*. Phillipsburg, N.J.: P & R Publishing, 2001.
Juel, Donald. *Messiah and Temple*. SBLDS 32. Missoula, Mont.: Scholars, 1977.
Kampen, John. "The Eschatological Temples of 11QT." In *Pursuing the Text, Studies in Honor of B. Z. Wacholder*. JSOTS 184. Sheffield: Sheffield Academic, 1994.
Keener, Craig S. *Revelation*. The NIV Application Commentary. Grand Rapids: Zondervan, 2000.
Keil, Karl Friedrich. *The Book of the Prophet Daniel*. Edinburgh: T & T Clark, 1884.
Kerr, Alan R. *The Temple of Jesus' Body*. JSNTS 220. Sheffield, Sheffield Academic, 2002.
Kiddle, Martin. and M. K. Ross. *The Revelation of St. John*. Moffat New Testament Commentary. London: Hodder and Stoughton, 1940.
Kittel, Gerhard and Gerhard Friedrich eds. *Theological Dictionary of the New Testament*. 10 Vols. Grand Rapids: Eerdmans, 1964–76.
Kline, Meredith. *Glory in our Midst*. Overland Park, Kans.: Two Age Press, 2001.
Kline, Meredith G. *Images of the Spirit*. Grand Rapids: Baker, 1980.
Koester, Craig R. *Revelation and the End of All Things*. Grand Rapids: Eerdmans, 2001.
Kraft, Heinrich. *Die Offenbarung des Johannes*. Handbuch zum Neuen Testament 16a. Tubingen: Mohr Siebeck, 1974.
Krodel, Gerhard A. *Revelation*. Augsburg Commentary on the New Testament. Minneapolis: Augsburg Publishing House, 1989.
Kuyper, Abraham. *The Revelation of St. John*. Translated by John Hendrik de Vries. Grand Rapids: Eerdmans, 1963.
Lacocque, Andre. *The Book of Daniel*. London: SPCK, 1979.
Lacy, T. A. "The Two Witnesses." *Journal of Theological Studies* 11 (1910): 55–60.
Ladd, George Eldon. *A Commentary on the Revelation of John*. Grand Rapids: Eerdmans, 1972.
Ladd, George Eldon. "Why not Prophetic-Apocalyptic?" *Journal of Biblical Literature* 76 (1957): 192–200.
Lang, George H. *The Revelation of Jesus Christ*. London: Oliphants, 1945.
Leivestad, Ragnar. *Christ the Conqueror*. London: SPCK, 1954.
Lenski, Richard Charles Henry. *The Interpretation of St. John's Revelation*. Minneapolis: Augsburg Publishing House, 1963.
Levenson, Jon Douglas. *Theology of the Program of Restoration of Ezekiel 40-48*. HSMS 10. Missoula, Mont.: Scholars Press, 1976.
Lind, Millard. *Yahweh is a Warrior*. Scottdale, Pa.: Herald, 1980.
Lindsay, Hal. *There's a New World Coming*. New York: Bantam, 1975.
Lioy, Dan. *The Book of Revelation in Christological Focus*. Studies in Biblical Literature 58. New York: Peter Lang, 2003.
Lohmeyer, Ernst. *Die Offenbarung des Johannes*. Handbuch zum Neuen Testament 16. Tubingen: Mohr Siebeck, 1970.
Lohse, Eduard. *Die Offenbarung des Johannes*. Handbuch zum Neuen Testament 16; Tubingen: Mohr, 1970.
Longman, Tremper III. *Daniel*. NIV Application Commentary. Grand Rapids: Zondervan, 1999.
Longman, Tremper III and Dan Reid. *God is a Warrior*. Grand Rapids, Zondervan: 1995.

Longman, Tremper III. "Form Criticism, Recent Developments in Genre Theory, and the Evangelical." *Westminster Theological Journal* 47 (1985): 46–67.
Longman, Tremper, III. "The Divine Warrior: The New Testament Use of an Old Testament Motif." *Westminster Theological Journal* 44 (1982): 290–307.
MacKay, T. W. "Early Christian Millenarianist Interpretation of the Two Witnesses in John's Apocalypse 11:3-13." Pages 222–331 in *By Study and By Faith*. Salt Lake City: Deseret Book Co., 1990.
Maier, John and Vincent Tollers eds. *The Bible in its Literary Milieu*. Grand Rapids: Eerdmans, 1979.
Malina, Bruce J. *On the Genre and Message of Revelation: Star Visions and Sky Journeys*. Peabody, Mass: Hendrickson, 1995.
Marshall, I. Howard. "Church and Temple in the New Testament." *Tyndale Bulletin* 40 (1989): 203–22.
Mathewson, Dave. "Revelation in Recent Genre Criticism: Some Implications for Interpretation." *Trinity Journal* 13 (1992): 193–213.
Mazzaferri, Frederick David. *The Genre of the Book of Revelation From a Source-Critical Perspective*. Berlin: de Gruyter, 1989.
McComiskey, Thomas E. "Alteration of OT Imagery in the Book of Revelation: Its Hermeneutical and Theological Significance," *Journal of the Evangelical Theological Society* 36/3 (1993): 307–16.
McNicol, Allan. "Revelation 11:1-14 and the Structure of the Apocalypse." *Restoration Quarterly* 22 (1979): 193–202.
McKelvey, R. J. *The New Temple*. Oxford: Oxford University Press, 1969.
Meeks, Wayne A. *The Prophet-King: Moses Traditions and the Johannine Christology*. NovTSup 14. Leiden: Brill, 1967.
Metzger, Bruce M. *Breaking the Code: Understanding the Book of Revelation*. Nashville: Abingdon, 1993.
Metzger, Bruce M. *A Textual Commentary on the Greek New Testament*. London: United Bible Societies, 1971.
Meyers, Carol. "Temple, Jerusalem." Pages 359–60 in *Anchor Bible Dictionary* 6, 1992.
Meyers, Carol "Lampstand." Page 546 in *Harper's Bible Dictionary*. Edited by P. J. Achtemeier. San Francisco: Harper & Row, 1985a.
Meyers, Carol. 'The Tree of Life.' Page 1094 in *Harper's Bible Dictionary*. Edited by P. J. Achtemeier. San Francisco: Harper & Row, 1985b.
Michaels, J. Ramsey. *Revelation*. IVP New Testament Commentary Series. Downers Grove, Ill.: IVP, 1997.
Michaels, J. Ramsey. *Interpreting the Book of Revelation*. Grand Rapids: Baker, 1992.
Miesel, John. "The Two Witnesses: Revelation 11:3." Ph.D. diss., Grace Theological Seminary, 1957.
Miller, Patrick D., Jr. *The Divine Warrior in Early Israel*. Vol 5, Harvard Semitic Monographs. Cambridge: Harvard University Press, 1973.
Minear, Paul S. *I Saw a New Earth: An Introduction to the Visions of the Apocalypse*. Washington: Corpus, 1969.
Minear, Paul S. *I Saw a New Earth*. Washington: Corpus Books, 1968.
Minear, Paul S. "The Cosmology of the Apocalypse." Pages 23–37 in *Current Issues in New Testament Interpretation*. Ed. William Klassen and Graydon F. Snyder. New York: Harper, 1962.

Morris, Leon. *The Revelation of St. John: An Introduction and Commentary.* Tyndale New Testament Commentaries. London: Tyndale, 1969.
Motyer, J. Alec. *The Message of Zechariah.* The Bible Speaks Today. Downers Grove, Ill.: IVP, 2003.
Morray-Jones, Christopher R. A. "The Temple Within." Pages 400–31 in volume 1 of the *SBL Seminar Papers, 1998.* 2 vols. Society of Biblical Literature Seminar Papers. Chico, Calif.: Scholars Press, 1998.
Morton, Russell. "Revelation 7:9-17: The Innumerable Crowd Before the One Upon the Throne and Lamb." *Ashland Theological Journal* 32 (2000): 1–11.
Moule, Charles F. D. "Sanctuary and Sacrifice in the Church of the New Testament." *Journal of the Evangelical Theological Society* 1, 34 (1950): 29–41.
Mounce, Robert H. *The Book of Revelation.* New International Commentary on the New Testament. Grand Rapids: Eerdmans, 1977.
Mounce, Robert H. *What Are We Waiting For? Commentary on Revelation.* Grand Rapids: Eerdmans, 1992.
Moyise, Steve. *The Old Testament in the Book of Revelation.* Sheffield: Sheffield Academic, 1995.
Mulholland, M. Robert. *Revelation.* Grand Rapids: Zondervan, 1990.
Munck, Johannes. *Petrus und Paulus in der Offenbarung Johannis.* Teologiske Skrifter 1. Copenhagen: Rosenskilde og Bagger, 1950.
Murphy, Frederick James. *The Structure and Meaning of Second Baruch.* Atlanta, Ga.: Scholars Press, 1985.
Osborne, Grant R. *Revelation.* Grand Rapids: Baker Academic, 2002.
Patte, Daniel. *Early Jewish Hermeneutic in Palestine.* Pages 129–208. Missoula, Mont.: Scholars Press, 1975.
Pattermore, Stephen. *The People of God in the Apocalypse.* Society for the New Testament Studies 128. Cambridge: Cambridge University Press, 2004.
Paul, Ian. "The Use of the Old Testament in Revelation 12." Pages 256–76 in *The Old Testament in the New Testament.* Edited by Steve Moyise. Sheffield: Sheffield Academic, 2000.
Peterson, Eugene H. *Reversed Thunder: The Revelation of John and the Praying Imagination.* San Francisco: Harper & Row, 1988.
Peterson, Rodney Lawrence. "Preaching in the Last Days: The Use of the Theme of 'Two Witnesses,' as Found in Revelation 11:3–13, with Particular Attention to the Sixteenth and Early Seventeenth Centuries." Ph.D diss Princeton Theological Seminary, 1985.
Porteous, Norman W. *Daniel.* Philadelphia: Westminster, 1965.
Poythress, Vern S. *The Returning King: A Guide to the Book of Revelation.* Phillipsburg, N.J.: Presbyterian and Reformed, 2000.
Poythress, Vern S. "Counterfeiting in the Book of Revelation as a Perspective on Non-Christian Culture." *Journal of the Evangelical Theological Society* 40/3 (1997): 411–18.
Poythress, Vern S. "Genre and Hermeneutics in Rev 20:1-6." *Journal of the Evangelical Theological Society* 36 no. 1 (1993): 41–54.
Poythress, Vern S. *The Shadow of Christ in the Law of Moses.* Phillipsburg, N. J.: P & R Publishing, 1991.
Poythress, Vern S. "Hermeneutical Factors in Determining the Beginning of the Seventy Weeks (Daniel 9:25)." *Trinity Journal* 6 NS (1985): 131–49.
Poythress, Vern S. "The Holy Ones of the Most High and Daniel vii." *Vetus Testamentum* 26 (1976): 208–13.

Prévost, Jean-Pierre. *How to Read the Apocalypse*. New York: Crossroad, 1993.
Rad, Gerhard von. *Holy War in Ancient Israel*. Reprint, Grand Rapids: Eerdmans, 1991.
Rahlfs, Alfred ed. *Septuaginta*. Stuttgart: Wurtembergische Bibelsant, 1971.
Ramsay, William M. *The Letters of the Seven Churches of Asia*. New York: Armstrong, 1905.
Reader, William. "The Riddle of the Identification of the Polis in Rev. 11:1-13." *Studia Evangelica* 7 (1982): 407–14.
Resseguie, James L. *Revelation Unsealed: A Narrative Critical Approach to John's Apocalypse*. Leiden: Brill, 1998.
Rissi, Mathias. *The Future of the World: An Exegetical Study of Revelation 19.11-22.15*. Naperville, Ill.: Alec R. Allenson, 1972.
Rissi, Mathias. *Time and History: A Study on the Revelation*. Richmond, Va.: John Knox, 1966.
Rissi, Mathias. "Das Judenproblem im Liche der Johannesapokalypse." *Theologische Zeitschrift* 13 (1957): 241–59.
Rowland, Christopher. *The Open Heaven: A Study of Apocalyptic in Judaism and Early Christianity*. London: SPCK, 1982.
Rushdoony, Rousas John. *Thy Kingdom Come, Studies in Daniel and Revelation*. Nutley, N.J.: Presbyterian & Reformed, 1971.
Russell, David S. *Daniel*. Philadelphia: Westminster, 1981.
Russell, James Stuart. *The Parousia*. Bradford, Pa.: International Preterist Association, 2003.
Rusten, Elmer M. *A Critical Evaluation of Dispensational Interpretations of the Book of Revelation*. 2 Vols. Ann Arbor, Mich.; UMI, 1977.
Ryken, Leland. "Revelation." Pages 458–69 in *A Complete Literary Guide to the Bible*. Ed. Leland Ryken and Tremper Longman, III. Grand Rapids: Zondervan, 1993.
Schmitt, John W. and J. Carl Laney. *Messiah's Coming Temple*. Grand Rapids: Kregel, 1997.
Seiss, Joseph A. *The Apocalypse*. 3 Vols. New York: Charles C. Cook, 1917.
Shea, William H. "The Chiastic Structure of Revelation 12:1-15:4; The Great Controversy Vision." *Andrews University Studies* 38 (2000): 269–92.
Smalley, Stephen S. *The Revelation to John: A Commentary on the Greek Text of the Apocalypse*. Downers Grove, Ill.: IVP, 2005.
Smith, Christopher R. "The Structure of the Book of Revelation in Light of Apocalyptic Literary Conventions." *Novum Testamentum* 36, 4 (1994): 373–93.
Smith, Christopher R. "The Portrayal of the Church as the New Israel in the Names and Order of the Tribes in Revelation 7.5-8." *Journal for the Study of the New Testament* 29 (1990): 111–18.
Smith, Ralph L. *Micah-Malachi*. Word Biblical Commentaries 32. Nashville, Tenn.: Thomas Nelson, 1984.
Spatafora, Andrew. "From the 'Temple of God' to God as the Temple." *Tesi* Gregoriana 27 (1997): 72–73.
Steinmann, Andrew E. "The Tripartite Structure of the Sixth Seal, the Sixth Trumpet, and the Sixth Bowl of John's Apocalypse (Rev 6:12-7:17; 9:13–11:14; 16:12–16)." *Journal of the Evangelical Theological Society* 35 (1992): 69–79.
Stefanovic, Ranko. "Finding Meaning in the Literary Patterns of Revelation." *Journal of the Adventist Theological Society* 13 (2002): 27–43.
Stefanovic, Ranko. *Revelation of Jesus Christ*. Berrien Springs, Mich.: Andrews, 2002.

Strand, Kenneth A. "'Overcomer': A Study in the Macrodynamic of Theme Development in the Book of Revelation." *Andrews University Seminary Studies* 28 (1990): 237–54.

Strand, Kenneth A. "The Eight Basic Visions in the Book of Revelation." *Andrews University Seminary Studies* 25 (1987): 107–21.

Strand, Kenneth A. "An Overlooked Old Testament Background to Revelation 11:1." *Andrews University Seminary Studies* 22 (1984): 317–25.

Strand, Kenneth A. "The Two Olive Trees of Zechariah 4 and Revelation 11." *Andrews University Seminary Studies* 20 (1982): 257–61.

Strand, Kenneth A. "The Two Witnesses of Rev 11:3-12." *Andrews University Seminary Studies* 19 (1981): 127–35.

Strand, Kenneth A. "Chiastic Structure and Some Motifs in the Book of Revelation." *Andrews University Seminary Studies* 19 (1981): 401–408.

Strand, Kenneth A. *Interpreting the Book of Revelation*. Naples, Fla.: Ann Arbor, 1979.

Strand, Kenneth A. *Interpreting the Book of Revelation: Hermeneutical Guidelines, with Brief Introduction to Literary Analysis*. Worthington, Ohio: Ann Arbor, 1976.

Swete, Henry Barclay. *The Apocalypse of St. John: The Greek Text with Introduction, Notes and Indices*. 3rd ed. London: Macmillan, 1908. Grand Rapids: Eerdmans, 1968.

Swete, J. P. M. "Maintaining the Testimony of Jesus: the Suffering of Christians in the Revelation of John." Pages 101–17 in *Suffering and Martyrdom in the New Testament: Studies Presented to G. M. Styler*. Cambridge: Cambridge University Press, 1981.

Swete, J. P. M. *Revelation*. SCM Pelican Commentaries. London: SCM Press, 1979.

Talbert, Charles H. "The Christology of the Apocalypse." Pages 166–84 in *Who do You Say That I am? Essays on Christology*. Edited by M. A. Powell and D. R. Bauer. Louisville, Ky.: Westminster John Knox Press, 1996.

Talbert, Charles H. *The Apocalypse: A Reading of the Revelation of John*. Louisville: Westminster John Knox Press, 1994.

Tan, Christine Joy. "The Identity of the Two Witnesses in Revelation 11." Ph.D. diss., Dallas Theological Seminary, 2002.

Tenney, Merrill C. *Interpreting Revelation*. Grand Rapids: Eerdmans, 1957.

Terrien, Samuel L. *The Elusive Presence: Toward a New Biblical Theology*. New York: Harper, 1978.

Thomas, Derek. *Let's Study Revelation*. Edinburgh: The Banner of Truth Trust, 2003.

Thomas, Robert L. "Literary Genre and Hermeneutics of the Apocalypse." *Masters Seminary Journal* 2 (1991): 79–97.

Thomas, Robert L. "The Literary Unity of the Book of Revelation." Pages 347–63 in *Mappings of the Biblical Terrain*. Edited by Vincent L. Tollers and John Maier. London: Associated University Presses, 1990.

Thompson, Leonard L. *Revelation*. Abingdon New Testament Commentaries. Nashville, Tenn.: Abingdon, 1998.

Thompson, Leonard L. *The Book of Revelation: Apocalypse and Empire*. New York/Oxford: Oxford University Press, 1990.

Torrey, Charles C. *The Apocalypse of John*. New Haven: Yale, 1958.

Trites, Allison A. *The New Testament Concept of Witness*. Cambridge: Cambridge University Press, 1977.

Trites, Allison A. "Ma,rtuj and Martyrdom in the Apocalypse: A Semantic Study." *Novum Testamentum* 15 (1973): 72–80.

Ulfgard, Hakan. *Feast and Future: Revelation 7:9-17 and the Feast of Tabernacles."* Coniectanea Biblica (New Testament Series) 22. Stockholm: Almqvist & Wiksell, 1989.

Villiers, P. G. R. de. "The Lord was Crucified in Sodom and Egypt: Symbols in the Apocalypse of John." *Neotestimentica* 22 (1988): 125–38.

Voorwinde, Stephen. "Worship, the Key to the Book of Revelation?" *Vox Reformata* 63 (1998) 3–35.

Waal, Cornelis van der. *Openbaring van Jezus Christus: Inleiding en vertaling.* Groningen: Vuurbaak, 1961.

Wall, Robert W. *Revelation.* New International Biblical Commentary. Peabody: Hendrickson, 1991.

Wallace, Daniel B. *Greek Grammar Beyond the Basics.* Grand Rapids: Zondervan, 1996.

Walvoord, John F. *The Revelation of Jesus Christ.* Chicago: Moody, 1966.

White, R. Fowler. "Reexamining the Evidence for Recapitulation in Revelation 20:1-10." *Westminster Theological Journal* 51 (1989): 319–44.

Wilcock, Michael. *I Saw Heaven Opened: The Message of Revelation.* Downers Grove, Ill.: InterVarsity, 1975.

Wong, Daniel K. K. "The Two Witnesses in Revelation 11." *Bibliotheca Sacra* 154 (July 1997): 344–54.

Yarden, Leon. *Tree of Light: A Study of the Menorah, the Seven-Branched Lampstand.* Ithaca, N.Y.: Cornell UP, 1971.

Yeatts, John R. *Revelation.* Believers Church Bible Commentary. Scottdale, Pa.: Herald, 2003.

Young, Edward Joseph. *The Prophecy of Daniel.* Grand Rapids: Eerdmans, 1949.

Zimmerli, Walther *Ezekiel.* Vol 2. Philadelphia: Fortress, 1983.

Zimmerli, Walther *Ezekiel.* Vol 1. Philadelphia: Fortress, 1979.

www.ingramcontent.com/pod-product-compliance
Lightning Source LLC
Chambersburg PA
CBHW051949160426
43198CB00013B/2375